ADVANCED FLY FISHING FOR
STEELHEAD

Deke Meyer

Frank Amato Publications
Portland, Oregon

Dedication

Dedicated to Barbara, a best friend when they
can be hard to come by.

Cover: Robert Owens and a steelhead. Photo by Steve Probasco
Fly Plate Photos — Jim Schollmeyer
Photo Credits: Bill McMillan — Page 1, 4 and 5, Frank W. Amato — Page 2 and 3.
Illustrations by:
Vic Erickson — Pages: 133, 134, 140
Tony Amato — Pages: 11, 55, 57, 60, 78, 122, 123, 125, 126, 127, 132
Book Design: Kathy Johnson
Printed in Hong Kong

3 5 7 9 10 8 6 4 2
ISBN NUMBER: Softbound 1-878175-10-6, Hardbound 1–878175–11–4

Table of Contents

Acknowledgements

In the hopes that I don't overlook any of those people who contributed to the success of this book, I would like to thank the following: Harry Lemire, George Cook, Gary Alger, Lani Waller, Walt Johnson, Bob Ververka, Dave McNeese, Joe Howell, Leroy Hyatt, Bob Wagoner, Bill Chinn, Mark Bachmann, Dave Hall, Bill Black, John Shewey, Forrest Maxwell, Dan Callaghan, Alec Jackson, Lee Wulff, Joan Wulff, Leon Chandler, Lora Hall, Howard West, Carol Bystrzycki, Bruce Richards, Bob McEnaney, Patrick McHugh, Scott Swanby, Ken Groslick Jr., Bob Clay, Jim Gourlay, Marty Sherman, Joyce Sherman, Frank Amato, Joyce Herbst, John Hazel, Bill McMillan, Don Green, Boyd Bush, Hollie Hokrein, Denise Trowbridge, Vic Brockett, George Cronk, Cal Hudspeth, Don McNeil, Al Buhr, Jeannie Hellmann, Bill Chase, Dave Hannes, Doug Smith, Gary Hewitt, John Leane, Larry Dahlberg, Linda Martin, Mike Maxwell, Denise Maxwell, Kit Shitanishi, Patsy Noble, Polly Rosborough, Steve Parton, Bill Black, Dave Lambroughton, Elsie, Holly Hokrein, John Randolph, J.D. Love, Jim Teeny, John McCall, Lawrence Feller, Cathy Rosenthal, Richard Bunse, Gene Trump, Dick Wentworth, Lee Clark, Dick Nelson, and Jim Stovall.

Photo By Brad Jackson

Introduction

This book was conceived as a follow-up to Bill Stinson's Fly Rod Steelhead, and as such I don't address the basics of steelheading that he covers in his text. This book assumes that you can wade, cast, tie on flies, and are comfortable on the river. You've caught steelhead and are eager to catch more. You will.

You will learn how to read water tailored to more challenging and rewarding methods than a simplistic chuck-it-and-chance-it approach. You will annex new strategies that incite steelhead to take your fly on top. You will see how the latest winter techniques work and how you can catch steelhead year round.

You will read about how fly design affects how the fly works in the water. You will learn how to match specific types of water with proven methods for catching steelhead.

You will see how it's all pinned to the underlying theme for *Advanced Fly Fishing For Steelhead:* proper presentation of the fly is the cornerstone for success.

Technique is the key: recognizing prime holding lies; determining factors such as water depth, current speed, water clarity and temperature, and how they effect steelhead; matching fly, fly line, and rod to the best strategy; and most importantly, controlling the "action" of the fly by controlling the fly's drift speed, depth in the water, and position in the river.

Advanced Fly Fishing For Steelhead builds on the work of previous authors and the countless days spent astream by sung and unsung fishermen. This book embodies some of the traditional approaches to steelheading, but it also sails against the tide of some long-held beliefs. I propose that you use a steelheading strategy because it works, not because it is the accepted method or because it is the only method.

Fly fishing gear is part of the sport. We need it, and besides, the tools of fly fishing can be as satisfying as the fishing itself. Quality gear magnifies and intensifies the fun but can also add just that much more tinder to the mystique of fly fishing. Specific tackle will be included only when specific to a strategy or technique; gear will not be included just for its own sake. Sometimes, simple is best.

Monmouth, Oregon, August 1990.

Steelhead Fly Design

I

The first steelhead flies were often crude patchwork trout flies used by fly fishermen when the angling world said steelhead wouldn't take a fly.

But pioneering fly rodders persisted in tying their own steelhead patterns, developing flies that appealed to the tyer and caught steelhead. They designed durable flies that held together through extended hours of steelhead fly casting—sweptback wet flies that cleaved the air when cast. Delicate trout patterns were replaced by hairwings like Enos Bradner's Brad's Brat, 1937; Umpqua Special, circa 1935; and Jim Pray's Thor, 1936. (*Steelhead Fly Fishing And Flies*, 1976, by Trey Combs is a fascinating account of much of our steelheading heritage.)

There are literally hundreds of steelhead hairwing pattern recipes that use calf tail, squirrel tail, deer hair, bucktail, and polar bear when available. These traditional steelhead streamers are blendings of bright oranges, reds, and yellows with subdued black and purple, many with names associated with the fishermen and rivers that are part of our steelhead tradition.

Hairwing patterns evolved mainly in conjunction with the classic wet fly swing presentation. From the first, steelheaders discovered that sea-run rainbow find a wet fly swinging in front of them to be irresistible, and bucktails are excellent wet flies for steelhead. A prime example is probably the most famous of the hairwings, the Skunk, with its red hackle fiber tail, black chenille body ribbed with silver tinsel, black hackle, and white bucktail wing.

Combs wrote, "The Skunk is the best known of all the dark patterns. It is also the most popular steelhead fly by far in the Northwest. It has been around for perhaps 30 years or more and would presently make almost any 'dozen favorite' steelhead fly list. Yet its originator, even its general geographic origins, are unknown. It was probably the product of time and many tiers. My intuition places its beginnings on the North Umpqua, but I have no concrete evidence to support this possibility."

Author Polly Rosborough told me: "The original Skunk was tied by Clarence Gordon, who operated the old North Umpqua Lodge, but it was a little bit different. It didn't have any tail; you see, neither Gordon nor Ward Cummings believed in putting tails on their flies because they thought they got short strikes. They were probably the first to tie with a short wing, just the length of the hook.

"Gordon's Skunk was tied with a short yellow egg sac, then the rest of the body was black, with no tinsel. It had the black hackle and a two-toned wing, black and white. That's where it got the name Skunk because it had a white underwing and a black top."

Gordon's Skunk was probably developed in the 1930's, but we may never be able to pin down the origins of the Skunk widely used today. In effect, the present dressing for the Skunk may have been developed on another watershed altogether, with the same color scheme reflected in the name—the white wing over a black body could easily inspire the moniker of Skunk.

Polly Rosborough is most noted as the author of *Tying and Fishing the Fuzzy Nymphs*. In his 1982 book *Reminiscences From 50 Years Of Flyrodding*, he relates how he caught his first steelhead late in the summer of 1933 on the Klamath River. It weighed four and a half pounds and the "fish's stomach held two big crayfish and one very fresh field mouse." Among other things he describes the origins of the Orleans Barber steelhead fly and the Jack Horner tale about Cole's Comet. He also relates taking a bus from Portland to Camas, Washington

---

Polly Rosborough is most noted as the author of Tying and Fishing the Fuzzy Nymphs. *In his 1982 book* Reminiscences From 50 Years Of Flyrodding, *he relates how he caught his first steelhead late in the summer of 1933 on the Klamath River.*
Facing page: *The wet fly in bright red was more than this steelhead could refuse, even in 40 degree water. Photo by Frank Amato*

Bill McMillan says, "Large, brown-toned caddis are common on Northwest streams — especially in the fall. Steelhead seldom require exact imitations so I decided to develop a sparse, muddler-like fly that would keep up on the surface, creating the illusion of the general shape, color, and fluttering activity of the larger Northwest caddisfly species. The result was the Steelhead Caddis."

FLY PATTERNS OR RECIPES VERSUS FLY DESIGN

Hairwing patterns are the most commonly used steelhead flies, but a pattern in itself is a recipe—a selection of colors and materials. The type of fly deals more with design—how the fly will act in the water, closely melded with tactics and how the angler wants to present the fly to the fish. It's enjoyable to tie steelhead flies that are pleasing to the eye, which also leads to one of angling's supreme moments—hooking, fighting, and landing a steelhead on your own fly. There is certainly nothing wrong with concocting a fly based on the tyer's whims, but the design of any steelhead fly and the components affecting its construction and resulting union between the river current, the fish, and the angler's tactics bears directly on how the fly is tied.

HOW STEELHEAD VIEW THE FLY

As we construct a fly in the vise or as we tie the fly to the tippet, we tend to view the fly sitting upright, with the lines of the hook, body material, and wings and hackle all flowing nicely to the rear, based on the horizontal plane that we experience during everyday life. It's a balanced view, formed from our walking on terra firma in the upright position, and we tend to view all the events on our planet from the same perspective. It makes for a sane world. But matters change drastically for the fly, and particularly for the wet fly, when it's pitched into a steelhead river.

Because there is more steel at the rear of the fly in its bend, hook gape, and barbed point, the wet fly abandons its horizontal plane. When drifting downriver on a slack line, the fly sinks butt first, with the hackles and wing tending to point almost straight up. In his steelhead videos for Scientific

Trey Combs, author of Steelhead Fly Fishing And Flies, *1976, presents a fascinating account of much of our steelheading heritage. Photo by B. J. Meiggs*

Anglers, director John Fabion included footage of a dead-drifted wet fly, which is probably as close as we'll come to a steelhead's-eye-view of the drifting fly. The video shows the fly canted, with the hook bend lower than the front of the fly.

The degree of angle imparted to the free-drifting wet fly is affected by the amount of current; tension on the fly via the

in the summer of 1943 to hike three miles up and three miles back to fish the Washougal River for steelhead.

Rosborough told me this story: "The Umpqua Red Brat hooked but didn't land my first Umpqua fish, estimated at ten pounds, in 1946. The fly is a copy of one tied by a guide on the Umpqua who later drowned, named Davis. A lot of guys drowned in those days; they didn't have Korkers, you know. I didn't know him, but Vic O'Bern (known as 'Umpqua' Vic O'Bern) drowned after guiding over 40 years on the river.

"I arrived on the river on Labor Day weekend and went to the old lodge where the Forest Service building is today, and talked to Clarence Gordon. He told me to take the trail along the south side of the river and I would not have any trouble finding a spot to fish. I went down and wound up at the Ledges.

"The river was very low. There was a 'V' in the underwater rock and the fish was laying right in that 'V'. It wasn't really a long cast, maybe 60 or 70 feet. I had the Umpqua Red Brat on and made my first cast and he flashed under it.

"I thought, aw hell, that's just a little one, nothing important. He wouldn't look at it again, so I put on a Jock Scott, no dice, I tried another fly, then I sat down for a bit, then I put the Red Brat back on. And I mean he nailed it right now.

"I still thought it was a small fish from the speed he had, but he stayed on the bottom, back and forth across the river, which should have told me something different. Finally, he come up right in under me in about six foot of water—that son-of-a-gun was 30 inches long, a big 'ol buck.

"There was a skinny little island in the middle of the river that was only about three foot wide and it had a bunch of willows on it. I was just using a number 6 hook—he went around the backside and I tried to stop him and the hook pulled out. That's the story of the first steelhead I hooked on the Umpqua, over 45 years ago."

The Jock Scott, an Atlantic salmon fly, was a Haig–Brown favorite for steelhead. This one was tied in Great Britain about 1870, just after the American Civil War.

tippet, leader, fly line, and fly rod; tippet stiffness and diameter; type of knot used; and materials used in the fly—whether they are naturally buoyant, contribute to sinking, or are neutral density. Even though these variables are independent elements, to a great extent they interact with each other. That a wet fly on a slack line drifts butt-down is interesting, but not nearly as important as other presentation variables such as sink rate, position of the fly in the water column, or how fast the fly is scooting crosscurrent.

The speed and amount of river current affects the fly's horizontal angle during its drift. For example, in very heavy current a wet fly drifts in a more horizontal plane because the additional weight at the rear of the hook has less time to affect the fly than if it is drifting in slow water. However, the crucial component of most wet fly presentations centers around the speed of the current and has more to do with sinking rate than at what angle the fly maintains to the horizontal while drifting downstream.

When tension is applied to the fly via the rod or the fly line, the fly tends to regain its horizontal plane. Light tension

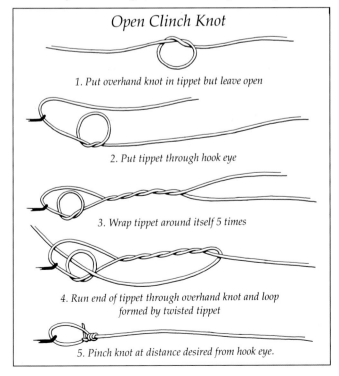

Open Clinch Knot

1. Put overhand knot in tippet but leave open

2. Put tippet through hook eye

3. Wrap tippet around itself 5 times

4. Run end of tippet through overhand knot and loop formed by twisted tippet

5. Pinch knot at distance desired from hook eye.

in stiff current or severe tension in meager current will bring the fly to a more horizontal axis. Due to the extra weight in the rear of the hook, the fly will still tend to drift with its butt lower than the rest of the fly. With tension applied, the wings, hackle, and tail tend to flow in the current at about a 45 degree angle.

A stiff or thick tippet will cause the fly to be less responsive to the whims of the current. This is particularly true when the fly is attached with an improved clinch knot. A double turle knot helps to keep the fly in the upright position, but like the improved clinch knot, it's a fairly stiff knot. The advantage of the open clinch knot is that it allows the wet fly to sway in the current with a maximum latitude of movement. (See the illustration below.)

The angle of the fly to the horizontal during a greased line presentation follows the same criteria as for a wet fly, with the butt of the fly slightly lower because of the extra weight in the rear of the fly. That can be offset by designing the fly to float in the surface film by adding a deer hair tail or a palmered hackle, but I seriously doubt that a steelhead would not hit a fly because the butt end is lower.

Buoyancy versus the weight of the rear of the hook is more critical for a skating or dry fly presentation than for any other type of steelhead fly tactic. If insufficient buoyancy is built into the fly to compensate for that extra weight in the hook bend area, even though the fly looks fine at the vise it will tend to drag its rear end under water on the stream, particularly when fished skating under tension. Overcoming the extra weight of the hook bend is a very real design problem because a dry fly will try to sink below its lateral plane when fished against the river current.

Weight added to the fly can change the angle to the horizontal considerably. For instance, if you add lead eyes to a Steelhead Woolly Bugger the fly tends to drift front-end-down on a slack line. When you apply tension to the fly with short quick pulls on the fly line, the fly follows those spurts of force with an equally quick up-and-down movement in the water. (The Woolly Bugger design is not generally used by steelheaders but is an effective fly for those jumbo rainbow for the same reason it is deadly on browns, brookies, and bass: the fly is tied "in the round," emanating the same "bugginess" at all angles. The lifelike animation of the palmered hackle and soft marabou bewitches predatory game fish, including steelhead.)

And that illustrates the main point behind this discussion—there are times when the angle of the drifting fly to the horizontal is either a crucial part of the presentation tactic or directly affects it. For our purposes, there may not need be any other justification in exploring the angle of the dangling fly to the horizontal other than that of simply examining another aspect of presenting a fly to a steelhead.

FLY DESIGN—HOW THE FLY "WORKS" IN THE WATER—WHAT STEELHEAD SEE— "STRIKE TRIGGERS"

One of the most important facets of steelhead fly design is determining how you want the fly to work in or on the water. And a major factor closely linked to both fly design and fly presentation is how the steelhead sees the fly. So how the fish sees the fly and how the fly is made to act in the water is the basis of steelhead fly design.

In the classic wet fly presentation, the angler casts the fly upstream or straight across to allow the fly to sink before the actual wet fly swing begins to bring the fly crosscurrent. As the fly sinks and glides downstream dead-drift, the hackle, tail, and wing point almost straight up as the fly drifts butt-down. Unless the wet fly is cast so it immediately begins its crosscurrent swing, the first part of the wet fly presentation is actually similar to a dead-drift nymph-like presentation. A steelhead holding downstream from the fly will see it drifting butt-down, and since the fly is gliding without tension, the steelhead might see the fly in any of its four "sides"—the top, the underside, or either of the lateral sides that would face you while the fly was in the vise.

Once on the North Umpqua, a companion watched me cast a Black Gordon hairwing to a steelhead that we had spotted. I had confidence in the fly because of its tradition: Clarence Gordon developed his wet fly in the 1930's for the Umpqua's wild summer steelhead. I cast straight across and mended the line so the fly would have time to sink to the fish's holding level in the river. Several times I cast and mended, letting the fly swing crosscurrent in front of the fish. After exhausting my patience and not hooking the fish, I joined my companion on a rock that overlooked the river. He told me that on one of the dead-drift segments of the fly's downstream drift, a steelhead had eased out from under a rock ledge, glided over and inhaled the fly.

Even though I was watching my line, I never had a clue that a fish had taken the fly on the dead-drift. I suspect that the steelhead had ghosted down with the fly, clamping down without telegraphing any motion up the fly line. At least that is what I think happened. My observer said he yelled at me when the fish took the fly, but I didn't hear him because I was concentrating on the wet fly swing, never considering that a fish would hit the fly before the swing.

Once the wet fly swing starts, the fly will briefly present a broadside view to a steelhead holding downstream from the fly; it only lasts a moment as the fly alters from a dead-drift to an active crosscurrent swing. As the fly starts crosscurrent on the typical tight-line swing, the fly responds to the tension on the line by turning so the head of the fly points upstream. The only parts of the fly that a downstream-holding steelhead can see are a bit of the wing, some of the body and the hackle, and the butt of the fly. That's possibly why the Green Butt Skunk is so effective—the fish respond to the wet fly, but particularly to the dab of fluorescent green on the butt of the fly right in the fish's face.

The probable originator of the Green Butt Skunk for steelhead is Dan Callaghan. His vivid photographs have complemented several books, including Charles Brooks's *Fishing Yellowstone Waters*, Ernest Schwiebert's upcoming *Where Flows The Umpqua*, and a cookbook centering on the North Umpqua, *Thyme And The River*. Although addicted to the pursuit of fine photographs, Callaghan is in love with the North Umpqua and its wild steelhead, an affair spanning over 30 years.

Callaghan says, "I first tied the Green Butt Skunk for the Umpqua in 1957 or 1958, for fishing the Camp Waters and the Kitchen Hole. I tied the butt with fluorescent green chenille. At first I tied the fly with a white deer hair wing, then went to polar bear. I don't remember exactly how big the fish was, but the first steelhead I caught on a Green Butt Skunk came from the Kitchen Pool. I believe I used a nine foot, nine weight "Jimmy Green Special" fiberglass rod with ugly green tinsel wraps and a Pflueger Medalist reel."

If a steelhead is holding even or slightly downstream from the drifting wet fly as it starts its crosscurrent swing, the fish will see the fly in a broadside view. Steelhead will often attack a fly that they see from a broadside view when they wouldn't have responded to the rear-view of the fly simply because they can see more of the fly. That's why the riffle hitch is effective—the knot "bends" the fly in the stream. The hitch causes the fly to swing crosscurrent with its lateral sides holding against the current, presenting a broadside view of the fly to the downstream-holding steelhead.

Sometimes steelhead will glide down with the dead-drifting wet fly and nail it when it "activates" on the

The author's definition of the strike zone is very simple: it's how far the steelhead will move to take the fly. That zone can vary considerably, depending on numerous factors. Photo by Frank Amato

One of the most important facets of steelhead fly design is determining how you want that fly to work in the water. So, how the fish sees the fly and how the fly is made to act in the water is the basis of steelhead fly design. Photo by Scott Ripley

crosscurrent swing, just as the fly swings up and across the current. (The amount of current and tension on the line determines whether the fly will stay at the same depth when it crosses the current on the wet fly swing.) The most common strike to the wet fly swing occurs when the fly is coming across in front of the fish. In most cases the fish has already seen the fly on previous crosscurrent swings. Although the butt of the fly and other parts of the wet fly in themselves provide a visual triggering device to the steelhead, the repeated presentations of the wet fly are a part of the "strike trigger," whether they stir up latent feeding instincts or territorial aggression.

Steelhead will also follow the wet fly across the current, then nail it when it completes its swing. We can guess that the fish sees the fly dangling in front of its nose, taunting it, and further stirring aggression. In his Scientific Anglers videos, Lani Waller emphasizes letting your fly hang in the current for a bit after the wet fly swing. Sometimes a following steelhead will hesitate, then nail the fly as it hangs in the current. Waller aptly calls it the "Hang Down" technique.

I believe that the most important triggering component of the greased line technique is presenting a broadside view of the fly to the steelhead. However, there are successful steelheaders who will argue that the most important component for them is the surface film presentation of the greased line fly, primarily because the visual thrill of the steelhead taking the fly on top is tremendously exciting. Investigating how steelhead see the fly and how that affects fly design, I've come to the conclusion that a greased line approach will sometimes move steelhead to a strike when a wet fly would not, primarily because the fish are responding to a broadside view of the fly.

Skating dry flies show the steelhead the butt end of the fly, much like a dry version of the wet fly. The steelhead not only see just the butt, however, but also the wake of the skater in the surface film, which undoubtedly triggers strikes. The most effective design for skaters puts most of the fly in contact with the surface film so the steelhead see more of the fly. And

Lani Waller emphasizes letting your fly hang in the current after the wet fly swing. Sometimes a following steelhead will hesitate, then nail the fly as it hangs in the current. Waller aptly calls it the "Hang Down" technique. Photo by Dick Evans

whether the fly skates across the surface or burrows a wake in the surface film, you are changing how the steelhead views the fly by imparting motion.

The dead-drifted dry fly elicits the least number of strikes for two reasons: anglers seldom fish a dead-drifted dry fly for steelhead; and the dead-drifted dry fly offers the least number of "strike triggers" to the fish. To the steelhead the dry fly is motionless; steelhead see it as a blurred form sitting on top of the water; and finally, a dry fly demands that the steelhead rise to the surface to take. But there are times when steelhead take dead-drifted dry flies and there are variations you can apply to the motionless dead-drift that excite steelhead into striking. (See the Dry Fly Chapter)

So one of the most important aspects of designing a fly is to determine how you want to present the fly to the fish and how the steelhead will view it. Sometimes a change in tactics is more valuable than just changing flies, because although a change in fly coloration is sometimes effective, more often it's a change in how the fish sees the fly.

FLY COLORATION & COLOR THEORIES

The particular coloration of any specific steelhead pattern has probably engendered more speculation about why steelhead take flies than any other element in fly design. For example, we've all heard the old theories about dark day, dark fly, bright day, bright fly, versus dark day, bright fly, bright day, dark fly, or that orange is the "hot" color for one river or purple colored flies are the only way to go for another river. In many instances, an angler will justify any particular theory because he will invariably fish a favorite pattern that inspires confidence, mainly because that is the fly that worked on previous trips. So when the angler catches yet another steelhead on a pet pattern, the theory is reinforced. In all probability, the angler fishing just downstream has hooked steelhead on a fly of a completely different color, so his strongly held convictions probably contradict the other angler's theories. In most circumstances, I believe that color in itself is of secondary importance to other factors, such as presentation, brightness and size.

HOW STEELHEAD SEE COLOR

By examining and dating fossil evidence from ancient seabeds in northern Australia and other places, scientists have determined that the first fish-like ancestors of steelhead and other modern fishes developed some 500 million years ago. The fossilized heads of those creatures had eye sockets, so we can surmise that sight was an early ability. If you give credence to the general evolutionary theory that life on earth evolved from the sea, it stands to reason that our eyesight evolved originally from the predominant life in the sea, the fishes. (Today, there are about 30,000 different species of fish swimming the three quarters of the earth that is covered with water.)

The basic construction of our eyes and the steelhead's are very similar, consisting of a closed sphere with a transparent opening that contains a lens on the front and a light-sensitive lining at the rear, with optic nerves connected to the brain to decipher what the eye sees. There are two types of receptors at the back of the eye: rods are specialized cells that receive light energy and transform it into a signal the brain can "see"; and cone cells that tell the brain the color of the light received. The rods and optic nerves can handle the difference in light intensity between noon on a sunny day and starlight on a clear night— a factor of 10 billion to one! Cones don't function in low light conditions, so we can't see color at night; on a moonlit night we can only see in pale shadowy tones—areas of light and non-light. Although steelhead can see well enough to swim upstream on a moonlit night, they probably see shades of light and dark as we do.

About 400 million years ago, the fish family split into two camps; the sharks, rays, and sturgeon that have a cartilage skeleton instead of bones, and the bony skeleton fishes.

There is another basic difference between the cartilaginous fish and bony fish that bears directly on fly fishing for steelhead. Sharks, rays, and sturgeon do not have cone cells in their eyes so they can't recognize color. That may be one of the reasons why these fish are drably colored, in browns, grays, olive greens, and grayish blues.

Bony fish have cone cells in their eyes and can readily see color, just as we do. In fact, biological evidence proposes that in many respects our eyes are akin to a fish's. That may explain why it's hard, if not impossible, for some of us to kill a fish while looking in its eye. That innate bond that threads the common filament of life on this planet is no where more apparent than in the eye.

One of the evolutionary advantages of color vision comes into play during the spawning cycle. In almost all species of birds and fish, the male parades the predominant flashy colors while the female exhibits subdued coloration. When the hen steelhead arrives in fresh water, her flanks are silvery, her dorsal areas are dark iron green, and she has faint pearl red on her cheeks. She blends in well among the interplay of light and shadow near the bottom cover of the stream. She seeks her gravel spawning area while awaiting the male who will triumph over his competitors. The buck steelhead comes in bold, striped with wide red slashes of hormonal readiness, randy and aggressive, primed to nip and bite his rivals with his overdeveloped, kyped jaw.

The coloration of the male in particular is quite a contrast from the steelhead's ocean-going pigmentation. In the sea both genders are silver with iron gray gunmetal backs and pale white bellies because that is the ideal camouflage while swimming in the sea. A predator viewing a steelhead from above does not see the charcoal back of the fish against the darkened depth of the ocean. A predator looking up finds it hard to distinguish the white belly against the sky. A side view of the fish reveals a muted reflection of scattered light, hard for the predator to pin down.

From the side steelhead look silvery because their scales are made of small, thin, flat shining crystals, about six million per square inch. The scales are stacked on the fish's sides so that light is reflected to the side and not upwards, much like a venetian blind. The scales on the fish's back are tipped so light doesn't reflect, but passes through to the dusky pigment cells underneath.

When entering fresh water, changes in steelhead coloration are determined by the time of the year the fish enters the natal river and the composition of the mother stream. For instance, in a winter-swollen river, the protective coloration of the ocean also works well in the deep green winter river. A fish entering a river at summer level will take on more trout-like coloration because the more pronounced side stripe and darker coloration is an advantage for camouflaging the fish in the lower, clearer flows of summer and early fall when the coloration of the river bottom is more pronounced.

Studies have shown that the way we see color and the way fish see color varies with water depth, amount of sunlight, and clarity of the water. The determinant factor is the wavelength of light reflected by specific colors; light with long wavelengths is absorbed more quickly than light with short wavelengths. The wavelengths that we see as colors ranges from 1/33,000 to 1/67,000 of an inch. The spectrum of light that we see is as follows: red has the longest wavelengths, then orange, yellow, and finally, the shortest wavelengths are green

Hard core steelheaders all seem to have their own pet fly patterns with varied color schemes, but it's surprising how many of those flies are variations of basic black. Photo by Frank Amato

and blue. When we see a color such as red, what we see and what steelhead see is the light reflected that is in the red spectrum, or the red wavelength. The object that reflects the red absorbs the other wavelengths.

As steelhead fly fishermen, we aren't as concerned with color factors at depths over 10 feet, but we are concerned with color factors in low light conditions of dawn and dusk, and during turbid river flows.

For example, as light fades in the evening, the first color to "shut off" is red, then orange, yellow, and finally green and blue. By that time, steelhead have switched off their cone cells and don't see color anymore; their rod cells see everything in shades of white and black, or light and non-light. White isn't really a specific color exactly, but it's what we see when all the wavelengths are reflected, or a mixing of wavelengths. When none of the wavelengths are reflected we see black.

In the early morning the pattern is reversed: when the cone cells activate in the steelhead's eyes, color vision enhances the strictly light/dark rod vision. The first visible colors are green and blue, followed by yellow, orange, and finally, red.

The same chain of color recognition occurs in turbid water. As the water goes more off color, the first color to go is red, followed by orange, then yellow, and finally green and blue.

Justifiably, you might leap to the conclusion that an angler should try flies with color schemes matched to the available light and prevailing water clarity, but color is only one factor, and even color is affected by brightness of the color and whether fluorescent dye has been added to a particular color. Green's shorter wavelengths may partially explain the effectiveness of the Green Butt Skunk, but why aren't there more equally effective blue flies, a color not often associated with most steelhead flies?

COLORS THAT AREN'T REALLY COLORS

As mentioned earlier, white isn't a specific color. It's the overall color effect from an object reflecting all the wavelengths of colors at once. The brain translates that mixture of reflected wavelengths as the color white.

Black is what the brain "sees" when none of the color wavelengths are reflected, but are absorbed by the object we are looking at. So black is a sort of non-color, the result of a lack of reflected light. That is, assuming there is enough illumination to see, black is the color resulting from the absorption of visible light rays.

These two basic colors that aren't really colors present some interesting questions for fly design. What is the design rationale for the commonly used white wing on a steelhead wet fly? The possible triggering device inherent in white might stem from the fact that steelhead feed on white or silvery-white fish while juveniles in fresh water and while reaching adult size in the ocean. It's doubtful that steelhead can see a white wing against a clear sky, but the wet fly often swims steelhead waters under an overcast sky or in the early morning or late evening when white shows up well, even under water.

It also seems to make sense to use a white wing on a fly fished on or near the surface because the angler can readily see the fly and track its progress.

Serious steelheaders all seem to have their own pet fly patterns with varied color schemes, but it's surprising how many of those flies are variations of basic black.

Black flies have a density of tone. When fished they endow a blocky solidity that seems to stand out. The steelhead's world is one of flowing current and camouflage, a shifting montage of flecks and specks of subdued colors, a watery world of earthtones; in direct contrast, black is dense and hard. That quality of denseness contributes to the overall effectiveness of black flies, which stems from the basic nature of steelhead. In theory, two things seems to excite steelhead into striking a fly: the remembered feeding instinct that is dormant but not completely turned off; and the strong territorial urge to attack any intruder.

While it may be argued that a black fly might imitate a freshwater food like a stonefly nymph, it's doubtful that in the open sea steelhead feed on any saltwater prey that is black. In rivers with rich stonefly populations such as the giant *Pteronarcys* salmonfly on the Deschutes, dead-drifting a sizable Black Stonefly Nymph is a very effective tactic.

It's probable that steelhead hit a black fly because it represents an easily seen invader, a possible rival or usurper of spawning rights, the ultimate territorial imperative for fish. The same arguments might hold true for any number of brightly colored flies, which may or may not excite a latent feeding instinct, but are certainly likely to inspire an open-mouthed attack by territorial fish.

But black flies have an advantage over most bright patterns because they attract steelhead without spooking them. The hazard with fishing luminous flies is that they often scare as many steelhead as they attract. Black isn't flashy.

And unlike many drab patterns, black flies still show up well in off-colored rivers or on overcast days or in the first glimmer of dawn or fading shimmer of evening. Black flies also work well in brilliant sunlight because they have that quality of denseness without flashiness.

OTHER FACTORS THAT AFFECT COLOR

Brightness can affect a specific color. For example, orange can be rich but subdued, or it can be fluorescent, which is not only bright, but almost another color.

Although we can make calculated guesses, we will probably never determine exactly what triggers a specific steelhead to strike a particular fly. As rational beings we put forth what we consider logical explanations based on what we have observed steelhead do in the past, and then we form strategies for catching more fish.

We can be reasonably sure of some general assumptions, though, based on reactions of steelhead that we can readily observe. For instance, at times we can see steelhead flee from a bulky, glossy fly, particularly in low, clear water. And conversely, I've seen steelhead attack a bright fly in what appeared to be the identical circumstances that set them to fleeing the day before. The logical conclusion is that almost

The wings of the commonly called October caddis (Limnephilidae Dicosmoecus) look like a moth's wings; they are relatively drab, with dull black and gray overtones. But if you examine their wings in the sunlight you will see sparkles of what look like fluorescent particles of gold dust sprinkled on the wings.

all of our steelheading theories can be proved or disproved on any given day afield.

That's the beauty of it—because almost any theory is provable, almost any theory has some merit. But I believe many steelheaders may be missing out on some of the fun of fly fishing for these husky sea-strong rainbow because they adhere too strongly to firmly held beliefs.

It's impossible to solidly plug steelhead behavior into convenient theoretical pockets because steelhead swim in too many different types of rivers under tremendously varied conditions during all months of the year. Besides which, there are distinct races of steelhead, specifically tuned to each home river by thousands of years of genetic programming for the conditions found in that specific river. Steelhead are swimming upstream to mate, a mission charged with the evolutionary imperative to perpetuate the species. The spawning drive causes a host of chemical and physical changes in steelhead, including adapting from salt to fresh water, and homing in on the natal river, while suspending one of the strongest drives for life, the desire to feed.

FLUORESCENCE

Steelheaders have used fluorescent fly tying materials for a number of years now, mainly because the added brightness of fluorescent materials often makes the fly more effective in low light conditions and in murky water.

Fluorescent fly tying materials glow only when light is applied. Fluorescent materials glow during the day in full sun, but we don't see the fluorescence. It only becomes visible to us in dim light. An excellent example is the fluorescent dye in the finish of many of our fly lines. The advantage to the fisherman becomes obvious when fishing in the fading light of evening or in a deep canyon on an overcast day: because the line will fluoresce or glow a bit in the dimness, it's much easier to see, which allows the angler to quickly approximate where the fly is tracking the water. The same principle holds true for steelhead tracking a fly tied with fluorescent materials—the fish can see your fly from farther away—which can make an immense difference in subdued light or when water clarity is less than ideal.

To my knowledge, steelhead fly fishermen haven't experimented with glow-in-the-dark flies, possibly because few fly fishermen fish at night and possibly because no one has popularized any specific patterns.

Fluorescence may have an additional attractant quality for steelhead besides just looking brighter in the water. When you catch a steelhead, have you ever noticed how its red stripe or pearly cheeks seem to gleam in the dull light of a cloudy day or deep in a canyon or in the afterglow of the evening?

The red stripe breaks up the fish's outline in the water and contributes to its underwater camouflage, but the fluorescence in the red stripe and the cheeks may also be a triggering mechanism, an integral component of the spawning cycle. The predominant red stripe of the buck is a spawning flag designed to attract the female and to warn off other males. It makes sense that fluorescence would be a component of the spawning cycle because sometimes steelhead spawn in murky water, so the fluorescence would make the red stripe and cheeks more prominent. And it's quite possible that other steelhead detect that bit of fluorescence in the red as part of the spawning signal. Of course, even if we disregard this fluorescent theory, red will always be a basic color for steelhead flies because spawning steelhead exhibit red coloration, which excites aggression towards the fly.

There are numerous examples of fluorescence in plants and aquatic insects associated with reproduction in low light conditions.

Under dense canopies of Douglas fir and cedar, many flowers that flourish on the dim forest floor, such as violets and primrose, incorporate fluorescence in their flowers to attract pollinators like bees, wasps, and other insects. The wings of the commonly called October caddis (Limnephilidae Dicosmoecus) look like a moth's; they are relatively drab, with dull black and gray overtones. But if you examine them in the

Like fluorescent materials, phosphorescent or glow-in-the-dark fly tying materials are also fueled by light energy and they glow in dim light.

sunlight you will see sparkles of what look like fluorescent particles of gold dust sprinkled on their wings. These caddis don't hover in flight like bobbing mayfly spinners to attract a mate, but clamber about on the brush and trees, while hoping

to encounter a partner. I believe caddis can see that fluorescence and that it aids in attracting a mate.

PHOSPHORESCENT FLY TYING MATERIALS

Like fluorescent materials, phosphorescent or glow-in-the-dark fly tying materials are also fueled by light energy and they glow in dim light. But the major difference between fluorescent and phosphorescent materials is that the phosphorescent materials continue to glow for a few moments after the light source is taken away. So to that degree, phosphorescent materials are not dependent on the continuous application of light.

Glow-in-the-dark fly tying materials include body tubing and Flashabou. The tubing can be split out and unraveled to make wing and tail material, but it's coarser and stiffer than Flashabou. Glow-in-the-dark Flashabou is a bit coarser than regular Flashabou but still moves well in the water. Phosphorescent Flashabou wing and tail material is well complemented with more flexible materials such as marabou, Crystal Flash and regular Flashabou, particularly in pearlescent. The tubing comes in small, medium, and large, and both materials come in white, yellow, green, blue, orange, and pink. However, when energized with bright light, these glow-in-the-dark phosphorescent materials all glow with a yellowish green glimmer.

I was curious as to how glow-in-the-dark materials worked—how they store and release light over a span of minutes—but the supplier wouldn't tell me for fear of others copying what is a trade secret. At any rate, I suspect that light energy changes certain chemical properties of the material on a molecular level, and somehow that energy is retained a few minutes and then quickly dissipates. It's called cold light because unlike a light bulb, it generates no heat.

In the mid-1970's I fished the Nestucca River in Oregon with a friend who used conventional gear for May and June summer run steelhead. Arriving at dawn, he would shine his flashlight on his phosphorescent Corkie drift bobber to get it glowing in the dim light. He would consistently catch chrome bright steelhead, hard fighting wild fish just six miles from the ocean.

But to my knowledge, steelhead fly fishermen haven't experimented with glow-in-the-dark flies, possibly because few fly fishermen fish at night and possibly because no one has popularized any specific patterns. Another factor is that although it's legal to fish at night in Washington and Idaho, it's illegal in Oregon and California.

The beam from a flashlight just isn't intense enough to work well for glow-in-the-dark flies at night. One of the most efficient ways to energize phosphorescent materials for night fishing is to zap the fly with a camera flash. Flash units that are not built into the camera work best. One option is to purchase a used flash unit at a camera store, and the off-brands are just fine for this purpose. Tape some folded aluminum foil around the flash opening so the foil concentrates the light in an area just wide enough for the fly. Most flash openings are square or rectangular so the aluminum housing is maybe two inches high and molded into a square or rectangle that matches the flash opening. When fishing, you tie the fly on your tippet, drop the fly into the aluminum housing, cover the opening with your hand, point the flash away from you and fire. The phosphorescent materials will glow-in-the-dark for several minutes.

Phosphorescent materials glow under the low light conditions of evening or when fishing in a deep canyon on an overcast day, and they offer the advantage of providing the angler with the choice of energizing them to glow when needed.

Another option is to design a fly that incorporates a glow-in-the-dark Cyalume Lightstick, sold in sporting goods stores as "Lunker Lights" which include three lightsticks in either green, blue, or pink, with clear plastic tubing included. These lightsticks generate light from a chemical reaction caused when two solutions mix inside the lightstick. One of the solutions is stored in a very thin ampule. To start synthesizing light, you flex or bend the lightstick, which breaks the inner ampule, mixing the solution. Lightsticks are safe for normal use and like phosphorescent materials, are not a source of heat because they give off a cold luminescence.

The greatest advantage in using Cyalume lightsticks is that they don't have to be recharged, and in fact, they are not rechargeable. Another advantage is that the lightsticks glow in different colors such as yellowish green, pale blue, and pink.

The challenge in tying flies incorporating a lightstick is designing the fly so that the lightstick won't fall out when casting, won't impede the hook point from hooking the fish, and finally, allows for replacement of an expended lightstick with a new one.

The clear plastic tubing included with the Lunker Lights must be notched at one end of the tubing for a secure tie-down, and it should be tied in so the tubing can lay flat, otherwise the lightstick will impede hooking the fish. You can build up the head with chenille or yarn, which allows the lightstick to parallel the hook shank. (Lightsticks retard sinking because they are hollow, so you might weight the fly.)

Some novelty or party supply shops carry smaller lightsticks in green or blue, but without tubing; lightsticks can be ordered from Chemical Light Company, Chicago, 1-800-446-3200. Surgical tubing, aquarium tubing or gas line tubing for model airplanes will hold these smaller lightsticks.

BIOLUMINESCENCE

The glow-in-the-dark notion is not new; scientists call it bioluminescence, the emission of light by living organisms, caused by a conversion of chemical energy into light energy. Bioluminescence doesn't come from light absorbed by the organism or depend on light absorbed. It's a special kind of biological chemical reaction that produces a cold light without giving off heat.

The flash of the firefly, the brilliant "phosphorescence" of the ocean, or the glow of Jack-my-lantern or foxfire mushrooms in the forest at night are examples of bioluminescent organisms. Certain bacteria, fungi, worms, crustaceans,

Many early steelheaders were influenced by traditional Atlantic salmon flies and fishing methods.

insects, jellyfish, squids, shrimp, clams, and fish are bioluminescent. Some emit light to frighten or confuse predators, some to attract prey, and some to attract mates.

Bioluminescent fish include the dogfish shark, luminous shark, pony fish, flashlight fish, angler fish, dragon fish, viper fish, hatchet fish, and lantern fish.

In their travels in the ocean, steelhead may see some of these phosphorescent creatures. Possibly, a steelhead may strike a glowing phosphorescent fly because of feeding instinct. However, it's just as likely the fish bites the fly because it's an invader of spawning grounds or contested river bottom.

This Gordon double Atlantic salmon fly was tied around 1870, and was used by Al Buhr to catch an 18-pound Clearwater steelhead in the mid-1980's. It proved that steelhead find Atlantic salmon patterns provoking, but it's amazing that the silk gut eye held such a fish after over 100 years of aging.

NIGHT FISHING

It's debatable whether fly fishing steelheaders will embrace glow-in-the-dark flies for fishing at night or during the low light conditions of dawn or evening or during turbid water conditions. Many will be repulsed by yet another inroad into a traditional sport by more high tech "plastics". And there is no doubt that energizing flies with a camera flash or pitching a Lightstick fly at steelhead is a long cast from tradition.

Disregarding the use of a camera flash or Lightsticks though, it's not that far off the traditional track to fish with a fly tied with phosphorescent body tubing and wing material. The fly does show up better in dim light, possibly triggering steelhead to strike because of the additional "glow" factor. Fluorescent materials were just as much on or off the track when they were first used, depending on your point of view.

I haven't fished at night for steelhead, so using a modified camera flash to zap a phosphorescent fly or fishing with a glowing Lightstick fly seems alien. My friends and I have used glow-in-the-dark flies for night fishing for trout, bass, and saltwater fish. I've received letters from a sea-run cutthroat fly fisherman in Vancouver, B.C. and a salmon/steelhead fly troller from the Great Lakes region who both use phosphorescent flies, and from fly fishermen whose flies imitate phosphorescing squid that are prey for tuna off the coast of Hawaii.

I don't mind using glow–in–the–dark flies at night for black and copper rockfish off the jetties and docks of Oregon's saltwater bays. In fact, it's fun. (Although flies look so weird shooting through the dark while being cast that one friend suggested it looked like a UFO, while another said the glowing fly would make a great lapel button for the Chernobyl Chamber of Commerce.

Although steelhead fly fishing is a physical sport and can be rough-and-tumble at times, it still maintains an aura of aesthetics and even magic, if you will. Messing with camera flashes, Lightsticks, and glowing flies certainly doesn't appeal to the fly-fishing-as-art-and-beauty expression of our sport.

If you accept the notion that some of our steelheading heritage evolved from the Atlantic salmon traditions of the British Isles, there is some historical precedent for night fishing for Atlantic salmon and what the Brits call sea trout, an anadromous brown trout. In his 1984 book *Salmon Fishing*, Hugh Falkus quoted from A.H. Chaytor's 1910 book *Letters to a Salmon Fisher's Sons,*"...in the heavy streams and in big waters at dusk, or when it has grown quite dark, you may use your very largest fly, and may take fish that would not look at anything during the day." Falkus writes about fishing for Atlantic salmon at night and says that he and his friends have taken over 50 salmon at night on flies. In his 1986 book, *Fly Fishing for Salmon and Sea Trout,* Arthur Oglesby writes of catching both species at night on flies in lakes in the Hebrides.

Fly fishing for steelhead at night does sound interesting and I would like to try it sometime, but I suspect that for me, anyway, it would be a novelty and a chance to experience some different steelheading sensations. But I also suspect that it wouldn't compare to what I believe the true spirit of steelheading is, with the soul of the sport rooted in our visual contact with the river and its fish.

One of the truly fascinating aspects of fly fishing and tying is the constant carousel of changes in materials, tying techniques, and tactics associated with new approaches to fly fishing puzzles. I offer this information on phosphorescent materials and Cyalume Lightsticks for those who wish to use it for steelhead, largemouth bass, or any of the myriad saltwater species.

OTHER COMPONENTS OF FLY DESIGN

Color and its degree of brightness are the most obvious elements of a fly, but other aspects to consider in fly design are bulk, water absorbency, reflection, the type and size hook, and movement of the fly through the water.

The bulk of a fly directly affects sinking rate. For example, a fly with a tightly dubbed body sinks quickly when compared to a fly tied with a palmered hackle or a heavily dressed wing. Lead wire can make a small fly sink like a rock (and cast

"I'm a firm believer in soft hackles. Being from the north country of England, my style of tie is really a north country style that's been adapted for steelhead," says Alec Jackson.

only slightly better than said rock). Generally, slim sinks better than bulky.

Alec Jackson has a theory about the mass of a fly that bears directly on designing his versions of the Skunk. He says, "I'm a firm believer that a fish's eyes deteriorate along with body condition as they get farther from salt water. What I call my Coastal Skunk has a much slimmer body than my Inland Skunk." The underlying logic is that since the steelhead is losing its visual acuity, to a certain degree a bulkier fly will attract more strikes because the fish can see it more easily.

Jackson is originally from what he refers to as "the north country of England"; his flies reflect the influence of the soft hackle style of tying "in the round." Jackson has added his own wrinkle though—a special vise that allows him to rotate the fly very quickly. The tail on his Skunk is the usual red hackle fiber, but the greatest modification is in the body. He twirls body material around oval silver tinsel, using tinsel in the same manner as you would spin dubbing around tying thread. In the Coastal Skunk he spins peacock herl, which he calls "a magic material," around tinsel. For the Inland Skunk he spins black ostrich for the back half of the body and black seal for the front half, both around tinsel. The resulting bodies are underlaid with the subdued sparkle of silver tinsel while the peacock herl, ostrich, and seal project spicules of light reflection and lifelike animation.

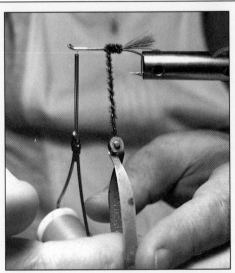

Alec Jackson's Fly Design

Alec Jackson twirls the body material around oval silver tinsel, using the tinsel in the same manner as you would spin dubbing around tying thread. In the Coastal Skunk he spins strands of peacock herl around tinsel; for his Inland Skunk he spins black ostrich herl for the back half of the body and black seal for the front half, both around tinsel.

Before Alec Jackson spins his bodies with several strands of ostrich wrapped around tinsel, he combs the ostrich out with a toothbrush so the ostrich will radiate out at right angles to the tinsel, freeing the ostrich fibers for more lifelike underwater movement.

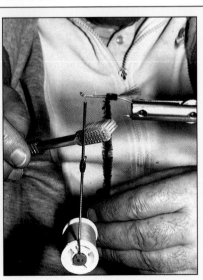

He uses soft black hackle and finishes the fly with a white wing. He says, "Polar bear is a magic material because of its translucence and the way it picks up light." Tied with 6/0 red fluorescent thread, his Skunks have a bit of red in the tail and in the head of the fly, which creates a balanced and pleasing effect.

Permeability of the fly's materials also affects sink rate. Bucktail is commonly used for traditional steelhead streamers, but it's hollow and retards sinking. Non-buoyant wing materials that move well in the water include monga tail, skunk, squirrel tail, kip tail, and marabou. These materials take dye well, too.

Tinsel, embroidery thread, and silk buttonhole twist are examples of fly tying materials derived from the millinery trade.

Tinsel particularly caught the eye of early tyers in the British Isles, which had a solid impact on our fly fishing tradition. Tinsel is a prime ingredient in most steelhead flies because it reflects flickers of light and endows, we think, the impression of life, possibly because rocks and drifting sticks and leaves do not reflect glints of light, whereas small fish and aquatic insects do have that quality.

In varying degrees of intensity, the use of tinsel, fine wire, Flashabou, or Crystal Flash adds flash and reflection of both light and color. The Golden Demon and Silver Demon were early steelhead hairwings tied with gold and silver tinsel bodies. The tinsel body on the Winter's Hope reflects the orange and yellow wing and blue and purple front hackles, suggesting life and providing color. Tinsel-bodied Steelhead Matukas offer the wing and tail silhouette that is so effective in that style of fly, while incorporating the reflective quality of the tinsel and a quality that is common to all tinsel-bodied wet flies—they sink quickly.

Lee Clark has developed a series of tinsel bodied dry flies that reflect the coloring in their yarn wings. The Clark

There are literally hundreds of steelhead hairwing pattern recipes that use calf tail, squirrel tail, deer hair, bucktail, and polar bear when available.

Stonefly was originally designed for trout but has proven to be an effective steelhead fly as well. The Muddler is another tinsel-bodied fly that was originally designed as a trout fly and has since established itself as a deadly steelhead fly.

THE MAGIC OF DEER HAIR

The slimness of the tinsel body that allows quick sinking is offset in the Muddler by the spun deer hair head; however, the bulk of the head creates a disturbance in the water that attracts steelhead, particularly in riffles. Using deer hair as a design component allows the tyer to build in a varying degree of buoyancy and bulk, besides simulating aquatic insect life or prey fish.

Guide John Hazel has developed the Purple Muddler shown in the color plates; it has no tail, a reduced head of spun purple deer hair, an underwing of purple Krystal Flash, and a body of purple plastic floss. He says, "I developed the Purple Muddler specifically for the lower Deschutes River in Oregon. The reasoning behind this was that the lower Deschutes often has turbid water with visibility less than five feet.

"To bring steelhead to the surface I needed a fly that I was sure they could see in turbid flows and purple shows well in dim light conditions. Hence, the Purple Muddler, and to be sure it showed well I simply added a hint of Krystal Flash material for that 'little extra'. I might also make note to the shape of the Purple Muddler's head. It is trimmed flat on top and bottom to keep the fly tracking in the surface film rather than bobbing up and down which the round type heads have a tendency to do.

"The Purple Muddler is highly effective on both sides of the Cascades and has proven to be one of my top favorites over the last ten years. The Muddler is keenly effective fished in the surface film with floating line techniques or with a deep wet fly presentation with sinking lines or heads. I prefer the floating line methods with this pattern, however. There really isn't any special water type in which the fly is more productive than any other. In fact I prefer patterns that are versatile in all surface presentations without regard to water type."

In his 1987 book, *Dry Line Steelhead*, Bill McMillan wrote: "In the fall of 1971 I began taking steelhead regularly on the surface using a Muddler. My steelhead fishing up to that time had primarily been with traditionally bright steelhead patterns fished just subsurface. Each year thereafter I began using the Muddler more and more until it was doing 80 to 90 percent of my fishing from June through October. However,

Guide John Hazel says, "To bring steelhead to the surface I needed a fly that I was sure they could see in turbid flows and purple shows well in dim light conditions." Photo by Randle S. Stetzer

despite the Muddler's effectiveness I couldn't keep it "waking" on top as often as desired. While the Muddler is effective at any depth, the surface rise of a 4- to 20-pound steelhead holds obvious attractions for the angler that no other level of presentation can equal.

"After reading Leonard Wright's *Fishing the Dry Fly as a Living Insect,* I realized that a Muddler held waking on the surface was likely a very good duplication of caddisfly surface activities. Large, brown-toned caddis are common on Northwest streams—especially in the fall. Steelhead seldom require exact imitations so I decided to develop a sparse, muddler-like fly that would stay up on the surface, creating the illusion of the general shape, color, and fluttering activity of the larger Northwest caddisfly species. The result was the Steelhead Caddis."

Observing that steelhead respond to adult golden stoneflies on the river, Mike Maxwell designed his Telkwa Stone.

Mike Maxwell has developed his own system of fly fishing for steelhead. Photo by Denise Maxwell

"On the first morning's fishing in September, 1975 I took a 16-pound steelhead on the Steelhead Caddis, and on a drizzling afternoon two days later I lost two even larger steelhead that lifted the surface with massive rises to the new pattern. By the end of that first season I had learned the line control techniques and strike reactions that best complement the pattern, and now the Steelhead Caddis does the majority of my steelhead fishing from May through October."

Harry Lemire has devised two flies that simulate the jumbo autumn caddis, the Grease Liner and Lemire's Fall Caddis. In 1962 he designed the Grease Liner with a cinched down deer hair wing, leaving the stubble intact over the fly's head. (His wing design predated Troth's Elk Hair Caddis with its stubble wing by many years.) When tying the Grease Liner the tan deer hair tail and wing remains a constant.

Lemire says, "In different rivers you find different colors of caddis so the fly's body color is changed to approximate the hatch. I use black, dark brown, gray olive, burnt orange, and yellow orange, with a sparsely tied barred hackle not tied dry but wet, with just a couple of turns to break up the color of the body and give it some little flowing legs.

"For a large river I also tie a Grease Liner as a searching pattern which is all black—tail, wing, and body. If you are fishing a new river and don't know where the fish lie, then you must search for them, at that time I'll use a size 4 in black.

That allows me to find the fish better. Sometimes they'll only boil at it, then I'll go to a smaller size and concentrate on that one fish."

Developed in 1986, Lemire's Fall Caddis has a reduced spun deer hair head with a few sparse deer hairs flowing backwards from the head that simulate legs and trailing antennae. A more imitative tie for the husky autumn caddis, it includes flat orange monofilament ribbing and paired, mottled orangish-brown grouse feathers enclosing the burnt orange dubbed body.

When I asked Lemire to describe his favorite tactics for presenting these flies he said, "It depends on water flow. Consider you're fishing an average piece of water with a head, center, and tail. At the head there is bouncy, riffly water. I like to stand above and make my cast quartering down so I have good line control. After the cast I hold my rod tip high and bounce the fly along the top of the riffles, fluttering the fly on the surface. If the river is heavily fished or clear the fish will often hide in the riffles. They're like an ostrich; if they can't see you then you can't see them.

"As you work down into the center of the drift where the flow slows, then your mending changes. At the top of the riffle you start with an upstream mend and as you progress to the center and the flow slows you might not have to mend much. As the water slows more, switch to a downstream mend to speed the fly. You continue doing this through the drift, doing whatever is necessary to keep the fly swimming like an insect, keeping it broadside to the fish as it's swimming towards shore.

"When fishing a Grease Liner or Fall Caddis you're imitating an insect that is struggling in the current trying to get to shore or possibly laying eggs. You try to make a wake behind it because commotion attracts the fish. If you fish dead-drift there is nothing to excite the fish. You're trying to excite the fish into taking something that is trying to get away and this brings out the animalistic instinct to grab it."

In 1987 Lemire fashioned his Steelhead Sculpin with a reduced deer hair head, sparse deer hair overwing, Matuka-style feather wing, ribbed dubbed body, and red wool for gills.

He says, "I fish the Steelhead Sculpin under the surface as a wet fly, but swimming it the same way. I like to bring out the predatorial instinct in steelhead because I think that's the key. I fish dark or natural patterns. My style or technique is to imitate an insect or a fish, so it isn't just chuck-and-chance-it."

Mike Maxwell and his wife Denise (a Canadian fly casting champion) operate a lodge on the Bulkley River in British Columbia, where he has developed his Telkwa Stone.

Although not constructed with deer hair, the fly incorporates many of the same design principles as steelhead deer hair flies.

Maxwell says, "Steelhead are spawned and spend their juvenile years in the upper reaches of the river where they feed on many forms of underwater and surface insect life. To escape predation, their habitat is usually under or around rocks or large gravel, close to a food supply and with well oxygenated water. By a happy coincidence, large stonefly nymphs have exactly the same habitat and form a major portion of the juvenile steelhead's diet. This symbiotic relationship of large gravel, juvenile steelhead, and stonefly nymphs is extremely important when locating the resting or holding stations of the upward migrating steelhead and is now known as 'the juvenile habitat imprint'.

"Although the nymphal stage of the stonefly is significant to the maturing steelhead smolt, it is the effect of the flying stonefly adult that is important to the angler. After mating, the female flies upstream and deposits her eggs by fluttering down and dipping her egg sac into the water. Some stoneflies are blown sideways across the surface as they attempt to take off to fly upstream again. This process is repeated many times and is so clumsy that it creates a large disturbance above and on the water and proves irresistible to any nearby fish. (Unlike many other insects, stoneflies on British Columbia steelhead rivers normally do not swarm and cause feeding periods, as mayflies and caddis do, and are most often seen singly or in small groups, following each other intermittently.)

"The fact that steelhead smolts will rise to an isolated fly is extremely important in understanding its adult behavior and can be called 'the single fly feeding response'. The steelhead smolt must compete for food with many other species of fish and as one adult stonefly has an enormous food value, its appearance will trigger an immediate 'competitive feeding response' (some of the juvenile fish are not much bigger than

Perhaps the most radical deer hair fly used for steelhead is the fly Larry Dahlberg designed for bass, the Dahlberg Diver.

the fly). It is important to note that in most cases stoneflies have completed their egg laying and are not present during the upward migration of steelhead.

"Fly fishing in its purest form relies on motivating a fish to take an artificial fly which represents its natural food, and is presented to imitate the natural behavior of that food. Steelhead dry fly fishing for returning non-feeding fish depends on triggering the adults 'single fly' and 'competitive feeding' responses imprinted during its juvenile period.

"When an adult steelhead observes a well presented stonefly imitation floating straight down the river towards it, sometimes splashing and struggling, it will leave its resting hold and drift down behind to check it out. This close inspection can continue as the fly finally swings into shore and is stripped in for the next cast. Remember that this represents the natural female stonefly, fluttering straight downstream, being blown across the current as she tries to take off upstream again.

"Once the fly is directly downstream from its original position it will start to swing in towards the bank. The speed of the swing can be controlled by mending upstream or downstream. During the drift and the swing, mending should be as gentle as possible. The small amount of movement imparted to the fly activates it, imitating the struggling adult stonefly.

"Steelhead may come to a dry fly in many ways without getting hooked. This can vary, from pushing the fly upstream with its nose, to slapping it with its tail. If the fish is sufficiently motivated, it will make a closer inspection by taking the fly into its mouth. Do not strike the fish—the steelhead must be allowed to hook itself as it swims back upstream to its hold.

"The Telkwa Stone has all the characteristics required for the various stages of the natural presentation: it must closely resemble the predominant resident adult female stonefly in size, shape, and color; it must be visible enough to be seen 80 feet away and float high in the water without excessive false casting to dry it; it should be easy to tie and durable to withstand the munching of an aggressive fish; and the hook must be light enough to aid in floating and super sharp to assist the self-hooking process."

Possibly the most radical deer hair fly used for steelhead is the fly Larry Dahlberg designed for bass, the Dahlberg Diver. In the spring of 1967 Dahlberg was stalking a largemouth that he was determined to take with a fly. He says, "The bass would follow a popper, but it wouldn't take it. I needed to devise something that I could get to dive under the water and come back up. I changed the shape of the deer hair to make the fly do what it needed to do and I caught this particular fish, a 6-pound 7-ounce largemouth.

"The Dahlberg Diver will do something that is real different: it will actually go below the point at which the leader ties onto the tip of the fly line. It will actually go below that level, whether it's from the surface and down a few inches, or a foot and a half, or whether the fly line is on the bottom, the fly will want to go to the bottom and a little beyond.

"What I look for is the broad application of *what it does* in all the flies and everything I try to do in fly fishing. In a real broad application—*what is the general purpose of this thing and then allow room to vary*—make it bright, make it dark, make it long, make it short, make it fat, make it thin, make it sink fast, make it float, whatever, if it fits into the general dynamics of the thing.

"For the Dahlberg Diver you make the tail very long and of soft materials. I like rabbit and Flashabou for this particular fly because it gets soaked up real good. When you pull it the fly gets shorter and when you slow it down the fly gets longer because the vortex that the head makes causes the tail to get sucked up. If you tie the tail too short it won't even run because the whole tail gets sucked up in the vortex, so you have to make it long enough to escape that vortex.

"The idea is that you're using a floating fly and a fly that has a negative pull rather than a positive one. The fly will dig in a little bit, but it will still come out of the water so you can cast the thing; that's kinda the trick. You can fish it with a floating line and a split shot where legal or a fast sinking line with a reasonably short leader. Cast down and across and let the thing swing down; you have to be patient enough to let the line get to the bottom. Then you just tease it and ease it, across back and forth, back and forth, constantly backing up in front of the fish. A lot of times they'll take it right away; a lot of times you have to walk it down the pool, like a Hot Shot in a drift boat."

In the mid-1960's Dahlberg designed a deer hair fly for bass, the Flashdancer, which preceded his diver. as my effort at imitating the spinner. I had an old uided that had trouble catching fish and she ets with the others and always lose them. I felt it. She couldn't cast and it was dangerous to boat with a fly rod. I put a spinner on her line r quiet, and I told her to just hold it. I would ck and forth across the river and that would cept she kept trying to cast the spinner and lives.

ea dawned on me to just tie some reflective wing of a fly and see if it would go. I found e stuff straight on, like in the form of a Mick-'t do much. But I found if I tied a little deer it, it created a turbulence, a bubble chain, d work real well if it was made of the right nd flexible. Metallic didn't work as well as ay I created this little fly and it turned into uth fly. The old lady started catching 16 went into the money."

the Flashdancer "is pretty much the same ometimes I'll weight it. I also use it with The deer hair head may seem incongru- but the deer hair is needed to create tur- Flashabou into action." He's tried vari- but has found gold, silver, and some- abou work the best.

the Flashdancer like a spinner: down t on an up to downstream cast. It's h on or it turns a fish off and it's best way to *pulse* a system, too, and look aught steelhead on it in fast riffled spinner in; just swing it across and ing you fish in a slow pool and just pe they'll bite it."

ASTICS

e most innovative field of fly tying rend will undoubtedly continue many traditional natural materi- protected by law from importa- ch as jungle cock and polar bear; for new materials is man-made designed or modified for fly synthetic dubbing and yarn, new "plastics" to make a home d by Crystal Flash, Cactus Che- ous braided nylon body mate-

revolution in plastic fly tying use it's limp enough to move le lots of reflective color and

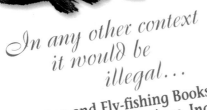
flash. It's major drawback is that for many applications it's too flashy and bulky. But for flies that you desire to be visible in clouded water conditions or when you need a lot of gaudy bulk to get the fish's attention, Flashabou is great stuff.

Crystal Flash is similar to Flashabou in that it's limp enough to move well in the water and it gives off lots of flash. Crystal Flash is crimped, which imparts a toned down effect, a more muted underwater flash than Flashabou. Whereas all the colors of Flashabou are bright, Crystal Flash colors can be either bright or somber—such as black, olive green, and blood red. In that regard you can tie a toned-down fly but add some subtle shimmer with strands of Crystal Flash. One of the advantages of Crystal Flash is that because of the crimping of the material, sparkles of light are reflected in all directions. Flashabou only reflects light from its top and bottom planes because it's flat.

Plastic chenilles, like Crystal Chenille, Cactus Chenille, and Spectra Chenille combine the reflective properties of a plastic material that is similar to Crystal Flash with a woven cotton string core as found in regular chenille. The fibers radiating out from the core are a dyed translucent plastic material that is crinkled, but it's a different material than Crystal Flash. Flashabou and Crystal Flash don't affect the sinking rate of a wet fly because these materials absorb such a small amount of water. However, even though the string-like core of the plastic chenille absorbs water, the numerous miniature blades of the plastic material slow down the sinking rate of the fly.

John Shewey ties his Summer Fling, which incorporates plastic materials, while at the same time retaining a touch of tradition by including hackle, floss and tinsel.

The overall effect of the plastic chenille is a variable, however. For example, if you use it as ribbing over a body material such as yarn, dubbing, or tinsel and use only a few turns of plastic chenille, the sink rate is similar to a fly without it. If the fly is tied with a floss body covered with tight wraps of plastic chenille, the fly sinks more slowly than a standard wet fly because the overall surface area of the blades of plastic slows the fly's sinking rate considerably.

There are several types of woven plastic body material available for tying bodies of steelhead flies. Some of these braided materials are opaque enough to mask the color of the hook. Others are translucent and when tied on the fly show the hook through the body material, so they require an underbody of floss, dubbing, or thin yarn. When tied over silver or gold tinsel, the translucent materials gleam with a subdued sparkle of reflected light, giving a nice effect, such as the floss-over-tinsel in Walter Johnson's Lady Coachman, Migrant Orange, and Evening Coachman. It looks lovely to us, anyway, and I suppose we naturally speculate that steelhead might find it attractive as well.

As shown in the color plates, examples of flies incorporating plastic materials include Dave McNeese's Deschutes Madness and John Shewey's Marabou Madness and Summer Fling. While these flies embrace plastics, at the same time they retain a touch of tradition by including hackle, floss, and tinsel. Another approach is to modify a traditional fly such as the Polar Shrimp with plastics, as in McNeese's version, the Plastic Polar Shrimp, or Bob Wagoner's Polar Shrimp tied with Edge Bright.

I look forward to the day when some as yet unknown plastic material will replace polar bear, calf tail, squirrel tail, deer hair, and bucktail for wing material on steelhead wet flies. Polar bear is the best material for steelhead flies, but the bears need our protection. Calf tail or kip tail is coarse and the tips don't stack nicely. Squirrel tail is fine for small flies, but is limited because of its coarseness and the black barring makes for difficult dyeing. Skunk tail fibers are too delicate; they break when you tighten the thread. Monga ringtail is also short and delicate and we should protect those animals, too. Deer hair and bucktail are commonly used because they are readily available, take dye well, are inexpensive, and stack easily. Besides tending to flair out when tied, the main drawback to deer hair or bucktail in a wet fly is that the material is hollow and retards sinking.

There are some nylon wing materials available, but they are not yet up to snuff for steelhead flies. These plastics are functionally able to stand in as wing material on wet flies because the nylon moves well enough in the water and the material is available in various colors. The main drawback is aesthetics—the ends of the nylon material are scraggly and not tapered, making it tough to make a pretty fly with what is presently available.

Plastic materials used for fly tying are by-products of other industries. Although dear to us, the fly tying market is so limited that manufacturers don't make thread, floss, Flashabou or Crystal Flash for fly tyers. Our materials are primarily discovered and converted from the manufacturing world by fly tyers. In this vein of discovery, I hope that an investigative fly tyer will soon find a plastic hair wing material to replace many of the natural materials that we now use.

If you were to look in the fly boxes of ten different fly fishing steelheaders, I would guess that you would find nine out of the ten had at least one fly in his or her box tied with "plastics". And in most cases, there would be numerous flies tied with plastic materials for summer and winter steelhead. One thing is certain: "plastics" are here to stay and more plastic materials will be introduced in years to come. While some tyers will undoubtedly reject these new synthetics, the majority of steelheaders will enjoy experimenting with these new materials, for developing innovative tying techniques and in creating new flies.

HOOKS ARE THE MOST IMPORTANT COMPONENT

Flies look differently when tied on a different style of hook, and swim differently according to fly shape, hook shape, weight of the hook, and weight and configuration of the completed fly. Fly design rests on this premise: what do you want the fly to do in the water, and how will the materials that you select contribute to that fly design, centered around the most important component, the hook?

Mustad and Eagle Claw hooks have changed very little over the years, with this exception: Mustad has its "Accu-Point" and Eagle Claw has its "Lazer Sharp" series; both of which are chemically sharpened hooks that are much sharper than their previous hooks. Mustad's Accu-Point hooks feature a smaller barb and they claim they are also 20% stronger than their standard hooks. Eagle Claw has added a cryogenic treatment to some of its Lazer hooks. The hooks are immersed in a super cold bath of liquid nitrogen for several hours, then returned to room temperature. The hooks are marketed under the name "Diamond Point" to illustrate the fact that the metal in the hook will stay hard longer. Both of these manufacturers have improved their products but still subscribe to the business attitude of making as many hooks as possible as cheaply as possible. If you want an inexpensive steelhead hook, look to Mustad or Eagle Claw.

The least changes have taken place at Partridge, which still offers hand made hooks. They are reasonably sharp, expensive, traditional, and often hard to get in the United States. Their "Low Water" hooks are some of the most gorgeous hooks in steelheading.

Partridge is currently making Alec Jackson's Spey Fly Hooks in a modified Bartleet style in several different sizes and finishes. The hooks are beautiful in the classic Atlantic salmon style of the Bartleet hook that originated in the 1800's in the British Isles. (Contact Alec Jackson, Box 386, Kenmore, WA 98028, 206-488-9806.)

The greatest change occurred when the Japanese started making hooks that are chemically sharpened, well designed, and well manufactured. These hooks are expensive but most serious fly fishermen have welcomed this new standard of excellence in hooks. Steelheaders in particular are using these new hooks because it only makes sense—when you travel a great distance, cast for hours, and finally get that longed–for hookup to a fish that may weigh from 6 to 16 pounds, you don't want a cheaply made hook of poor quality.

At this point, Tiemco is leading the field for fly tying hooks in general and steelhead hooks in particular. It will be interesting to see what happens as more Japanese hook makers send their wares to America, including Gamakatsu, Owner, Dai-Riki, Daiichi, and others. It would be great if an American manufacturer seized the opportunity and began

In his book, The Western Angler, *1939, Roderick Haig-Brown wrote: "Good wet flies for summer steelhead are, as are good wet flies for Atlantic salmon, dependent upon the fancy of the angler rather than upon the preferences of the fish."*

making superior hooks for fly fishing, but I don't see that happening in the near future.

The traditional steelhead hairwing streamer and most other steelhead flies are tied on a long shank hook, with the main differences being whether the eye is up or down or looped, or whether the hook wire is heavy or extra heavy.

The main advantage to the looped eye is that it offers a smooth loop of steel for attaching the tippet. The Tiemco looped eyes and most of the Partridge looped eyes taper nicely at the rear so the tyer can form a smooth fly. Mustad looped eye hooks are blunt at the end of the loop, causing an unnecessary tying hassle.

The quality of the finish and the closure of standard round hook eyes varies greatly between manufacturers—the cost of the hook is an appropriate gauge as to the overall quality of the finish. I believe I once lost a steelhead on a size 6 Dark Caddis, an effective Mike Kennedy pattern, because I tied the fly on an Eagle Claw 1197B hook and didn't close the eye of the hook with tying thread. I had just tied on the fly and had a fresh tippet, but the fly broke off when the fish started running downstream. After it happened I tried to determine what had gone wrong. When I checked my other flies tied on the same type of hook, I noticed that the eye closure on all the flies was rough, and rough enough on some of the flies to saw through a tippet. If there is a moral to this story, it's this: you can tie with inexpensive hooks and you can catch fish with inexpensive hooks, but you need to pick up the slack at the tying bench to overcome rough eyes or blunt looped eyes.

The only advantage to a lighter wire steelhead hook is when designing a pattern for surface work. Also, in years past a light wire steelhead hook was often much sharper than a standard or heavy wire steelhead hook and some steelheaders favored that quicker penetration by the more slender hook. That's not necessarily the case now; in fact, the Tiemco 7999 steelhead hook is just as sharp as the lighter wire Tiemco 7989. (I discuss hooks and fly design for greased line presentations in the "Greased Line Steelhead" chapter, and for surface flies in the "Dry Fly Steelhead" chapter.)

Combining steelhead wet fly design with non-traditional hooks is discussed in the "Winter Steelhead" chapter, primarily because of the winter steelheader's need for a hook that is less snag-prone than the standard steelhead hook. Although included in the winter techniques chapter, some of those flies are also effective under more hospitable water conditions as well. They include the Black Stonefly and the Steelhead Shrimp tied on the Tiemco barbless English Bait Hook with 2x heavy wire, the 207BL. A short shank hook such as the Tiemco 800B lends itself to the Steelhead Woolly Bugger or to Bill Black's Buster Leech tied with rubber legs. Both types of flies use lead eyes, which flip the fly upside down, reducing snags. Drifting egg patterns tied with yarn on bait-style hooks for dour summer run fish often provokes a strike.

DIFFERENCES IN TYPES OF WET FLIES BASED ON DESIGN

There are several distinct wet fly types that display a different action in the water or a different silhouette to the fish because of a variation in fly design.

The most common steelhead fly is the hairwing streamer, consisting of a tail, body, ribbing, front hackle, and a wing. Modifications in color combinations in the tail, body, hackle, and wing abound, but changing colors isn't a change in fly design. An example of this is found in the 1976 Trey Combs

Del Cooper—Mike Kennedy
 Tag: Flat silver tinsel
 Tail: Red hackle fibers
 Rib: Narrow silver tinsel
 Body: Purple wool
 Hackle: Red
 Wing: White bucktail

Surgeon General—Robert Terrill
 Tag: Fine oval silver tinsel
 Tail: Fluorescent red hackle fibers
 Rib: Silver tinsel
 Body: Purple yarn
 Hackle: Fluorescent red
 Beard: Guinea fibers
 Wing: Fluorescent white bucktail

The Matuka style of wet fly adapts readily to steelhead fishing because these giant rainbows are predators and the Matuka design mimics the outline of a baitfish.

1. Attach thread, tie in ribbing, and dub body.

2. Tie in matched hackle tips at the front of the fly. (Look for hackle that is wide and straight; curved hackle is difficult to work with.)

3. Secure the hackle to the body by wrapping the tinsel forward, through the hackle. (Moistening the hackle and stroking it forward helps, and a bodkin or needle will help keep the hackle from being trapped under the ribbing.)

4. Tighten the ribbing, tie down at the head of the fly and trim excess.

5. Tie in front hackle, wrap hackle, tie down and trim excess. (You can add on optional facing hackle, such as guinea.) Whip finish and cement head.

Rob Dougherty with a steelhead he hooked with a Matuka. The Matuka style looks different in the water because the wing and tail silhouette is radically dissimilar from the conventional hairwing pattern. It has a lot of built-in action and may trigger a remembered feeding response by steelhead to prey fish.

book, *Steelhead Fly Fishing and Flies,* where he lists the Del Cooper and the Surgeon General.

Some examples of other variations on the standard steelhead hairwing include substituting marabou for the tail hackle or the wing material, or substituting Flashabou or Crystal Flash for the wing, or going with plastic chenille ribbing over a body of floss, chenille, yarn, or dubbing. The color or flash effect may be different, but the fly design is still a basic steelhead hairwing streamer, and other than color or flash, all hairwings behave similarly in the river when fished.

THE STEELHEAD MATUKA

The Matuka style of wet fly adapts readily to steelhead fishing because these giant rainbows are predators and the Matuka design mimics the outline of a bait fish, particularly with the spiked-hackle simulation of the dorsal and caudal fins. The Matuka hackle swims well underwater, adding a sense of movement and life to the fly. Although you can fish the Matuka in the standard wet fly swing, the strong point of the Matuka is its broad outline when viewed from the side, so that in turn is the best way to present it to steelhead—in a slow crosscurrent greased–line presentation. You want just enough tension on the line to cause the fly to swim across the river while maintaining its broadside vector to the fish.

The Matuka style looks different in the water because the wing and tail silhouette is radically dissimilar from the conventional hairwing pattern. The Matuka style has a lot of built–in action and may trigger a remembered feeding response by steelhead to prey fish that exhibit a pronounced dorsal and caudal fin outline.

One such prey fish is the stickleback, a small bait fish that inhabits freshwater rivers and estuary systems that steelhead negotiate on their way to the salt as juveniles and again when the steelhead return as adults. Undoubtedly, juvenile steelhead prey on stickleback and sometimes returning adults do, as well. The stickleback has a prominent dorsal and caudal

fin configuration, which is well matched by the upright hackles in the wing and the vertical tail of the Matuka style.

One fall Dave McNeese was fishing a small steelhead stream in the Alaskan panhandle. He says, "I caught several steelhead that were stuffed with sticklebacks. I could tell they were feeding heavily because their bellies were bulging and some of the sticklebacks fell out of their mouths. I even saw a sculpin fall out of the mouth of one of the steelhead. And the funny thing was, the surface of the stream was completely calm—we had no idea all that feeding was going on. You would think that you would see some of those little fish jumping out of the water trying to escape or swirls from the steelhead chasing them."

McNeese says that on one 4th of July in the Redman Creek area of the North Umpqua he caught a 7-pound steelhead that had eaten several steelhead smolts—prey that a Matuka would imitate well.

I seldom see fly fishermen using Steelhead Matukas, possibly because the fly is considered hard to tie. The only mildly tricky parts are selecting two sets of matched hackles that are mounted on top of the fly, with concave sides facing each other, and sandwiched so they blend together to form a single thick wing and tail hackle, and then wrapping the rib-

Forrest Maxwell designed his Purple Matuka in the late 1970's for the North Santiam. It has since proven to be an effective fly on a number of steelhead rivers.

bing material forward from the rear of the fly through the hackle. It takes patience but no special skill; moistening the hackle and then guiding the ribbing with a bodkin through the hackle helps.

In his Scientific Anglers video, "Tying Attractor Flies", Doug Swisher demonstrates tying a trout Matuka. He trims the bottom of the wing hackle, but I leave it on for Steelhead Matukas because I favor a more full-bodied wing. If you use the full hackle, you need to tweak and tease the wing hackle into the upright position. I also add a front hackle for more underwater movement. Whether that front hackle simulates pectoral fins or gill covers on a prey fish is debatable, particularly since my favorite Matukas, the Halloween Matuka and the Purple Matuka, are tied with black bodies and fluorescent orange and fluorescent purple hackles, which are radical tints for bait fish colors.

You can also tie a Steelhead Matuka by using a stacked wing array using the same materials that you might use for wings on conventional steelhead streamers, such as calf tail, squirrel tail, monga tail, skunk, and marabou. You tie in a clump of wing where you would normally tie in the tail, wrap dubbing in front of that wing, add another wing that extends almost as far back as the first wing, add more dubbing, then another wing clump, then more dubbing, until you reach the head of the fly. Then you wrap a front hackle if desired.

Many early steelheaders were influenced by Atlantic salmon flies such as this Smith, tied around 1900.

In that same video Doug Swisher demonstrates tying an Aztec, a synthetic yarn fly very similar to the Matuka. In 1976 Dick Nelson invented the Aztec by using acrylic knitting yarn to form the Matuka-style spikey wing. The yarn is looped to the body of the fly, then combed out to form the silhouette that is the key to the Matuka.

In an article in *Outdoor Life* that same year, Nelson wrote, "The most important characteristic of the Aztec is its motion in the water. The flexibility of its acrylic fibers causes it to quiver with every subtle variation in the current, and to respond to any vibrations induced by the retrieve.

"The only tying material that can be compared with these acrylic fibers is marabou. But marabou has serious short–comings. It is expensive, collapses in the water and only expands during a pause in the retrieve, and it is extremely weak. The acrylic fibers, on the other hand, are inexpensive, maintain their expansion when they're in the water, and are strong. Because of the unusual properties of the acrylic fibers, the Aztec blooms in the water. It becomes a much larger fly, even though the fibers provide this body without weight."

I don't necessarily agree that marabou is expensive or that the collapsing–expanding properties of marabou are a disadvantage; in fact, that "breathing" action is a true asset in numerous flies. However, marabou is delicate stuff when put through the paces of steelhead fly fishing.

Acrylic yarn Aztecs offer distinct advantages: the yarn is inexpensive and readily available in dozens of luminous and subtle colors; it remains intact even after hours of strenuous casting; the Aztec retains its Matuka-like shape in all but the stiffest currents; when wet the Aztec stays the same size as when dry, so you know what size Aztec you're fishing; and finally, because acrylic yarn absorbs little water, the Aztec can look bulky in the water without being heavy. For more information on his Aztecs and tying kits contact: Dick Nelson, 14748 Golf Links Drive, Los Gatos, CA 95030.

SPEY FLIES

The Spey style of steelhead wet fly is best suited for slower waters in the throat of the run and in tailouts, before the current quickens. The long undulating Spey hackle displays maximum movement in slower water—water that is too fast "collapses" the hackle around the body of the fly, diminishing the effect of the leggy Spey hackle. By contrast, in slower currents the standard steelhead hairwing streamer looks stiff when compared to the wispy Spey wet fly.

Steelheaders have adjusted to the lack of heron and Spey cock feathers by substituting pheasant rump and duck flank feathers for Spey hackle. Some of the most intriguing Spey designs use marabou, that master material for maximum movement in minimum currents.

Gary Alger combines the body and hackle material in his Marabou Spey series by wrapping the marabou as both the body and the Spey hackle. Inspired by traditional Atlantic salmon flies that use eagle marabou, Dave McNeese and Forrest Maxwell have substituted the commonly available turkey marabou to fashion bright flies that undulate nicely in the current, attracting steelhead to strike. (The Spey style of steelhead fly merits its own chapter, "Spey Flies Go West".)

STEELHEAD WET FLIES THAT RESEMBLE AQUATIC INSECTS

Dave Hall, a guide on the North Umpqua who has averaged over 120 days a year on the river since 1980, uses three flies that suggest aquatic insects, the Golden Stone Tie–down, October Caddis Tie–down, and A.P. Flash Black Nymph. He says, "I theorize that after steelhead re-enter freshwater they regain and rely on certain instincts that were very important in their early development. I think the fish *key in* with their freshwater surroundings to some extent, and large aquatic insects are part of those surroundings.

"These flies represent insects that are prevalent in the North Umpqua river system that steelhead are familiar with

Dave Hall, a guide on the North Umpqua who has averaged over 120 days a year on the river since 1980, uses three flies that suggest aquatic insects, the Golden Stone Tie–down, the October Caddis Tie–down, and the A.P. Flash Black Nymph. Photo by Pete Anderson

Early October on the Clearwater River in Idaho. Each year about 20,000 summer steelhead (mostly of hatchery origin) return beginning in late September and continuing through winter. The water is broad but wonderfully suited for wading and long–casting.
Photo by Frank W. Amato

because they were part of their diet when they were juvenile fish. But I'm not trying to match the hatch in any kind of traditional sense. I started fishing *natural buggy* patterns when the standard traditional patterns were not producing.

"I have been using the Tie–down patterns for trout for years with great success. All I did was enlarge them to accommodate steelhead and varied some techniques in their presentation. The Flash Black Nymph was a fairly standard A.P. pattern (from Andre Puyans, a noted California tyer who developed the series of A.P. Trout Nymphs). All that was needed was a touch of pearl Flashabou that I use on many of my nymph patterns.

"I use soft hackle for the long legs; and the tied-down thorax and flared wing makes a wonderful silhouette in the water. You can weight these flies for subsurface fishing or skate them unweighted. I always fish the Flash Black Nymph subsurface.

"For presentation techniques, I use a straight floating line: cast, mend, swing; or a dropper system using two of the same pattern, with the dropper fly weighted and the trailer fly unweighted. This approach makes the trailer fly very active. I will also vary the size of the two flies. I also use weight forward sinking lines and sinking shooting heads with a bounce technique and the wet fly swing. The bounce tactic involves a dead-drift approach where I lift the rod tip as the fly drifts, bouncing it off the bottom so it won't snag. I also skate the unweighted tie-down patterns with a floating line and very long leaders. This can be deadly, but it takes patience and lots of adjustment in leader length to get maximum skating distance from one side of the pool to the other."

Hall has also developed a Natural Crawler and a Black Crawler that feature hackle from chicken tail feathers, as found on the rump section of the saddle. Hall prefers natural black feathers, but it's the lifelike animation of the hackle that makes these flies effective.

Hall says, "The long soft legs give the fly as much action as any fly I've ever used. The feathers are tail pieces that are very seldom used, but I found them to be much better than rubber legs, which I can't stand. They are as good a silhouette pattern as I have found.

"These Crawlers can be weighted and fished deep, with a standard cast, mend, and swing technique, or bounced along

Soft hackle and Spider steelhead flies have their roots in the very beginnings of fly fishing. They are very similar styles of flies, particularly from a fly design standpoint.

Turning the Silver Hilton into a Spider type of soft hackle fly is a logical extension of the Hilton's mallard tail and black and gray mottling. Instead of grizzly hackle, the use of mallard, pintail, or gadwall flank feather as the front hackle enhances the built-in movement and gray subtlety of the pattern.

The traditional Silver Hilton is probably the only flared-wing steelhead fly still in wide use. The Silver Hilton might be considered a wet "Steelhead Adams".

the bottom. I like to fish them lightly weighted in deep tailouts and pump them through the water—they pulsate like crazy. I also fish them unweighted on a floating line with a long leader, swung just under the surface and agitated."

SOFT HACKLES AND SPIDERS

These steelhead flies have their roots in the very beginnings of fly fishing. Soft hackles and Spiders are very similar styles of flies, particularly from a fly design standpoint. In fact, they are so similar that I consider the terms as synonymous.

In his book *Steelhead Fly Fishing and Flies*, Trey Combs credits Al Knudson as the first to use Spider flies for steelhead in the 1930's. Flies dressed with soft webby hackle date back to ancient times, to the very inception of fishing with an artificial fly. In his massive book *Trout*, Ernest Schwiebert quotes from a second century Roman author, Claudius Aelianus: "The fisherfolk wrap ruby-colored wool about their hooks, and wind about this wool two feathers, which grow under a cock's wattles and are the color of dark wax."

We can easily infer that the first flies were wet flies because even today it takes generations of controlled breeding and specialized care and feeding to raise roosters that sport hackle stiff enough to support a dry fly. Also, the hooks of yesteryear were too coarse to afford proper dry fly lightness.

In *The Practical Angler,* 1857, W.C. Stewart wrote, "We think the cock hackle by no means deserving of so much attention as is bestowed upon it, being too stiff and wiry." Stewart wrote of tying flies in his hands, without a vise, twisting the silk thread and the soft hackle of the Spider style of the fly together, so the thread would reinforce the hackle. Of using a pliant feather he wrote, "So soft are they, that when a spider is made of one of them and placed in the water, the least motion will agitate and impart a singularly life-like appearance to it, whereas it would have no effect upon a cock-hackle."

Since the chief criterion of the feather is that it be supple and snakey while underwater, there are numerous feathers that fall under the category of soft hackle or Spider hackle. Stewart wrote, "Amongst those most serviceable to the angler are the small feathers taken from the outside of the wings, as also from the neck and shoulders of the following birds: the starling, landrail, dotterel, mavis, grey plover, golden plover,

partridge, and grouse." Stewart listed six patterns in his book and had nine patterns in the color plates that were soft hackles or Spiders. Even though he was writing of trout fishing in the British Isles over a hundred years ago, we can still glean the soft hackle concept for designing steelhead flies.

Effective soft hackle steelhead flies use marabou, grouse, partridge, pheasant rump, hen hackle, or duck flank feathers such as mallard, pintail, widgeon, shoveler, or wood duck.

The Spider variation can also be applied to many traditional hairwing patterns by using a wide webby front hackle instead of a stiff rooster feather. Consider for example the traditional Silver Hilton, which is probably the only flared-wing steelhead fly still in wide use. The Silver Hilton is a salt-and-pepper pattern, consisting of a mallard flank fiber tail, black chenille body ribbed with silver tinsel, flared out grizzly hackle tips for the wing, and grizzly front hackle. The combination of basic black set off by a bit of reflective tinsel and the breakup contrast of the grizzly and mallard has hoodwinked many a steelhead into striking, particularly in low, clear flows when a subtle fly is often most effective. The Silver Hilton might be considered a wet "Steelhead Adams." Turning the Silver Hilton into a Spider type of soft hackle fly is a logical extension of the Hilton's mallard tail and black and gray mottling. The use of mallard, pintail, or gadwall flank feather as the front hackle enhances the built-in movement and gray subtlety of the pattern. Wood duck, widgeon, bronze mallard, or shoveler flank feathers give a more brownish overall effect for the alternative dressing, the Gold Hilton, which has a gold tinsel ribbing.

When we choose a fly to fish for steelhead we often follow such scientific factors as hunches, attractiveness of certain colors, and the name of the fly, much like those who bet at horse races. There is certainly nothing wrong with that, and when you catch a fish, your hunch is confirmed. Changing from a large fly to a small fly or from a brilliant fly to a somber fly or vice versa is often as systematic as we get.

The next time your usual wet fly approach doesn't pan out, try changing to a fly of a different design—one that offers the fish a different action or silhouette in the water, and vary your presentation to make the fly seem totally different than your previous offerings.

Spey Flies Go West

II

The exact origin of the first Spey fly is lost in the mists of the fly tying and fly fishing folklore of the last century. We know that the style originated on the Spey River in northeastern Scotland and is characterized by long flowing hackles. The first Spey flies were tied with feathers from a specific rooster, the Spey-cock, that lived in the Spey River valley. This chicken has since attained a certain mystical quality because it is now extinct.

The Spey rooster was a jumbo capon, a neutered bird of about 15 pounds, which was raised for its hackles. The feathers used for Spey flies were the dozen or so large saddle hackles that formed part of the tail fan. Spey roosters grew hackle in a variety of colors: dun, black, brown, reddish brown, and variegated. Unfortunately, the last Spey roosters died before World War II.

Many Spey flies were also tied with feathers from the great blue heron, a bird now protected under international law. Early Spey flies such as the Grey Heron, Gold Heron, Black Heron, Carron, and Lady Caroline were tied with palmered heron hackle.

In the Scottish highlands where the Spey style originated, the gillie not only guided his sportsman, but often supplied the flies. All over the world, fly tyers tend to make use of materials readily at hand. So it's not hard to imagine a stone cottage braced against Scotland's cold wetness, with wood smoke wisping from the chimney, and the gillie tying flies. By kerosene lamplight, his rough but dextrous hands built a fly using saddle hackle from a favorite rooster or a heron feather found along the river's edge the day before.

It seems fitting—herons are of the river and a fly tied with heron already has the kiss of good luck. Spey flies share a bond with their gaudy Atlantic salmon brothers-of-the-fly in that they are historically rooted in Atlantic salmon fishing tradition. They are less colorful than most Atlantic salmon patterns and less complicated to tie. But the beauty of the Spey fly lies in understatement; they are built with materials of subtle coloration that are intertwined with glints of floss and tinsel.

In addition to heron or wide saddle hackle, traditional Spey patterns included yarn, seal fur, floss, tinsel, and feathers from ducks such as mallard, teal, and European widgeon. Most Spey flies were tied with a dark brown wing of either bronze mallard flank feather or oak turkey.

Even with a name like the Purple King, Spey flies were somber; the body of the Purple King is a rich king's-robe purple yarn, plush with subtlety. The classic Lady Caroline Spey was tied in earthtones of olive and brown, palmered with gray heron hackle. The original dressing, as far as we know, included a tail of reddish-brown golden pheasant breast feather, which is unusual because most Spey patterns don't include a tail.

In *Salmon Fishing*, by Eric Taverner, 1931, he quotes one of the earliest works on Atlantic salmon flies. The *Driffield Angler* was published in 1808 by Alexander Mackintosh, who wrote: "I caught one (Atlantic salmon) when angling with the fly at Castle-Menzies in the year 1765, that weighed fifty-four pounds and a half." Mackintosh listed seven flies, including the **Black Dog,** which had this dressing:

Wing: bluish feather from a heron wing intermixt with spotted reddish ones of a turkey's tail
Body: lead-colored pig's wool from under the ear; ribbed small gold twist
Throat and hackle: large black cock's hackle
Head: dark green mohair spun on dark green silk

Taverner mentions that Mackintosh recommended a four piece 18-foot rod with an interchangeable tip that was used for spinning. The end of the tip incorporated six to nine inches of whalebone to absorb the fish's strike. Mackintosh also wrote: "Remember, with all your dubbing to mix bear's hair and hog's wool, which are stiff and not apt to imbibe water, as the fine fur of most other kinds of dubbing do."

It's interesting to note that 100 years before the American Civil War, Mackintosh was catching Atlantic salmon with a fly tied with large rooster saddle hackle for the throat and hackle and heron feather for the wing. It's easy to speculate that tyers would begin using heron feathers for the body hackle, as well.

Syd Glasso tied this Silver Doctor in 1979.
Facing Page: *The steelhead is now a resident of a few rivers in South America where ocean feeding sometimes makes them exceptionally fat for their length. Photo by Frank W. Amato*

Many early Spey flies were dressed on a long shanked Dee hook, influenced by Dee strip wing patterns from the Dee River country, the rivershed just south of the Spey Valley. Spey flies also lend themselves to an extended hook to show off their wide hackle, but the wings on Spey flies have a more hooded effect, often tied to form a humped style of wing over the body of the fly. The Dee strip wing looks totally different, being split to form two wings straight back over the body.

However, Dee and Spey flies show a great deal of similarity in their characteristically leggy hackle. It's debatable which style originated first; both styles may have grown in an organic fashion, with gillies and fishermen exchanging ideas and flies between neighboring river valleys.

Autumns On The Spey, written by A.E. Knox in 1872, lists 16 patterns developed in the Spey River Valley, including several series of flies such as Speals, Reeachs, Kings, and Herons. None were actually named Spey flies, so we might assume that the term Spey fly came to denote a style characterized by the fly body palmered with wide saddle hackle or heron.

Spey fly circa 1870 from Great Britian tied with a twisted silk gut eye.

Just four years later in 1876 in *A Book Of Angling,* author Francis Francis listed the Spey Dog: "This is usually dressed large for the spring, the long-shanked Dee hooks being preferred. Body, black pig's wool; up this is then wound some broad silver tinsel in widish rings; over the tinsel is laid on a large black feather (it can hardly be called hackle) with a lightish dun tip, taken from the side of a Scotch cock's tail. The feather is dressed the wrong way, so that the hackle stands out abruptly, and is carried round the opposite way to the tinsel, as some of the tinsel crosses it; over this hackle is wound some gold tinsel, not side by side with the silver, but quite independent of it. This aids in the glitter of the fly, and strengthens and keeps the hackle secure. At the shoulder a teal hackle; wing, a good wad of gold pheasant tail, with two long strips of grey mallard with brownish points over it. The fly can be varied by using a brown hackle and turkey instead of gold pheasant tail; add also orange silk between the tinsels."

Some Spey flies were tied so that the hackle was bound down by counter winding tinsel through it, while others were tied so the tinsel was laid next to the hackle stem as it was wrapped along the body. Spey flies were also tied using feathers from both rooster and heron; the effect was either a hooded shrimp-like fly or a spread-out Woolly Worm type.

Francis also included portions of a letter he received from Mr. C. Grant of Aberlour about two of Mr. Grant's favorite Spey flies: "The hackles are got from the common Scotch cock, and lie on each side of the tail, at the tip of the wings. The cock is rarely to be met with except with Spey fishers, who breed them for the sake of their feathers." Mr. Grant also wrote, "Without having any prejudice against gaudy flies, I would prefer Purple and Green Kings with their numerous offspring, provided I could get proper hackles to tie them, to any flies that could be used on the Spey." In *The Art Of The Atlantic Salmon Fly,* 1987, the late Joseph Bates included a color plate with three flies that honor members of the Grant family, of Castle Grant, on middle Spey: the Mrs. Grant, Glen Grant, and Miss Grant. The Glen Grant and Miss Grant exhibit that unique characteristic of the Spey fly, long heron hackle palmered up the body.

The late angling author Roderick Haig-Brown was one of the first to present a Spey fly to steelhead. He was born and raised in England, schooled in the wiles of brown trout and Atlantic salmon and the flies used to fool them. In the 1920's when he first opened his tackle bag to fish his adopted waters in British Columbia, his predilection was to use Atlantic salmon flies for steelhead.

In his book, *The Western Angler,* 1939, he wrote: "Good wet flies for summer steelhead are, as are good wet flies for Atlantic salmon, dependent upon the fancy of the angler rather than upon the preferences of the fish. One could fish satisfactorily through a season with a range of full-dressed Jock Scotts, on hook sizes from 1 or slightly larger up to 12. Most of the flies tied for Atlantic salmon will catch fish.

"Like most fishermen, I generally carry with me a tremendous diversity of flies; but if some unkind realist ordered me to confine myself to three wet flies only I should choose without hesitation the Silver Lady, Jock Scott, and the low-water Lady Caroline.

"For greased-line fishing, I think only two flies are necessary, the Blue Charm and the Lady Caroline; even the Blue Charm is probably superfluous, but on a really dark day it is possibly a little more effective than the Lady Caroline. Steelhead like the Lady Caroline surprisingly well, whether she is fished as a simple wet fly or by the greased-line method."

It's not surprising that Haig-Brown found the Lady Caroline Spey an effective fly; the seductive hackle of the Spey style gives the fly a maximum of underwater movement with a minimum of bulk. The fly is non-fouling; it doesn't wrap its

A picture of the late Syd Glasso with his Wheatley fly box and four favorite flies he originated and tied.

hackles and wing around the shank of the hook and distort its underwater movement.

Steelhead responded by biting the fly, probably for two reasons: the Spey resembles shrimp to a degree, triggering the latent feeding instinct of the returning steelhead; and secondly, many steelhead attack flies because the fly is intruding on contested territory—the run up the natal river is a spawning run, even though most steelhead will be in the river several months before they actually spawn.

One color plate in the Bates book shows a Black Dog tied by the late Syd Glasso in 1975, with a bright mixed wing that is representative of the Atlantic salmon flies tied in the late 1890's. Although the fly resembles the Mackintosh Black Dog of 1808, the Syd Glasso Black Dog is tied in the Spey style, which may have been a personal adaptation by Glasso.

Bates told me: "The Black Dog is typical of many of the older patterns in that it has been varied by a hundred different people. It depended on their whim. They thought they could improve it or they didn't have the right feathers so they used substitutes. Syd Glasso varied it into a steelhead fly."

SYD GLASSO'S OLYMPIC TORCH STILL GLOWS

Inspired by the rivers he fished on the Olympic Peninsula, Glasso was the first to adapt the Spey style for creating a series of Spey steelhead flies: Sol Duc Spey, Sol Duc, Sol Duc Dark, Polar Shrimp, Courtesan, Orange Heron, Gold Heron, Brown Heron, and Silver Heron. (These patterns are listed in *Steelhead Fly Fishing and Flies*, 1976, by Trey Combs, which is a fascinating account of much of our steelhead fly fishing heritage.)

Syd Glasso taught junior high school in Forks, Washington, eventually retiring as principal. He also taught fly tying and fishing to interested students, including Dick Wentworth. Dick says, "Mr. Glasso was always throwing a challenge out to us. He would tie a fly and when he and I would get together he would challenge me to do it just a little bit better. So I would either add a little or take away a little. He would instill the challenge in me by saying, 'What do you think of this, Dick?' I would then go home and try to do it a little different, like placing a Durham Ranger wing in the Sol Duc fly. Or maybe I would dye a pheasant crest hot orange. But you know, he could always tie them just a little bit better."

Wentworth inherited much of Syd Glasso's fishing tackle and a number of Syd's flies. Dick says, "Syd Glasso was like a father to me. In fact, in many ways he was more of a father to me than my own father. Syd and I first started fishing together in 1958 when I was 18 years old. I'm not ashamed to say it, but when Syd died on September 6, 1983, it was like someone carved away part of my heart.

"We always called him Mr. Glasso because everyone respected him. He just brought that out in people. Even after fishing with him since the late 1950's, there I was in my late middle age calling him Mr. Glasso. Sure, there were times when I called him Syd, but to me he was always Mr. Glasso.

"When Mr. Glasso got out of school he would go down to the river; I wouldn't get off until 4:30 or 5 and even though I would have all my gear laid out I would rush down to the river and many a time Syd would already have two steelhead on the beach. It was nothing in the 50's and 60's to catch 30 steelhead a year on flies."

When Wentworth first met Mr. Glasso as a junior high school student in 1954, Syd was already tying Atlantic salmon patterns. Dick says, "I would go over to Syd's house in the evenings after school and his wife Evelyn would be knitting. I particularly remember Syd trying to adapt a Green

Highlander to steelhead. I remember thinking that was the most beautiful fly I had ever seen."

In 1959 Syd Glasso placed fifth in the *Field & Stream* fishing contest with an 18-pound, 12-ounce steelhead caught on a Sol Duc fly on its namesake river on February 22, 1959. He was using a 9-foot, 9-weight Orvis Battenkill cane rod balanced with a Hardy Perfect.

Glasso also refinished bamboo rods for fishing friends like Wes Drain. But the real legacy of Syd Glasso lies in his adaptation of Atlantic salmon Spey flies to steelhead patterns, and in the development of his own series of unique steelhead Spey patterns.

Syd Glasso's Bogdan with flies he tied: Dark Sol Duc on top, Orange Heron in the middle, and Black Heron on the bottom.

THE MR. GLASSO SPEY FLY

In honor of Syd Glasso, Dick has developed his own Spey pattern called the Mr. Glasso. On March 14, 1981 Wentworth caught a 21-pound, 8-ounce steelhead on the Sol Duc River on 8-pound tippet with his Mr. Glasso fly, using a special sinking fly line that he and Glasso had developed for winter steelheading. Dick was using a 9-foot, 9-weight Orvis Battenkill cane rod he built from a blank in 1960 and a Bogdan "Steelhead" model reel.

Wentworth says, "I committed myself to fly fishing in 1958 or 1959 because it just got too easy fishing with hardware for steelhead. I just wanted to do it with a fly—I just wanted to do it the hardest way I knew how. Of course, I had a good teacher in Syd Glasso. He kept me on my toes, throwing that challenge in front of me to keep doing it better.

"At first," Wentworth continues, "when I was fishing with him, Mr. Glasso let me fish through the water first. Then after awhile, it was like a graduation when the time came: Syd said, 'You take the lower drift and I'll take the upper.'

"In those days we were using a Gray Orange or Grizzly Orange fly, which turned out to be the forerunner of Syd's Orange Heron," Wentworth says.

The Gray Orange and Grizzly Orange are also echoed in Wentworth's tribute to Syd Glasso, the Mr. Glasso Spey fly.

Wentworth ties the Mr. Glasso fly with wine colored 6/0 thread on a size 1 or 1/0 Low Water Veniard hook, with a silver rib, fluorescent orange floss, hot orange seal fur, natural or dyed black heron hackle, hot orange guinea throat hackle, and four matched hot orange hackle tips for the wing, topped with a dyed hot orange pheasant tippet.

Not all of these materials are readily available, therefore substitutions are in order: Alec Jackson's Spey hook or the Partridge Low Water Salmon hook or the Tiemco 7999; a fur dubbing with guard hairs, such as dyed rabbit with Antron added for sparkle; and wide hackle dyed black, such as duck flank feathers, pheasant rump, or saddle hackle. To get the black color, Wentworth first dyes the feather with dark brown RIT, then overdyes with black RIT.

Wentworth says, "Syd and I had a way of doing the body that's our trademark. First came two turns of some type of fluorescent floss, then we would split the floss and put the seal in it and twirl it in our fingers. Wayne Buszek first did it that way. It gives the seal a halo effect that is mirrored in the tinsel. The floss marries into the seal; the seal actually covers a bit of the body floss a little. It's not a distinct junction where the floss and the seal meet, but a gradual buildup of the forward body so everything looks sleek and isn't choppy looking.

"I strip the heron and tie it so the natural curve of the feather flows to the back of the hook. For the guinea I use as fine stemmed a feather as I can find and wrap maybe one and a half turns, maximum. I prefer black guinea with small speckles so that when I dye it hot orange, I get tiny orange speckles in the hackle.

"I like to fish the Mr. Glasso in low, clear water in March and April, especially on the Sol Duc River. I fish it on a wet fly salmon swing, 3/4 down and across, and keep the fly sunk on a fast sinking line. I try to get above the steelhead and let the fly swing so the fly comes straight down to the fish.

"In March and April when cottonwoods were just starting to bud out," Wentworth says, "Glasso liked to take a bit of a cottonwood bud and rub it on his rod handle and it would smell good, fresh like the season, and I still do that when I'm out on the river. It's a tradition that I picked up from Syd. That is the neatest time on the river, especially when a fresh run of steelhead is in."

Syd Glasso is gone but the Sol Duc River on the Olympic Peninsula still flows much as it has for the last millennia; Quillayute Indians power four-wheel-drive Broncos and Blazers; and Atlantic salmon Spey flies adapted to steelhead by Glasso and his protege Dick Wentworth still swim Olympic Peninsula rivers.

WALTER JOHNSON SPEYS

Glasso influenced other pioneering steelhead fly rodders like Walt Johnson: "When I started fishing with Syd Glasso on the Peninsula for winter run steelhead in the early 1950's and saw how effective his Spey flies were, I got the idea for my Deep Purple Spey.

"This is beyond doubt my most consistent producer, particularly on rivers with a light bottom such as the North Fork of the Stillaguamish. It took many years before steelhead anglers accepted purple as a viable color in a steelhead fly. Actually, the only one in use back in the 40's and 50's was Ken McLeod's Purple Peril, both wet and dry versions.

"Upon this foundation I devised my own version using the Spey tie with red golden pheasant body feather for wings and Chinese pheasant rump feather for body hackle. The beauty of this pattern is that it can be effective in all conditions of light and water.

"I have probably had more success with this pattern, particularly for summer run steelhead, than any fly I have

Walter Johnson fishing in August 1969, using his favorite style of fly, the Spey. One of the first to use Speys for steelhead, he also originated a series of Spey flies. Photo by Craig Shreeve

used over the ensuing years. Now it is over 30 years later and I still reach for this fly when the going gets tough."

In the 1950's Walter Johnson developed another Spey pattern, the Red Shrimp, after a trip to the steelhead waters of the upper Columbia with Ralph Wahl. Since then Wells Dam has forever inundated the Columbia at Pateros, Washington.

Walt says, "We had some spectacular steelheading at the mouths of both the Entiat and Methow rivers. Most of the anglers at that time were not fly fishermen, however, we befriended a couple of locals who were kind enough to give us some tips on the best water. One such angler was an auto mechanic from Chelan by the name of Ray Olsen. He took most of his fish on a simple fly with red chenille body and hackle.

"As the Columbia had a dark colored bottom in that area I surmised that a red fly showed up better under this condition. This prompted me to return home and devise the Red Shrimp with the Spey style of tie to give it the most action possible in the big river."

On both the Red Shrimp and the Deep Purple Spey, Johnson uses brown Chinese pheasant rump feather as the Spey hackle. He says, "I don't like the greenish shade of feather for these flies. I believe Spey flies give an added attraction whether fished sunk or greased line as the long undulating hackles provide extra enticement to excite steelhead into striking."

OTHER STEELHEAD SPEYS

Steelheaders continue to craft their own Spey flies. Keith Mootry's Purple Spey is deadly on steelhead in the North Santiam River in Oregon. Mootry ties his Spey with an orange floss butt, purple seal body ribbed with flat silver tinsel, black heron Spey hackle, guinea front hackle, and matched purple hackle tips for the wing, an approach inspired by Syd Glasso's Orange Heron and the Sol Duc Spey.

Dave McNeese modified the Purple Spey by using golden pheasant tippets dyed purple for the wing and added purple dyed heron breast feather in front of the guinea throat. He does his own dyeing with acid dyes in special combinations that render exquisite fluorescent colors.

Dave recalls that Ralph Wahl once told him, "I always liked purple because it's dark, but still has color to it."

Bill Chinn ties two versions of his Pink Shrimp Spey as shown in the color plates. He dyes much of his own materials with Veniard dyes. The larger one is tied on a 1/0 Bartleet hook with 1/3 hot pink seal, 2/3 claret seal ribbed with oval silver tinsel, gray heron Spey hackle dyed hot pink, and a wing of bronze mallard. The smaller one is tied on an old style size 2 down eye English salmon hook, hot pink seal ribbed with oval silver tinsel, white heron breast feather dyed hot pink, and bronze mallard wing.

Joe Howell of the Blue Heron Fly Shop on the North Umpqua River, has designed four favorite Spey flies for his home river: Silver Streak, Black Phase Spey, Red Phase Spey, and Feather Strip Wing Spey.

Howell says, "Spey flies seem to produce best for me on the Umpqua in the fall and winter months. The movement provided by the extra long hackle 'trailers' aids in the fly's appeal, both to fish and fishermen alike.

Joe Howell, of the Blue Heron Fly Shop on the North Umpqua River, fishes Spey flies on his home river, particularly in the slower stretches of current that allow the maximum movement of the long hackle.

"While I do fish them blind, I prefer to spot the fish first, then use a slow strip retrieve, which often spurs dour steelhead into action. I just start a slow strip when the fly is about four feet from the fish. As the fly begins to pulsate and move away, steelhead will often charge the fly wildly. I've also had them follow for 20 feet before finally accepting or rejecting a stripped Spey fly."

SIMPLIFIED SPEYS

Simplified Spey flies depart from the traditional trail of their ancestors by incorporating materials that are easily obtained, particularly for the Spey hackle. One of the advantages of using heron hackle for Spey flies is the elegant length of the heron hackle, matching even the largest of steelhead hooks. Simplified Speys are usually tied on smaller hooks because alternative feathers are not as wide or as long as heron. These alternatives include pheasant rump, guinea, extra large rooster hackle, some turkey feathers, domestic goose flank feathers, and many of the duck flank feathers from mallard, widgeon, gadwall, pintail and others.

Found heron, pheasant rump, rooster hackle, and turkey feathers make fine Speys in their natural colors and are easily dyed. Duck flank can also be used in its natural state, but waterfowl feathers are too webby for most Spey applications, even when only one side of the feather is used.

BLEACHING FEATHERS BY BURNING

To modify these webby feathers for use as the palmering hackle on a Spey, you can use two different bleaching methods. When the feather is bleached to remove excess webbing in the feather, it's called "burning" because the bleach actually dissolves the feather by "burning" away organic feather fibers. If left in the bleach too long, the feather will completely "burn up." The disadvantage of burning the excess webbiness from the feather is that it makes the hackle brittle and stiff to a degree, depending on the density of the hackle and how much it's burned. The second method of bleaching is actually a whitening process that lightens the color of the feather for dyeing—it bleaches the color out of the feather.

To burn hackle, pour household bleach mixed in a ratio of about 1/2 cup of bleach in a quart of water in a bleach-proof container such as a white plastic bucket or a stainless steel or white enameled pan. (I wouldn't recommend using regular kitchen utensils for promoting marital bliss. Thrift stores often have inexpensive containers that are ideal for bleaching and dyeing feathers.) Empty metal coffee cans or tall metal juice cans work, but the disadvantage with cans is that it's difficult to see the feathers in solution. Cans work better for dyeing feathers. You will also need a pair of tongs to pluck the feather out of the bleach to check its "doneness" and for retrieving the feathers from the bleach solution when the feather is burned. You can also use tweezers or forceps but most are too short and not as handy as plastic salad bowl tongs.

There is no hard and fast rule for the absolutely correct mixture of bleach to water, but bear in mind that the rate of burning increases with added bleach and with a higher water temperature. If you mix bleach with warm tap water, the feathers will burn much quicker than with cold water—with hot water the burn is very quick—too quick, in fact, for adequate control over the process. Adding more bleach does the same thing. The burning proceeds faster but allows you less time between burning the webbiness from the feathers and total annihilation of the material. Other variables that affect burning time are the amount of natural oil in the feather, its webbiness, and the thickness of the hackle fiber. Burn just a few feathers at a time, and when you first try burning feathers, experiment with just one expendable feather.

The idea is to just remove the webbiness, so the instant the feather starts to "fan out" in the solution and begins to look thinner, immediately immerse the feather in a container with water mixed with vinegar, baking soda, or baking powder to stop the bleach-burn. (Agitate the baking soda solution ahead of time so it's well mixed.) Swish the feathers around in the baking soda solution, then rinse them thoroughly under tap water. It's helpful to process feathers of similar density together, as they tend to be ready at the same time. Otherwise, it's too easy to excessively burn feathers left in the bleach solution while rinsing the less webby feathers you've done first. If you get pressed for time, simply leave the already burned feathers in the baking soda solution while waiting for the other feathers to finish burning. When burning a feather, watch the webby flue at the base of the feather because it will be the first to burn—when it starts to fan out or thin, immediately remove the feather and dunk it in the baking soda solution. The webby flue fibers act as indicators of the burning rate. Afterward, to reduce brittleness in the burned hackle, you can put hair conditioner on the feathers.

I recommend burning feathers in a well ventilated area; if you do it in the kitchen sink, turn the exhaust fan on high and open a window. Wear a pollen or dust mask because bleach fumes can be real nasty. Wearing eye protection, old clothes and an apron is also appropriate. (I have a favorite pair of comfortable pants that I can't wear to social occasions because drops of bleach solution splattered onto a conspicuous part of the pants.) Wearing rubber or plastic kitchen gloves makes sense and cover the kitchen work area with newspapers.

BLEACHING FEATHERS FOR DYEING

Many feathers tie nice Spey flies in their natural coloration, such as pheasant rump, burned teal or mallard. This second bleaching procedure ushers in a vast panorama of Spey flies tied in all the dyed "flavors" available to the avid colorist because this bleaching method lightens the color of the feathers to better accept the dye.

First, remove the fluff from the bottom of the feathers because it needlessly soaks up the lightening bleach. Because waterfowl feathers are so oily and all feathers retain a certain amount of dirt unless washed beforehand, it's beneficial to soak the feathers in a mixture of warm water and a strong dose of dish soap such as Ivory liquid before bleaching. Several hours are sufficient for upland game bird feathers, but waterfowl require an overnight soaking. After washing the feathers, rinse them thoroughly so all soap is removed, then gently squeeze excess moisture out of the hackle by stroking the feather between your thumb and forefinger, working from the base to the tip of the feather (without breaking the fibers, particularly with pheasant rump). Burned feathers don't require prewashing because the bleach has removed any dirt and oil. This method of bleaching feathers to lighten them is effective on dry or wet feathers.

The commonly available 10 volume hydrogen peroxide that you find at the supermarket is safe to use and will lighten feathers. Twenty volume hydrogen peroxide is available at most drug stores and beauty supply houses and works much better. The most effective lightener is basic white powder bleach hair lightener found at a beautician's supply house. By mixing a twenty volume hydrogen peroxide such as Clairol's "Clairoxide" liquid developer and "professional powder bleach for hair", you can lighten most feathers. Only the darkest won't bleach out to a creamy white.

The basic formula is one tablespoon of powder for each ounce of peroxide, but you may need a stronger mixture for darker feathers. You can remove the feathers from the solution after an hour, but half a day to an overnight soaking might be necessary for darker feathers and waterfowl feathers. After rinsing in water, the feathers are ready for dyeing and the bleach solution can be stored for future use. (The whitening solution may not be worth saving, though, because it quickly loses its effectiveness with each use.) This bleaching process tends to make the hackle a bit brittle, but not nearly as brittle as burning it.

DYEING FEATHERS

There are two basic ways to dye feathers for steelhead flies. The brilliant fluorescent colors you find in hackles at fly shops are obtained by acid dyeing, which should be left to professionals because it involves special dyes and hydrochloric acid, which eats containers, kitchen sinks, and plumbing.

In keeping with the philosophy of using readily available materials, most home dyeing is done with RIT or Veniard dyes, although dyes used for organic rug material like wool also work. RIT and Veniard dyes can be hot or cold-dyed. The resulting colors can be intense, but are much more subtle than acid dyed colors.

There are some problem colors, too, such as black and purple. The Veniard colors seem more true to fly tyer's desired colors, but Veniard's dyes can be hard to find. Black is always a problem because if you use straight black, you get a dark brown or a purplish black. Those can be useful colors, but to get a denser black you may need to mix black and brown dye or you can first dye with brown, then overdye with black. Purple and gray turn out with a grayish blue tint to them, so you need to add brown. By itself, brown turns out with pinkish overtones, so you can add black to darken the brown. Experimentation is easy and the materials for simplified Speys are inexpensive.

HOT DYEING

Just as when lightening with bleach, the hackle should be pre-washed and fluff removed because it needlessly soaks up dye. The rule with dyeing is that you can add dye to make a color darker but you can't make a color lighter.

For hot dyeing I use two tall metal juice or coffee cans because I don't need to clean the container after dyeing or worry about harming it. (A stained container is still suitable because seeing the feather change color isn't nearly as critical as the timing involved with burning hackle.) You will also need tongs and a colander. Hot dyeing instructions are usually included with the dye, but there are some basic differences between hot dyeing with powder RIT or Veniard versus liquid RIT.

To dye with powder the water is brought to a boil, then the dye is added at about one teaspoon of dye for a quart of water, stirred well. Then either turn the heat down or add a dab of cold water to lower the water temperature below boiling. Then add the feathers (but never to boiling water as it will harm them), stirring the feathers to soak the dye into the fibers evenly. Add 1/4 cup vinegar to the mixture to set the dye or the color will wash out when the fly is fished. (Cover the kitchen work area with newspapers.)

You can judge the resulting color of the dyed feather by removing it from the dye bath with the tongs and checking the color of the hackle stem, which will be pretty close to the color of the feather. It's not an exact gauge, but it gives you a fairly reliable approximation of the dyed color. The other rule when dyeing is that the color of the wet feather is always darker than when dried.

To further darken the feather in a hot powder dye bath, you have two options: increase the time the feather stays in the dye bath; or increase the amount of dye in the bath. To add dye with a powder solution, first remove the feathers, then bring the water back to boil. Add more powder to the boiling water, stirring well. Then cool the water and add the feathers.

Tongs work well for removing the dyed feathers if you are only doing a few at a time. Playing tong-and-feather in a

---

Facing Page: Speys are popular with steelheaders because they are pleasing to the eye, pleasing to fish and accommodate almost any steelheading tactic. You can fish Speys with sinking, sinktip or floating lines, in the classic wet fly swing, dead-drifted nymph style or with the greased line. Photo by Scott Ripley

This male fish from the Klickitat River was taken in the fall and reflects the coloration of a summer–run steelhead resident in the stream for probably two months or more. Coloration of steelhead as well as body conformation is sometimes quite different from stream to stream, reflecting age–old genetic traits. Photo by Frank Amato

batch of dye can lose its appeal, so I recommend the following method when dyeing feathers of similar density and webbiness. Next to the dye container, have another empty container with a colander resting on top of it. Make sure the second container is at least as big as the dye container. When the feathers are done pour the dye solution and feathers into the empty can, collecting the feathers in the colander. Tongs are handy for retrieving feathers that get stuck against the walls of the can.

The main difference between powder RIT or Veniard and liquid RIT dye is that you can add liquid RIT to hot water without boiling the resulting dye mixture. You can use hot tap water or warm the water on the stove, add the dye (after shaking the RIT bottle) at about 1/4 cup dye for one quart of water, add 1/4 cup of vinegar, and then add the feathers, stirring well. If you need to dye the feather darker, you can either leave it in the bath longer or add more dye. I prefer to use liquid RIT but you can't always find it in the colors you need.

Powder or liquid dye mixtures can be stored and they keep fairly well in airtight containers. The dye tends to drift to the bottom so the solution needs stirring before reuse. Each time you dye a feather, some of the dye is imbedded in the feather. Without adding more dye, the dye batch gets weaker. When you take the dye batch out of storage, you may want to add extra dye.

COLD WATER DYEING

Cold dyeing requires the least amount of effort, but produces more subtle colors unless the feathers are left in solution for several days to a week. You can use powder dye but the powder must be boiled and mixed beforehand; liquid RIT is best for cold dyeing. The feathers must be thoroughly cleaned and rinsed ahead of time; it doesn't matter if they are wet or dry. The flue should be stripped from the stem to conserve the dye.

You need a closeable container such as a wide mouth peanut butter or canning jar. Shake the RIT bottle vigorously, then pour the liquid dye into your container. Add 1/4 cup vinegar to set the dye, add the feathers, then fill the container to the top with water. Put the lid on tight, then shake the container well. Occasionally during the next few days, vigorously shake the container to further mix the dye with the feathers and the vinegar.

You can get a pretty fair approximation of the color of the feather by the color of the hackle stem. When you have the proper shade, simply remove the hackle and rinse it under tap water. You can store the dye in the same container for reuse at a later date.

DRYING HACKLE

One of the easiest ways to dry hackle is to first gently squeeze out the excess moisture by stroking the feather between your thumb and forefinger, working from the base to the tip of the feather. With the excess water removed, place the hackle on several layers of newspapers out of harm's way. Every so often, turn the feathers over and lay them on a dry spot on the paper, replacing the paper when it gets too wet. Another easy method is to place several layers of newspaper in the bottom of a cardboard box. That way the feathers won't blow away or become misplaced while they dry. If you have a lot of commotion in your drying area, use a cardboard box with a lid on it. It takes more time for the hackle to dry in the closed box, but the feathers will eventually dry without getting lost.

Be careful not to store your feathers in an airtight container before the hackle is dry because the feathers might rot.

Once completely dry, airtight containers such as jars are ideal because the hackles are safe from insects and will stay clean and dry, ready for tying.

Tight storage containers eliminate the need for moth balls. Naphthalene definitely won't do your lungs any good and might repel steelhead as well—steelhead zero in on their home river by "smelling" a specific molecule or set of molecules among millions of other molecules suspended in water, which is certainly more subtle than the odor of moth balls.

TWO TYING METHODS FOR HERON SUBSTITUTES

Dave McNeese has developed two methods for tying steelhead flies that look like Spey flies but are not tied in the usual manner. The first method uses pheasant tails from the Chinese, Lady Amherst, Golden, or Silver Pheasant. The tails are slightly burned as previously described to remove some of the natural fuzziness of the tail feathers. Then the feathers can be dyed any number of colors for the Spey hackle, including purple and black.

To tie in the hackle, Dave first spins on a little dubbing, then as he takes a wrap around the bare hook with the thread, he inserts several hackle fibers under the thread as you would on the throat or beard of an Atlantic salmon fly or a trout nymph. He then moves the hackle around so the fibers point out to the sides and bottom of the fly (if you are tying in a wing, if not, then move the fibers so they point out in all four directions). He then spins on another turn of dubbing, and then more hackle until the body and the Spey hackle are complete.

One of the advantages of this system is that you can use several different colors of hackle in one fly. Dave says one of his favorites has orange, purple, and blue pheasant tail fibers for the Spey hackle. Also, hackle fibers from the tail of most pheasants are much stronger and more durable than pheasant rump feathers.

Keith Mootry takes two lengths of two-pound monofilament, each several feet long, and secures one end in a vise. He then twists the monofilament several turns, inserts a hackle fiber, twists several turns, inserts another hackle fiber, and so on, leaving a space between the individual hackles. He uses two vises so he can secure the monofilament while he inserts the hackle. When hackle is mounted in the whole length of monofilament, he puts a drop of super glue every few inches

Dave McNeese is an accomplished and innovative fly tyer. He prepares many of his own materials with acid dyes in special combinations that render exquisite fluorescent colors.

to secure the monofilament hackle string. After sitting for an hour or so, the Spey hackle string is ready for tying. The method for tying in the hackle string is the same as for regular Spey hackle, except you rib with the hackle string first, then dub forward, covering the monofilament. This method is more complicated than the McNeese method, but the resulting Spey looks very similar.

The second tying method creates what could be called a Hair Spey. McNeese uses floss as the tying thread. After tying in the butt of floss he splits and coats it with Pliobond, then inserts polar bear, underfluff included. The polar bear/floss is then wrapped forward as you normally would. The underfluff of the polar bear hair forms the dubbing for the body of the fly and the longer hair fibers radiate out from the fly just as Spey hackle does.

Just as with using individual pheasant tail fibers, one of the advantages of using hair for the Spey hackle is that you can incorporate hair that is dyed different colors. In the Polar Bear Spey in the color plates the tag is flat silver tinsel, the butt is hot orange floss, the rear half of the dubbing/polar bear Spey hair is purple and the front half is hot orange. The wing is purple mallard topped with a golden pheasant crest dyed purple, and the front hackle is a golden pheasant tippet that is bleached and dyed purple and wrapped as a hackle. Some polar bear substitutes for this method include black bear, brown bear, squirrel tails of different types, dyed monga ringtail, skunk body hair, possum body hair, and others.

Tying the Simplified Spey

Attach thread. Tie in ribbing (tinsel or wire) and tip of Spey feather. Dub body.

Bring Spey feather forward as a palmered hackle, tie off and trim.

Bring ribbing forward, tie off and trim. (Ribbing may be wound parallel to the hackle, overlapping stem slightly for reinforcement or wound in opposite direction as hackle, crisscrossing it for stength. A bodkin or needle helps keep the hackle fibers out of the way while wrapping the ribbing.)

Tie in a front facing hackle such as guinea or duck flank feather, take one or two wraps, tie off and trim. Whip finish and cement head.

The author's Halloween Spey is a Simplified Spey using goose flank feather burned and dyed orange for the Spey hackle and black hackle tips for the wing.

TYING SIMPLIFIED SPEYS

The tying philosophy of Simplified Speys for steelhead revolves around the theory of using readily available substitutes for heron and seal fur. Simplified Speys are usually tied on smaller hooks because the hackle fibers in pheasant rump and waterfowl flank feathers are not as long as most heron feathers used in traditional Speys.

Rabbit fur blends make a suitable seal substitute, particularly when Antron and sparkle yarns are chopped up and added to the rabbit dubbing. Blending spikey natural furs such as mink, otter, and muskrat adds more guard hair to the rabbit blend. The sparkley poly yarns reflect bits of light, while the guard hairs poke out tiny fingers of movement and trap reflective bubbles of air which reflect light. White or creme colored rabbit can be dyed any number of colors, and most fly shops offer a dazzling display of blended dubbings of different materials.

Simplified Speys tied on smaller hooks use floss and tinsel, with less dubbing, resulting in slim Speys that blend color, light reflection, and the water–movement of Spey hackle such as guinea, teal, mallard, and pheasant rump. Using hackle tips for the wing eliminates bronze mallard or dark turkey, which can be hard to find. Hackle wings allow the Spey hackle to move more freely, and you can use wing feathers of almost any color, from vibrant fluorescents to subtle pale hues.

Forrest Maxwell adapted his version of the Skunk to a Spey style with his Deschutes Skunk Spey because he likes the black and red in the Skunk but wanted the movement of the Spey hackle. The tag is flat silver tinsel, the tail is a golden pheasant crest feather that is bleached and dyed red, the butt is red floss, the body is black dubbing ribbed with oval silver tinsel, the palmered Spey hackle is Chinese pheasant rump, the wing is bronze mallard, and the facing hackle is teal. Because Chinese pheasant rump feathers are so short, Forrest uses one for the Spey hackle and another for the front hackle.

He often substitutes gold for silver tinsel and turkey can be used in place of bronze mallard. Although Maxwell sticks with the red floss butt, with the substitution of a fluorescent green butt, you can tie a Green Butt Skunk Spey.

Richard Bunse's Rooster Spey incorporates Chinese pheasant rump feather for the body hackle and orange hackle tips encased with iridescent black rooster chicken tail feather as the wing. (You can substitute bronze mallard or turkey for the chicken tail feather in the wing.) Bunse says, "The Rooster Spey is a fly that has all the qualities of a good steelhead fly—subtle colors, life-like motion of the hackles and the wing, and the sparkle of the dubbed seal body. It is a pattern I use with confidence, and confidence is an important part of fly fishing for steelhead." (You can substitute a rabbit blend for the seal with equally fishable results.)

The Halloween Spey uses burned domestic goose flank feathers dyed hot orange for the Spey hackle, black dubbing ribbed with oval silver tinsel for light reflection, matched black hackle tips for a wing, and unburned dark guinea for the facing hackle. The burned goose is stiffer than heron or pheasant rump, so the hackle tends to stand out from the body of the fly in heavy current; when the hackle in more traditional Spey flies "collapses" and possibly becomes less effective in stiff flows, the Halloween Spey is a prime alternative. Using hackle tips for the wing instead of a hooded type of wing such as bronze mallard also allows the goose Spey hackle more movement.

When palmering the orange goose feather as the Spey hackle you have several options: you can work the hackle stem into the dubbing, burying the orange into the black dubbing; you can leave the stem on top of the dubbing for a band of contrasting color against the black body of the fly; you can counterwrap the ribbing through the hackle, which reinforces the hackle stem; or wrap the tinsel along the stem, hiding the stem with the tinsel so it appears that the hackle springs from the dubbing. You can also vary the color scheme. For example, you can use an orange Spey hackle over an orange body with gold tinsel.

In *Steelhead Fly Fishing and Flies*, Trey Combs wrote: "No freshwater gamefish is so willing to involve itself in our personal fly designs as the steelhead. This has permitted anglers unlimited latitude in exploiting their weakness for all things fluorescent and bright, somber and dark, large and small, while simultaneously creating in the fly tying tradition. The anadromous rainbow has challenged our ingenuity and imagination, and steelhead patterns are today among the most beautiful in angling."

SPEY SPIDERS

The Soft Hackle Spider originated as a trout fly in the north country in the British Isles. Al Knudson is credited with first using the Spider Soft Hackle style of fly for steelhead in the 1930's with his Wet Spider. (I explore the origin and ramifications of the Soft Hackle Spider in the chapter "Fly Design".) For tying flies, Soft Hackle and Spider are interchangeable terms—they mean the same thing, use the same materials, and result in identical flies.

The Spider Soft Hackle style is similar to the Spey in that they both exhibit long flowing hackle that is so attractive to tyers and to steelhead. The main difference is in simplicity—besides the palmered hackle, the Spey style includes a wing and sometimes a topping, and often a front hackle and a facing hackle. The Spider or Soft Hackle is usually just a body and a wide front hackle.

Spey Spiders combine these two traditional types of flies into one simple but elegant fly design that captures the best of both styles. A Spey Spider has a body, a Spey palmered hackle, ribbing to reinforce the Spey hackle, and a Spider soft hackle in front, with no wing.

Besides being more simply constructed than the traditional Spey, the Spey Spider has some design characteristics that make it attractive to steelhead. By eliminating the wing, the resultant fly has a very visible body, without the hooding effect of the traditional Spey. In many cases, the traditional Spey body is almost completely cloaked in the wing and heavy front hackle. The hooding effect of the bronze mallard or turkey wing also hampers the movement of the Spey hackle, forcing the Spey hackle on top of the fly to lay flat and clump toward the back of the fly, minimizing the movement of the hackle. The more open Spey Spider allows more light reflection from the tinsel and just as importantly, the Spey hackle flows more freely in the current because it isn't captured beneath a traditional wing of bronze mallard or turkey. Without the constraints of a wing, the wide Spider hackle also sways easily in the current.

The Spey Spider I tied for the color plates is but one example of this style of fly. It has purple dubbing, silver tinsel rib, Chinese pheasant rump dyed black as the Spey hackle, and guinea dyed purple as the front Spider hackle. When tying Simplified Speys I first select the Spey hackle, then match the hook size to the materials available. To tie the Spey Spider you need to match the Spey hackle and the Spider hackle for a balanced fly. One of the fascinating aspects of these flies is that there are no traditional Simplified Speys or Spey Spiders so you can use any color combination you want and vary the dubbing, floss, tinsel, or other ingredients in any number of variations.

In a way, as steelhead fly tyers we are involved in semantics; we might find the differences between traditional Speys and Spiders and these modified Speys very interesting, but the steelhead don't really care, but react according to instincts honed over the thousands of years that passed before the first fly was ever tied. As steelheaders we might develop more confidence in one style or another, but it's debatable whether a steelhead would reject a traditional Spey such as the

---

Tying the Halloween Spey, a Simplified Spey using goose flank feather for the Spey hackle

Select a prepared goose feather sized to the hook. (Use one side of burned and dyed feather.)

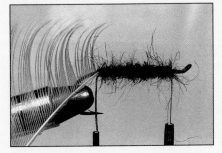

Tie in feather by tip, ribbing and dub body.

Bring feather forward, tie off and trim.

Bring ribbing forward, tie off and trim. (A bodkin or needle is helpful for keeping hackle clear of the ribbing.) Ribbing is wrapped in the opposite direction as the hackle, giving a cross hatch effect that helps protect the hackle.

Tie in matched hackle tips and trim. Tie in guinea hackle, wrap one or two turns, tie off the trim. Whip finish head and cement.

The greatest steelhead river of them all — each year the Columbia and its tributaries host about one half million summer and winter run steelhead. Here the river is shown near the mouth of the Klickitat River, Washington. Photo by Frank Amato

Lady Caroline and strike a Simplified Spey or Spider Spey, given the same set of circumstances and tactics.

Humankind as toolmakers, inventors, and tinkerers will continue to modify existing designs in all fields of endeavor, bulwarked with convincing theories. We will continue to remodel old flies and mutate new patterns because it's in our nature and is part of the fun of fly fishing.

Alec Jackson says, "I think all you need with a fly, to be honest, is a tail, a body, and a hackle. I'm not sure you actually need a tail when you get right down to it. The only reason you might need a tail on some flies is if you're using deer hair or something like that to hold the back end of the hook up. I think the fly needs to be a three dimensional fly rather than two dimensional. I'd call the classic flat, full dressed Atlantic salmon fly a two dimensional fly, and I'd call the Syd Glasso Spey or Al Knudson Yellow Spider three dimensional. That way, no matter which way the fish sees it, he gets a better chance at looking at it. It's like looking at a football instead of a knife blade. I think a three dimensional fly can be seen better and that's the way I tie my flies. I'm a firm believer in soft hackles. Being from the north country of England, my style of tie is really a north country style that's been adapted for the steelhead."

Alec Jackson's Pseudo Spey is an excellent example of what I call a Spider, although the blue eared pheasant that he uses for the front hackle flows back so far the result is very similar to a Spey Spider.

He says, "There's probably 18 or 20 different Speys that I tie with different coloring, trimming down the body or fattening up the body. I developed the Pseudo Spey as an easier way of tying Speys three or four years ago."

The Pseudo Spey in the color plates is tied on an Alec Jackson Spey hook size 1 1/2, silver finish, with a hot orange hackle fiber tail, rear half of the body is peacock herls twirled around oval silver tinsel, front half of the body is hot orange ostrich twirled around oval silver tinsel, then a hot orange hackle, blue eared pheasant hackle, then finished with another hot orange hackle.

(For more information on Alec Jackson's Spey hooks, contact The Yorkshire Flyfisher, Box 386, Kenmore, WA 98028, phone 206-488- 9806.)

To demonstrate how crazy semantics can become and also to illustrate the basic design differences between the traditional steelhead streamer, the Spider, the Spey Spider, and the Spey, we can examine Maxwell's Deschutes Skunk. The tag, butt, tail, body, and ribbing stay the same. With a front hackle of pheasant rump and a bronze mallard wing, the fly is a modified Skunk, one of the most widely used steelhead streamers. By eliminating the wing and adding a wide pheasant rump front hackle collar you have the Deschutes Skunk Spider. By eliminating the wing, keeping the broad front hackle, and adding a palmered pheasant rump hackle as the Spey feather, you have the Deschutes Skunk Spey Spider. With the palmered pheasant rump hackle as the Spey hackle, the pheasant rump front hackle, and the bronze mallard wing, you have the Deschutes Skunk Spey.

After meeting Syd Glasso and admiring his Spey flies, Gary Alger set about developing and perfecting Spey patterns of his own, such as the October Caddis Spey and the Golden Purple Spey. Alger's Golden Purple Spey is so named because of its purple dubbed body and the long reddish-brown golden pheasant Spey hackle and two smaller red phase golden pheasant feathers for the wing.

He says, "I believe the Spey fly is a superior design because it provides a silhouette that is consistent at all angles, giving the same appearance to the fish at whatever depth it is fished."

His Green Butt Spey in the color plates is an example of the traditional steelhead fly I most often see adapted to the Spey style, the Green Butt Skunk. His version has a flat silver tinsel tag, fluorescent green floss butt, black dubbing, oval silver tinsel ribbing, bronze mallard wing, blue pheasant Spey hackle, and guinea front hackle.

Alger's most radical Spey patterns are in his Marabou Spey series. The Purple Deceiver, Flame, Pink Prancer, and Marabou Paintbrush test our definition of a steelhead Spey fly. If our definition of a Spey is a fly with a wing and long leggy hackle that is palmered through the body and extends past the hook, then these are Spey flies. They have flat tinsel tags and bronze mallard wings, while the marabou forms the body and the Spey hackle at the same time because Alger wraps the marabou forward from where the tinsel tag ends. (George Cook's Popsicle fly looks similar, but isn't a Spey type because the marabou hackle is wrapped at the front of the fly in the conventional manner.)

Alger says, "I designed the Marabou Spey for fishing deep, slow holding water. I wanted a fly that would give me the most movement in the slowest water." The effect in the water is the same as with a Spey tied with heron, pheasant, or duck flank feathers—the hackle emanates from the body in extended leggy fingers, simulating life and stimulating steelhead to take.

Perhaps we should do as Atlantic salmon fishermen and name our flies according to the type of wing. But that would still not solve the problem of nomenclature because a bronze mallard wing would sit well on a standard steelhead streamer or a Steelhead Muddler or a Spey such as the Lady Caroline. It seems to me that steelheaders in general use the terms Spey, Spider, and Soft Hackle interchangeably to describe flies with extra long hackle. In spite of differences in construction between Spey flies and Spiders or Soft Hackles, I suspect that the terms Spey and Spider or Soft Hackle will continue to be confused with each other. One thing remains certain: the steelhead really don't care.

SPEY STEELHEADING TACTICS

Speys are popular with steelheaders because these flies are pleasing to the eye, pleasing to fish, and accommodate almost any steelheading tactic. You can fish Speys with sinking, sinktip, or floating lines, in the classic wet fly swing, dead-drifted nymph style, or with the greased line gambit.

Speys lend themselves better to medium current because heavy current will collapse the hackle around the body of the fly, decreasing its effectiveness. In slower current, however, Spey hackles undulate with every little whim of the river, attracting fish when other types of flies might be less appealing. Fishing a Spey on a floating line with just enough line tension to activate the hackle is a favored tactic.

Speys are particularly effective in the middle of the run or the throat, as current slows from the riffle or head of the run, but before the river accelerates into the tailout. Besides being attractive flies to fish and fishermen, Speys refuse to be stuck into a specific tactic—you can fish a Spey wherever you choose with whatever tactic you choose. Speys are accommodating in that regard, and as such, will always have a place in steelheading.

Whether tied with heron or pheasant hackle, Spey flies seduce steelhead throughout the Pacific Northwest. The gillies and fishermen in Scotland who developed the Spey fly style for Atlantic salmon in the 1800's had no idea that their flies would also catch steelhead in the twentieth and twenty first centuries, half a world away.

When fishing for steelhead sometimes we hook unexpected fish that add much warmth and interest to the day. Photo by Frank Amato

The Classic Wet Fly

III

The crosscurrent wet fly swing is many a fly fisherman's favorite because it is simple and straightforward. Using steelhead wet flies dusts the angler with a bit of tradition, too, because wet flies date back to the very beginnings of casting a fly for steelhead. Besides which, steelhead have shown a great affinity for a tremendous variety of wet flies, allowing any angler to construct flies based on his or her own whims, and then to go out and catch steelhead with those flies.

While it's true that a just-toss-it-out-there approach will catch fish, a fly fisherman will not only catch more steelhead, but enjoy it more fully if the fly is purposely presented in a specific manner, such as the classic, controlled wet fly swing. The object is to slowly slide the fly in front of the steelhead, exciting the fish to strike. The key is a *controlled* wet fly swing.

The trick to the wet fly swing is in controlling the speed and depth at which the fly crosses the current. The control factor includes the initial cast and mending the line to slow down or speed up the fly's swing.

Most wet fly swing casts are straight line, made directly across the river or down-and-across. If you want the fly to cross the current a little deeper, you can make variations of the straight across cast. These include an upstream cast, a pull-back or check cast, a slack or parachute cast, or a zigzag cast. All these casts give the fly varying amounts of time to sink before the current starts working the fly across the river.

The slack or parachute cast is tossed higher than necessary and with less force than a straight cast, so the cast loses power sooner than usual and the fly line lands in an uneven line across the surface of the river. The pull-back or check cast is thrown a bit harder than usual, then the rod is pulled back

or the line checked at the end of the forward cast, putting a pile of slack line close to the fly.

The zigzag cast consists of wiggling the tip of the rod while making the forward cast, which lays a series of waves in the fly line. Few trout fishermen and even fewer steelheaders use the zigzag cast because it is tiring if done more than a few times. The zigzag cast is particularly useful when you want the fly to sink but need to cast across conflicting currents of varying speeds. You then mend to maintain the slow crosscurrent passage of the fly.

Some advanced casters make aerial mends, throwing upstream slack in the line while the cast is in the air, but most of us make the necessary mends after completing a standard straight line cast upstream, straight across, or slightly downstream. (To help increase your casting and line handling proficiency I would recommend Doug Swisher's Scientific Anglers video "Advanced Fly Casting" or Mel Krieger's video or book, "The Essence of Fly Casting" or Joan Salvato Wulff's book *Fly Casting Techniques*.)

SLACK LINE OR "ON THE REEL"

My cardinal steelheading rule is to keep the line straight to the reel without holding slack line in my hand. In fact, once the fly is swimming properly I don't touch the line because the potential danger is that a steelhead will hit so hard and so quickly that three things might happen. First, the slack line might provide a loose cushion so the hook will not sink into the steelhead's mouth. Secondly, when the steelhead strikes the fly the hit is initially telegraphed to your hand holding the slack line—your immediate reaction is to tighten

---

Marty Sherman, editor of Flyfishing *magazine, with a prime summer steelhead he caught with a classic cane rod in a classic manner — with the wet fly. The trick to the wet fly swing is in controlling the speed and depth at which the fly crosses the current. The control factor includes the initial cast and mending the line to slow down or speed up the fly's swing.*
Facing page: *Charles Moos released this large native steelhead after it had taken a wet fly fished deep on a tributary of the Nass River. Photo by Frank Amato*

your hold on the slack line, snapping off the fly or ripping it from the fish's mouth. And lastly, a coil of slack line has looped around your reel or rod handle and the steelhead snaps the fly off on the strike.

I rely on the reel drag—it should be set tight enough to barb the fish and to prevent the spool from overrunning, which can cause a disastrous tangle. The drag should be loose enough to allow the fish to run and jump without snapping the tippet. One way to check your drag is to attach the fly to a stationary object, such as a tree, then bend your fly rod to see how much force it takes to pull line from the reel. Bear in mind that as the fly line and backing peel off downstream, drag increases because of the diminishing overall diameter of the backing remaining on the spool—tension increases on the line because the spool is spinning faster and faster in a smaller and smaller circle. A smooth and easily adjustable drag is crucial when fighting a strong fish.

However, as shown in his series of videos, expert steel-header Lani Waller holds slack line in his hand as his fly is drifting through steelhead holding water.

Waller says, "I like to keep a loop of 12 to 18 inches of line controlled under tension from my fingers. The reason I do that is sometimes when I feel a fish pull or strike or sometimes when I'm fishing certain techniques I want to give the fish time to turn and take the fly firmly in its mouth. As the fish turns with the fly, I let the line slide out under tension from

Deep in the back country of British Columbia, Mike Owen calmly watches as his steelhead bucks. Photo by Frank Amato

my fingers—I use that controlled loop to buy a little time on the fish's grab."

Another option is to fish the wet fly with the rod held at a 45 to 90 degree angle to the surface of the water, then drop the rod toward the fish when more striking time is needed. That's one of the truly fascinating aspects of steelheading—there is usually more than one way to do things.

Waller says, "A beginning steelheader has the need to focus in on a specific technique. The beginner has a need to narrow down the options, to simplify things, to make things less complicated, to do things in a particular way. But it's just the opposite with more experienced fishermen. The longer a person fishes, the less ironclad the person's rules become."

THE BEAUTY OF THE CONTROLLED WET FLY SWING

The elegance of the controlled wet fly swing lies in its simplicity. The fly crosses in front of the fish on a tight line and invariably, the steelhead hooks itself by biting the fly and then turning against a taut line, which sinks the hook into its mouth.

I believe that many "short striking" steelhead, particularly on rivers that hold quick, aggressive fish, are not "missing" the fly at all. Instead of not getting the fly completely in their mouth, I think what often happens is just the reverse: the fish has taken the fly, and has clamped down so hard that the fly is actually turned sideways in the fish's mouth. The fly is laying on its side on top of the fish's tongue so that the hook point has not pricked the fish at all. The fish charges downstream and the angler is "hooked up" until the fish opens its mouth and the fly falls out.

On the other hand, when the steelhead opens its mouth to breathe, the fish is often hooked because the drag of the fly line embeds the hook into the jaw of the fish. It's an interesting theory and hard to prove, although it does present one plausible reason for "short strikes."

Many anglers hold with the more traditional belief that the fish are biting just the tail of the fly. A steelhead merely nipping at a fly instead of attacking it might also cause a "short strike." When a steelhead nips at the fly, the hook often just barely catches the mouth of the fish, resulting in a fleeting tussle and a quick long-line release.

THE CRUX IS LINE CONTROL

More steelhead are caught on the fly by the classic crosscurrent wet fly swing than by any other method; as in all successful steelheading the key is line control. The crux is control over the drift of the fly, the depth of the fly, and the resultant "action" of the fly.

With experience you can visualize how your fly line will lead your fly through the water and what path it will take. There are some runs that, without mending, allow the fly to swing across perfectly.

Perfect would be the fly flitting crosscurrent at the speed of a lazy butterfly. The hackle, tail fibers, and wing of the fly move in the current, but the fly doesn't race across the stream. For the wet fly technique you want your fly presented so that it slowly undulates and dances in front of the steelhead. You want to tantalize and excite that fish into striking.

In most runs and riffles the current moves too fast; the fly is ripped crosscurrent too quickly for the fish to react. So you mend the line upstream to slow the fly's lateral progress. When the current is slow and the fly sinks and barely moves, a downstream mend with the current is necessary to speed the fly up to maintain enough tension to activate its hackle and wing.

OTHER FACTORS THAT AFFECT THE WET FLY SWING

Current speed, the type of fly, how the fly is dressed, and the type of fly line used all affect the depth of the swung fly. A fly that is cast downstream or down-and-across will swing across the current higher in the water column than a fly that is cast straight across or upstream because the fly has less time to sink before being swung back across the current. Upstream mends allow the fly to sink deeper, resulting in the fly coming crosscurrent deeper in the water, particularly when combined with further mending to slow the crossriver sweep of the fly.

Suppose you want to use a floating line to present your fly in a wet fly swing just below the surface in a tailout holding some skittish steelhead. Some variables: a lightly dressed fly would work if the current isn't too fast, because swift water causes the fly to plane in the current; if the current is too fast for a slim fly on a light hook, a slim fly on a heavier hook might work. A bucktail might work if its silhouette isn't so bulky it spooks the fish; a palmered hackle body fly might work because it would sink slowly and pulsate nicely in the water. These kinds of variables are part of the steelheading puzzle when fishing for summer and winter steelhead, but these variables also allow us to effectively use our favorite flies. And the wet fly swing is compatible with almost every style of steelhead fly.

Steelhead will also follow the wet fly across the current, then nail it when it completes its crosscurrent passage. We can guess that the fish sees the fly dangling in front of its nose, taunting it, further stirring aggression in the steelhead. Lani Waller emphasizes letting your fly hang in the current for a bit after the wet fly swing. Sometimes a following steelhead will hesitate, then nail the fly as it hangs in the current. Waller aptly calls it the "Hang Down" technique.

I witnessed a classic hang down by a fellow who frequently fished Dutchman's Flat on the Deschutes. He and his son-in-law would exchange places at the head of the riffle, effectively tying up the spot so only they could fish it. When the older man first took up his station he would make a few casts with his wet fly, but before long he would merely let his fly dangle in the current while he rested, leaning on his wading staff.

One hot September afternoon his son-in-law fell asleep in the shade of the willows on shore. The older man was also drowsy, nodding while he leaned on his staff, but he wouldn't relinquish his spot. After awhile his head no longer came up because the old man was snoozing while "fishing" mid-river.

When the steelhead struck his fly he came awake so abruptly that he teetered and almost fell in the river. The steelhead gyrated wildly out of the water, leaping on the tight line. About the time the man gained control of his wading staff, rod, and reel, the fish snapped off the fly. It was a fitting kiss-off by the steelhead gods.

I have met at least two steelheaders who regularly employ the hang down strategy: one plies the bubbly pocket water of the Clackamas for its summer runs, while the other uses the tactic along the ledgerock of the Deschutes. Both tie flies that can only be described as ugly. They use stiff dyed rooster hackle for their wet flies, tying the hackle oversize then cutting it short. When fished, the stubble of hackle resists the force of the river, making the dangling wet fly more active in the current. Though their flies are unattractive and the method is simplistic, the combination catches steelhead.

With the hang down technique you can often fish areas that are tough to probe with a proper wet fly swing. An angler on the North Santiam once told me, "I saw a spot between two big rocks that looked like it might hold a steelhead, but I couldn't swing a fly through there. So I just stripped line until my Black Woolly Bugger was hanging in the current between those two rocks. Wham, that steelhead smacked my fly. It was a nice 10 pounder that fought very well."

Hanging the wet fly beside and below obstructions like rocks and submerged logs is often the only way you can successfully fish those steelhead holding zones, partly because the conflicting currents make control over the wet fly swing an impossible task.

You can also probe riffles with the hang down strategy by casting downstream to the holding water and letting your wet fly dangle in the bubbly current. You can usually get some side-to-side movement of the fly by first holding your rod to one side parallel to the water's surface and 90 degrees to the direction of the current, then flip your rod 180 degrees over to the other side. By starting at the top of the riffle and letting out line after you execute several rod flip-overs, you can cover the whole riffle area.

Standard wet flies work well, but the Muddler is even more effective because the deer hair head creates additional disturbance in the water. With the nerves in its lateral line, steelhead may be able to detect some of the sound vibrations caused by the Muddler "fighting" the current, but more importantly, steelhead can see the bulk of the Muddler's head in the turbulent water.

The hang down can incorporate the wet fly or a skated presentation. For instance, when the Muddler is encompassed by the bubbly current, it's a wet fly hang down. But the deer hair head helps the Muddler scoot to the top, so the Muddler skates over the roof of the riffle, a different tactic. One of the advantages of a fly with a deer hair head like the Muddler is that you can trade tactics back and forth. While it's possible you may catch more steelhead with a wet Muddler, by ignoring the skating possibilities you may cheat yourself out of the heart-stopping surface explosion of a steelhead taking your top-prancing Muddler.

Most fly fishermen overestimate how deep their wet fly is swinging back across the river. In many cases, the fly is only just inches below the river ceiling. Of course, what this means is that the steelhead must move almost to the surface of the river to take the fly, which requires a fish that is active and willing to move.

At first you may desire to move the fish to the level in the water column that you prefer to fish. For example, the floating line is the most pleasant to use, and slimly dressed flies are some of the most beautiful. But if probing the top level of the water column with that combination proves unsuccessful and if you wish to keep fishing that spot with the wet fly swing, you have several choices. You can persist in plying the water with a close-to-the-surface method, searching the same water level but with flies that look different in the water, such as exchanging a hairwing for a Spey or a Matuka or a Steelhead Woolly Bugger. Or you can change the size or brightness of the fly. Or you can present the fly closer to where the steelhead are—that is, closer to the bottom of the river.

Or to put it another way—present the fly closer to the fish. I look at it like this: maybe the fish won't move all the way to the top of the river, but maybe the fish will move two or three feet. So I continue using a floating line but I might fish a fly that sinks deeper and stays deeper on the swing, coupled with a more upstream presentation and additional upstream mends of the line which give the fly time to sink before the wet fly swing begins to move the fly crosscurrent.

Flies sparsely tied on heavy wire hooks with non-buoyant materials such as tinsel bodied flies with only a turn of hackle or maybe no hackle and just a few tufts of marabou

Generally it is not necessary to run after a steelhead. Let it make its initial run, while holding your ground, and then as soon as it stops begin working it back to you. Photo by Frank W. Amato

swing more deeply across the river than flies dressed with buoyant deer hair or bucktail. Weighting the fly is an option, but I dislike using lead in a steelhead fly because it destroys some of the seductive movement that is a built-in factor of most flies. The greatest drawback when using weighted flies is that it hampers the fluidity of casting. When going to a heavier hook beware of those that are so thick in diameter at the point that it would take a sledgehammer to sink the hook into a steelhead's mouth. Better quality hooks are more expensive, but they will catch more steelhead for you. It makes little sense to invest the time, money and effort to hook a steelhead and then lose it for the few cents saved on a cheap hook.

Traditionally, most steelheaders fishing for summer runs use a floating line because it's the most pleasant to use and steelhead will often move up to take the shallow-drifting wet fly. But even on the warmest, brightest days of steelheading summer, a sinktip can often make the difference between just casting and catching fish. That's because the fly swings across closer to the bottom and to fish that may not be willing to rise very far.

I have been on both ends of the proverbial wading staff: I can clearly remember working through a run on the Deschutes in September with a floating line, then watching as a fellow worked through the same run behind me with a sinktip—he nailed a nice steelhead in the same water I had just fished with a floating line.

And I have reversed the coin. One day everyone was using a floating line but not catching steelhead, so when I

began fishing behind another angler who was using a floater, I went with a sinktip. About halfway through the run I felt a yank and a thrumming in the line—by the time I realized I had hooked a fish, 10 pounds of summer run blasted out of the water in an upstream arc. Then the fish came unpinned. Sometimes, to hook fish you just have to be willing to forego the easier casting floater.

We have a vast array of sinktip and full sinking fly lines of various densities to use; these tools allow us to pursue fish at almost any level. The sinktip is tremendously versatile, although not the answer to everything. Because of its floating portion, a sinktip line can be mended, and we can adjust the depth of the crosscurrent swing by using lines with tips of varying density and length, from slow to fast to super fast sinking, with tips available in 5, 10, 13, 15, 20 or 24 feet.

Full sinking lines can be used for steelhead, but are not nearly as versatile as sinktips, especially for summer and fall water conditions. (I cover sinking line tactics in the chapter on winter fishing. I cover shooting heads, including sinking shooting heads, in a separate chapter.)

There are two factors to consider with sinking lines. First, a denser, heavier line will sink faster and deeper than a lighter line. For example, a number 9 line will sink 33% faster than a number 6 line of the same type. The other important factor to bear in mind is that sink rates are only operative when there is no drag on the line—if the current takes hold, the line stops sinking and either maintains its depth or planes upward, depending on force of the current. So even with sinktips, mending tactics and upstream casts play a crucial role in controlling the depth of the crosscurrent wet fly swing.

READING THE WATER AND WET FLY TACTICS

Reading the water is of prime importance for all types of steelheading. Being able to pick out steelhead resting places is the key to catching fish. In his videos Lani Waller makes a distinction between resting and holding water for steelhead and explains why. I disagree with him in that I believe that steelhead will strike flies whether they are in resting or holding stations, and sometimes even when they are heading upstream in their underwater traveling lanes. In this book I use the terms holding or resting water to describe any place steelhead seek for protection from predators and respite from the relentless current that tries to drive them back to the sea. (Ironically, that same river force provides steelhead with the oxygen they need for life.)

Some examples of these holding areas include riffles, current seams, buffered areas above and below rocks, along ledges, sunken logs, brush piles, and the quickened current in tailouts. The advantage of learning how to recognize these preferred steelhead resting slots is that they attract and hold steelhead in any river system, so you can use known steelhead lairs as templates for picking out prime water on unknown streams.

A comment Mark Bachmann once made summed up the basic problem of all fishing, but with specific relevance to steelhead: "The hardest part of steelheading is finding out where the fish are, so you start at the head of the riffle and work the whole run, including the slow pools."

The wet fly swing is appropriate for almost all water types simply because steelhead are like giant trout and seem ready to respond to flies swung right in front of them. While it's true that fish may respond by fleeing the intruder or by rigorously ignoring the angler's flies, a steelhead is also very likely to strike that fly prancing in front of its snoot.

One reason the wet fly approach is so effective is that you can slice consecutive pieces of the holding water pie with each succeeding cast. So, in essence, you know that the water has been systematically covered. If each cast moves the arc of the swung fly only a matter of inches downstream each time, the steelhead undoubtedly sees the fly.

The wet fly swing is an excellent way to cover water where you hope a steelhead is hiding, but you can't see the fish. It works for fish spotted ahead of time, too. You can present the fly closer and closer to the fish until the fish hits the fly or you must admit that the fly is being ignored. And of course, sometimes the fish will spook out of its holding lie. If the fish doesn't spook, the angler can try a smaller or larger fly, a brighter or darker fly, or a different technique, such as a dead-drift nymph approach or a greased line presentation (covered in separate chapters).

One way to increase your chances for a strike to your wet fly is to use two flies at once. The advantages are that you can swing flies that are different sizes or a dark fly and a bright fly or possibly a fly tied with Flashabou or Crystal Flash or flies with a different silhouette or "action" in the water, such as a Skunk and a Spey. If the bottom fly is much larger or heavier than the top fly, the bottom fly will track crosscurrent more deeply than the dropper fly so you can cover different depths of the river.

The disadvantage of using two flies is that you must use a stronger rig to overcome the additional air resistance and weight of two flies. You also have twice the chance of dinging your rod during the cast and two flies tend to tangle more easily.

The greatest disadvantage becomes apparent when you hook a fish. Once on the Calawah River on the Olympic Peninsula, J.D. Love was using two flies and hooked a nine-pound steelhead. The river was so clear that we could easily watch the steelhead's underwater escape maneuvers. First the fish bolted downstream, swung across the stream to the other side, then raced upstream. J.D.'s line went tight—we could see the silver torpedo twisting this way and that, tethered to the bottom of the river. Within seconds the line went limp and the steelhead went free. The trailing fly had snagged something on the bottom—a virtual impossibility when the single fly is in the fish's mouth.

Sometimes steelhead will "boil" at the fly but won't take it. Theories contradict about how to catch those fish that swirl at the fly without taking it. Some guides say hit them immediately with a smaller pattern and some recommend resting the fish. I've tried both methods and sometimes the steelhead have thoroughly ignored my fly and sometimes I've caught fish. Since the guides I've talked to aren't in agreement, I usually try both approaches: first, I change to a smaller, darker pattern and make pretty much the identical cast. Then I'll make another cast or two in the same general area in case the fish has changed its holding station. If I have that section of the river to myself I'll probably rest it and try again later. When you come back for a rerun, you encounter the same dilemma—do you present the same fly the fish struck or do you try a smaller, darker fly or a fly with an entirely different silhouette? Do you try the exact same cast or do you surmise the fish might respond to a fly coming from a slightly different angle? Do you forgo the wet fly swing for a greased line or dead-drift nymph presentation?

That's probably why guides have different approaches—a fish may respond differently because of its individual

Some examples of steelhead holding areas include riffles, current seams, buffered areas above and below rocks, along ledges, sunken logs, brush piles, and the quickened current in tailouts. The advantage of learning how to recognize these preferred steelhead resting slots is that they attract and hold steelhead in any river system, so you can use known steelhead lairs as templates for picking out prime water on unknown streams. Photo by Scott Ripley

Joyce Sherman attempting to tease a fish up to the fly in the Deschutes.

predilection and because of the tremendously varying conditions of any river.

Any given presentation, including the wet fly swing, may have several different tactics associated with it. For example, let's say at the beginning of the wet fly presentation the line is cast straight across the stream. Then the angler throws a mend to allow the fly to sink a bit under the surface. At that point the fly is actually dead-drifting, a whole different tactic. After the wet fly has swung across the current and the wet fly presentation is essentially completed, the fly will often skate the last little bit of drift on the surface because the current is swift and the drag of the fly line has planed the fly on top of the water. So the final foot or two of drift of the wet fly technique may, in fact, be a skating fly technique. And a steelhead may strike during either the dead-drift or the skating part of the presentation.

It isn't usually important in itself whether the fish takes during the dead-drift, the wet fly swing, or the skating part; what's really important is that the fisherman knows what is happening and why. In other words, it's important that the angler knows where the fly is, how it's moving in the water, and what factors are causing the fly to move in that particular way. Besides which, fish that ignore the wet fly swing but take the fly during the dead-drift or the skated portion are telling you that is what they prefer—a change in tactics is in order.

THE STRIKE ZONE
AND "STRIKE TRIGGERS"

My definition of the strike zone is very simple: it's how far the steelhead will move to take the fly. That zone can vary considerably, depending on numerous factors. For example, in the cold flows of winter, the steelhead may not move at all or only a matter of inches to take the fly, so the strike zone on that day may be 12 to 18 inches, allowing for a buffer zone of 12 inches around the fish to prevent snagging. Under the right conditions, steelhead may move as far as 10 feet or more to take a fly. The average strike zone is from two to four feet, so most wet fly swings should come within that range.

Some of the variables that determine the size of the strike zone include water temperature, water clarity, aggressiveness of the fish, whether the steelhead are rested or not, whether the fish are being bombarded with lures and flies, time of the day in relation to sunlight or shadow, overcast versus a clear day, and amount of cover and security available.

As you might guess, we can get a handle on some of these variables, and some we can't. For instance, even though we fish for steelhead that are essentially on a spawning run, we aren't fishing for spawners. But these big rainbow are still in steelhead rut, bold with surging hormones that war with the fish's basic survival instincts to seek food and cover. It makes for a high degree of uncertainty, turning steelheaders into angling soothsayers that gamble on fly fishing hunches.

We can draw some general conclusions, though, which steelhead follow most of the time, but which may be disproved the next trip afield. The ideal water temperatures range from 45 to 65 degrees, with clarity favoring the fly fisherman, although ultra clear water may make the fish extra wary. Overcast days give the fish a reprieve from direct sunlight, which must be tremendously bright to steelhead because they have no eyelids or sunglasses. Steelhead generally seek shadowed areas and are more active on overcast days and during low light conditions of daybreak and after sundown.

The next time you are fishing the wet fly in mid-day with the sun at your back, turn around, pull off your sunglasses and look into the sun—you won't be able to take it, just as a steelhead is reluctant to look into the sun to see your wet fly. You will increase your chances of catching a fish by searching out water that allows you to swing the wet fly so that the fish aren't looking into the sun, whether it's water shaded by a canyon wall or under the protective canopy of a tall Douglas fir or where the river has turned so the sun is hitting at an oblique angle.

There is a common theory on the Deschutes that steelhead won't take in the middle of the day and you might as well only fish at dawn and after the sun has descended below the canyon ramparts. That isn't always true, however. You can disprove that theory by fishing water where the fish aren't looking directly into the sun. Sometimes that means finding a specific stretch of river that receives sunlight at an oblique angle and sometimes it means probing deeper runs that have boulders or ledgerock that offer the steelhead underwater shade from the sun—a wet fly entering the fish's protective shelter is likely to be met with an open-mouthed attack.

How well a fish is rested or how aggressive it might be are purely conjectural. I do know that steelheaders on the lower Deschutes will earnestly cast their flies in waters disturbed by jet sleds because that underwater noise and commotion stirs up the fish. The steelhead respond to the disruption of their aquatic world by swimming about; when the commotion subsides they reorient themselves, vying for the best resting spots and cover. While in this turbulent state of mind, so to speak, these fish become aggressive towards each other and towards an upstart little wet fly entering their territory. Steelheaders don't always catch fish in the aftermath of jet sleds, but it works often enough that some of this aggression-theory must apply.

And then there's the events we can't see on a wide river like the Deschutes but you can witness on rivers like the North Umpqua or Siletz where you can gain a view from atop a canyon wall or while concealed under the cover of alder and fir. For example, suppose there are two males next to a female or two females next to one male in a particular holding area. Although these fish aren't actually spawning, their survival-warfare instincts have been riled and are in high gear. You can picture in your mind those 30-inch torpedoes shifting this way and that, exhibiting brazen hostility by snapping their mouths open and closed while executing nip-and-bite swirling displays that signal rivals to stand clear. Into that arena of piscatorial tension saunters a spiffy little wet fly, undulating its hackle, wing, and slim body, teasing steelhead to aggressively bite it.

"Strike triggers" are the aspects of the fly and its presentation that entice the steelhead to strike. These include size, color, degree of brightness, built-in movement capabilities, and silhouette of the fly. (I go into detail about strike triggers in the "Fly Design" chapter.)

For the wet fly technique, the fly swinging in front of the fish is the main ingredient of the presentation and is the primary strike trigger. Repeated crosscurrent arcs of the fly in front of the fish further pull on that strike trigger as the fly comes closer and closer to the fish and its strike zone. Changing the angle of the arc of the fly and even more importantly, changing the depth of the fly tugs on the strike trigger and puts the fly closer to the fish and into the probable strike zone.

One September day on the Calawah River, J.D. and I saw the steelhead become overwhelmed to the point that it extinguished their strike triggers. It was early afternoon, we had landed several steelhead and lost others—it was a good day. I had just seen two steelhead move upstream to a holding station 45 feet away and swirl and nudge at each other in a courtship display. They weren't fighting, but looked as if they were almost playing. These were summer run fish, months from spawning. Steelhead are usually in a fly-biting mood when they display like that and aren't spooked by fishermen or boat traffic. Suddenly the wind came up and filled the clear fall river with twisting yellow and gold alder leaves. The fish "shut off" and we didn't get another bite that day.

My speculation is that the sudden appearance of thousands of twirling, twisting leaves in the current gave the steelhead a type of visual overload—why would these fish recognize, let alone bite a rather small wet fly in their world of swirling bright leaves? On the other hand, steelhead become accustomed to a certain amount of leaves drifting in the river on a day-to-day basis and ignore them. But a blast of wind that abruptly dumps great quantities of leaves in the river dampens the steelhead's strike triggers.

SIMPLE TECHNIQUE, SIMPLE GEAR

I love fly fishing gear. I love the rods of finely crafted bamboo and efficient graphite. I love the new race car tuned reels that perform flawlessly, and the sweet traditional Hardys. We have fly lines that come in a myriad of tapers that cast effortlessly and only need occasional cleaning to last a long time.

But if you're looking for a rationale to buy new gear, the wet fly method for steelhead just doesn't demand it. Almost any outfit will work if it's balanced for a 6, 7, 8, or 9 line and made of quality components. For smaller streams, shorter lightweight rods are appropriate; for bigger waters, the bigger outfits come into play. Some canyons can funnel tremendous winds at the angler, making a stronger rod necessary.

Trout anglers have no trouble owning several outfits, such as a No. 3 or 4-weight rig for little spring creeks, a 5 or 6-weight for streams, and a 7-weight for lakes and river fishing with larger flies. As a steelheader I have no trouble owning a lot of steelhead gear and I enjoy using it all. You just can't cover all steelheading situations with one setup, just as the trout fisherman can't do it. Some anglers operate on the single rig principle, but I think they miss out on some of the fun of steelheading with the fly.

Technically, the wet fly swing is the easiest, and consequently, one of the most effective ways to present a fly to steelhead, especially if it's done slow, slow, slow. The wet fly swing is deadly year round on steelhead wherever they swim. It's the method used for probably 80% of all steelhead caught on flies.

Once you have control of the fly line and the fly, you can effectively probe steelhead holding cover with the searching wet fly swing. You can tease the fly in and out of the steelhead's strike zone, sometimes slowly and sometimes not so slowly. So if you're looking to tangle with steelhead with a sense of humor like scrap metal the controlled wet fly swing is an excellent way to do it.

Greased Line Steelhead

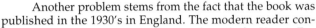

IV

There is probably more confusion about using the greased line technique for steelhead than any other method.

When I asked an internationally famous angling author of a dozen books if he was using the greased line method on a trip he had just completed on the Deschutes River, he said, "Yes, I was using a floating line."

A floating line is necessary for the greased line technique, but it's merely the tool, not the greased line presentation itself. And some anglers are under the mistaken impression that the wet fly swing with a tight floating line and a lightly dressed fly is the same as the greased line technique.

The term "greased line" refers to the greasing of the silk fly line in use when the greased line method was invented over 75 years ago. If the silk line wasn't treated it sank; so in that historical context, a line dressed to float was an important component of the greased line method.

There are several factors contributing to the confusion about this method, first presented to the angling public in 1931 in the chapter "Greased Line Fishing" by A.H.E. Wood in Eric Taverner's book, *Salmon Fishing* and further explained in the 1935 publication of the book, *Greased Line Fishing For Salmon.*

The first problem arises from the fact that although much of *Greased Line Fishing For Salmon* was compiled from the papers of A.H.E. Wood, who pioneered the method, the book was actually written by Donald G. Ferris Rudd under the pen name Jock Scott. The result is that much of the book is based on what Scott believed Wood meant; it's unfortunate that when Wood died in 1934 he hadn't written his book as he intended to do someday—thus, we have inherited Scott's second-hand impressions.

Another problem stems from the fact that the book was published in the 1930's in England. The modern reader contends with the King's English written in a stilted style popular over 50 years ago, which can be difficult to read and can cause the reader to misinterpret the author's intentions.

A further stumbling block is that Scott's overzealous adoration of Wood resulted in contradictory and inaccurate statements about the greased line method such as the one found on page 63, "...and finally it is applicable to almost any condition of water and weather." That simply isn't true for Atlantic salmon rivers in general or the rivers that Wood fished. When river conditions didn't warrant the greased line method, Wood used a modification of the classic wet fly swing, mending his line to allow the fly to sink, fishing it "down on the stones."

We certainly can't criticize Wood or Scott for not consulting a reliable crystal ball—how could they possibly know that the greased line method wouldn't be totally applicable for steelhead, a sea going rainbow half a world away. The greased line tactic for steelhead is limited because steelhead streams are tremendously varied with diverse types of holding water, as affected by rapids, obstructions in the river, stream gradients, water flow, and tendencies of individual races of steelhead. In fact, it's somewhat amazing and certainly fortuitous that the greased line method translates so well to steelhead fishing, because even though there are some similarities between Atlantic salmon and steelhead, there are just as many differences between the two races of fish and some of those differences are quite profound.

Greased Line Fishing For Salmon announced a radical departure from conventional Atlantic salmon methods,

---

The Matuka style of wet fly adapts readily to steelhead fishing because these giant rainbows are predators and the Matuka design mimics the outline of a baitfish, particularly with the spiked-hackle simulation of the dorsal and caudal fins.
Facing page: *The greased line method is appropriate in any stretch of stream that has medium depth, moderate current, and resting or holding places for steelhead. Photo by Brad Jackson*

presenting a tactic that placed the salmon fly in the surface film by building on the "hot" new tactic of mending the fly line and developing positive line control rather than the prevalent simplistic chuck-it-and-chance-it wet fly swing on a tight line.

Under the subchapter heading "The Birth Of An Idea," Wood wrote:

"One afternoon in July, 1903, I was fishing an Irish river. The weather for some time past had been exceptionally hot and dry, so that the river had dropped considerably and was very clear. I had had no sport all day and sat down to think beside a pool full of salmon that had steadily refused to look at a series of flies, presented to them, as I thought, in every possible way. Shortly afterwards, I saw one fish and then another rise to something floating down on the surface of the water. This continued at irregular intervals, and at length I was fortunately able to observe the cause; namely, a sort of white moth similar to those often seen amongst the heather.

"I went to the head of the pool, which consisted of an eel-weir, and there found a number of salmon lying with their noses pushed right up to the sill. As luck had it, I happened to have with me a White Moth fly; this I tied on the cast and sat on the plank-bridge over the weir. Then, holding the gut in my hand, I dibbed the fly over them. After some minutes, one of the salmon became curious enough to rise up to examine the fly, but at the last moment thought better of it; this I believe was due to its attention having been distracted by my feet, which were dangling over the plank, barely six feet away from the water. I changed my position, knelt down on the bridge and let down the fly. This time the fish came more boldly at the fly and it was followed by others; but I had pricked several before I realised that, because I was kneeling directly above them, I was, in striking, pulling the hook straight out of their mouths. So I changed my tactics, and, by letting go the cast at the right moment, succeeded in dropping the fly actually into the open mouth of the next fish that came to it. I then picked up my rod, ran off the bridge, and made all haste downstream. All this time the line and cast were slack and floating down; yet when I tightened on the fish, I found it had hooked itself. By the use of this trick I landed six fish, lost others and pricked more than I care to say, all in a few hours. After that experience, I discovered myself fishing on the surface or as near it as I was able. The final advance came, when I started using a greased line to assist in keeping the fly in the right position, and I thus evolved out of a simple experiment what has become a most interesting mode of salmon angling, the greased line method."

There is no escaping the fact that our knowledge of fly fishing for steelhead is rooted in the teachings of angling authors who have fished before us and who wrote of their findings after carefully examining the evidence compiled while afield. Thoughtful steelheaders embrace that accumulated knowledge and benefit from it on every steelheading trip.

My goal here is to simplify and clarify the greased line method as well as I can, translating the 55 year old text into American English circa late twentieth century, with a view towards the steelheading world as it exists now. The result will be my interpretation of Wood/Scott and their intent in *Greased Line Fishing For Salmon*. (The book is currently available from Frank Amato Publications, with a foreword and additional color fly plates by Bill McMillan.)

MENDING AND FOLDING THE FLY LINE

One of the first stream tactics taught to beginning fly fishers is how to mend a fly line to avoid drag. We take mending the line for granted now, but A.H.E. Wood will always be known to fly fishing historians as the inventor of the mending technique, both for slowing down and speeding up the drift of the fly.

Mending the line is a simple technique for steelheaders, particularly with long graphite rods. You can mend more line with a longer rod, but since the weight of the rod, the rod tapers, and the force of the casting stroke on the wrist and forearm are all factors in the overall enjoyment of fly fishing, most single hand steelhead rods run 9 to 10 feet. Two-handed graphite rods of 12 to 16 feet are becoming more popular because you can mend much more line than with a single-hand rod.

Wood emphasized not disturbing the fly's drift when mending the line because it put the salmon off. Steelhead don't necessarily spook from a fly because it suddenly jerks a bit through the water; in fact, that abrupt movement may trigger a strike. That strike-reaction to a sudden-movement fly reflects some of the trout-like traits in steelhead that are not present in salmon. A steelhead that is put off by an abrupt twitch in the fly is likely to come again to that same fly on a dead-drift presentation on the next cast or to a different pattern presented dead-drift—the point is, the fish moved to the fly. A reckless mend that disturbs the fly may spook fish in low clear water, particularly if the fish are already spooky. In a

Wood made a comment that is directly applicable to steelheaders: "Do not on any account acquire the habit of mechanically lifting over, no matter how the current runs. Always have some reason for doing it: to prevent drag, or, more often, to control the speed at which the fly crosses the river." Photo by Scott Ripley

Wood emphasized not disturbing the fly's drift when mending the line because it put the salmon off. Steelhead don't necessarily spook from a fly because it suddenly jumps a bit through the water; in fact, that abrupt movement may trigger a strike. That strike-reaction to a sudden movement fly reflects some of the trout-like traits in steelhead that are not present in salmon. A steelhead that is put off by an abrupt twitch in the fly is likely to come again to that same fly on a dead-drift presentation on the next cast or to a different pattern presented dead-drift —the point is, the fish moved to the fly. Photo by Frank W. Amato

situation like that, there are many things that might spook the steelhead, and a sloppy mend is only one of them.

If you want to present your greased line fly in the classic Wood manner, approach the mend more as a "folding" of the fly line, where you lift the rod and smoothly fold the line over as you would the cover on an envelope. Because graphite rods handle line more quickly than bamboo or fiberglass, we tend to flip the line in a mend rather than folding it. Another advantage to folding the line is that if a fish hits the sunken fly while folding the mend, you still have contact with the fly; if a fish hits while you execute a flipping mend, you may never know you had a strike.

To slow the mending stroke so it becomes a folding action, open up the loop of the mend, starting the mend slowly, then gradually accelerate the stroke. With practice you can judge how fast to speed up the mend so you won't over-accelerate the line, making an overly vigorous mend that disturbs the fly's drift. A small mend or one made close-in may not require any acceleration of the mending stroke. Speeding up the mending stroke is necessary when the line is tangled in conflicting currents or when you mend a lot of line. A combination of different folds are required when mending your line as the fly tracks across varying currents. In one drift you may need to mend both upstream and downstream and with folding strokes of varied strength.

About mending, Wood wrote: "The lifting over of a line is done to correct a fault, namely, to take the downstream belly out of a line and thus relieve the pull or pressure of the current on the line, which is communicated to the fly and exhibits itself as drag. But if the line is proceeding at an even pace and shows no sign of going to drag, there is no need to mend the cast. On the other hand, if the current continues to belly the line, but before it gets a drag, lift again and continue to do so as often as you can see a drag forming."

He continued with a comment that is directly applicable to steelheaders: "Do not on any account acquire the habit of mechanically lifting over, no matter how the current runs. Always have some reason for doing it: to prevent drag, or, more often, to control the speed at which the fly crosses the river."

Steelheaders seem to over-mend when fishing the wet fly swing more than with any other method because the continual cast, swing, cast, swing, becomes mechanical in its approach; the angler casts and automatically mends several times, no matter what the current speed. The greased line method, surface tactics with wakers and skaters, and dead-drifting the sunken fly all take more concentration on the angler's part, so the fisherman tends to make more precise mends and only as needed.

GREASED LINE AS CLOTHESLINE

When describing the greased line presentation I think of the fly drifting downstream while being tethered to the rod by the line in the shape of a clothesline. The line is not ruler-straight, but droops a bit from its own weight while suspended between the rod and the surface of the water. The fly is mostly dead-drifting, but there is still a light tension on the fly, via the line and the rod. That judicious application of line tension is one of the most confusing attributes of the greased line method. Some of the confusion results from the imprecise wording in the Wood/Scott book.

Over and over again Wood/Scott ádmonish the reader to eliminate drag on the line, which they also call "pull" on the line. The idea was to make the fly drift down sideways to the fish, as illustrated in the drawings in their book on pages 82 and 96 through 101.

One of the most important aspects of the greased line method is the broadside presentation of the fly to the steelhead. Wood/Scott wrote, "I find the best angle at which to present the fly is that which shows it broadside on to the fish."

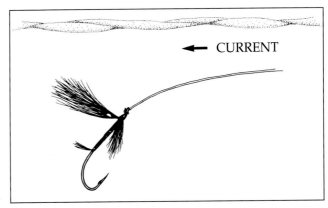

With no tension imparted to the fly, the standard steelhead wet fly drifts downstream with a butt–down axis, with its tail and wing canted up to about 45 degrees.

The challenge to the steelhead angler employing the greased line tactic is to impart enough tension in the fly's drift to cause it to drift downstream sideways, and yet allow enough slack so the fly drifts almost dead-drift, with the hackles,

The most appealing aspect of the near surface presentation of the greased line fly is that you can often see the steelhead take the fly. Photo by Bill McMillan

hairs, and body material in the fly reacting with lifelike movement to every whim of the current.

Wood/Scott wrote: "The basic idea is to use the line as a float for, and controlling agent of, the fly; to suspend the fly just beneath the surface of the water, and to control its path in such a way that it swims diagonally down and across the stream, entirely free from the slightest pull on the line."

If you allow too much slack in the surface presentation of the greased line fly, the fly will sink lower in the water column, turning indiscriminately on its butt-lowest axis because the extra weight in the hook bend will cause the fly to lose its broadside attitude in the stream. The presentation will then be much like a dead-drifted nymph; how much the fly tilts butt-down depends on how the fly is dressed and the amount of current bearing on the fly. There is nothing "wrong" with that—it just isn't what I believe Wood meant by the greased line method. (The butt-down axis of the drifting fly is shown in the Lani Waller Scientific Anglers steelhead videos. See illustration on previous page.)

Similarly, if the fly is tied with deer hair and floats in or on the surface film, a totally dead-drift presentation isn't a greased line strategy, but a dead-drift dry fly gambit. Nothing wrong with that either, and steelhead give their approval by sucking in dead-drifted floating deer hair flies much like giant trout feeding on surface insects.

Besides which, you must relay *some* tension to the drifting fly to bring it crosscurrent. If we rely solely on the current to bring the fly crosscurrent, we are left with only a few pools in which to fish the greased line method. Pools that have the ideal current lanes for a totally drag-free drift that brings the fly crosscurrent with absolutely no drag on the fly line are

rare. It's doubtful that Wood meant no crosscurrent steerage of the fly; I believe he tried to imply a difference between "pull" versus "drag" on the line, although the text isn't that explicit.

If your fly sinks or proceeds too far downstream from excess slack in the line, you can then impart more tension to the line, forcing the fly to the surface and crosscurrent at the same time. If you apply too much tension to the fly, instead of a broadside presentation, the fly will turn its head upstream and begin a crosscurrent wet fly swing. If the fly turns upstream from too much tension, simply lighten up a bit, fish the drift out, and try again. A steelhead holding downstream from the fly may not react to the narrow silhouette of the butt of the wet fly, but then again, the steelhead may nail the fly anyway. It's doubtful that a fish will be scared silly because the fly changed its axis in the river. However, if you rip the fly line and the fly from the water, you may scare the fish.

LEADING THE FLY

Besides mending the floating line to gain a broadside presentation, another critical aspect of Wood's technique was his "leading the fly." Instead of holding his rod at the customary 45 degree angle to the surface of the water and in line with the fly, Wood held his rod off to the side and pointed downstream from the fly. He varied the angle of the rod to the surface according to the speed of the current and to a lesser degree, the size of the fly. Using his 12-foot bamboo rod, he steered his fly in an arcing crosscurrent path, while combining mending tactics and the release of slack line to keep the fly broadside to the current.

When too much current speed develops or the line is too far downstream to mend properly, the greased line tactic actually gives way to the classic wet fly swing. There is nothing "wrong" with finishing out a greased line presentation with a wet fly swing, or a skated fly presentation for that matter. Some stretches of river lend themselves to a greased line presentation from start to finish, and some do not. The idea is to catch steelhead, and sometimes to catch steelhead in an interesting or challenging way. Besides which, the greased line method is an excellent way to bring a steelhead to the top—a sight that will remain forever emblazoned in your memory.

A steelhead coming to the top often excites the angler into making a mistake that is easily done when greased lining—striking the fish with a quick uplift of the rod. Unfortunately, jerking the rod just yanks the fly out of the fish's mouth.

Wood said, "When a fish goes for the fly, continue moving the point of the rod round as if no fish were there. Point the rod towards your own bank, but keep moving it. Do nothing more until you feel the fish, which will already have been hooked, because the stream has done the trick for you. If a fish misses the fly, I have often seen it come again; sometimes two or three times in the same cast, and finally hook itself. This would not have happened if I had struck or pulled the line. As you are clearly seeing all this taking place in front of your eyes and are in consequence very apt to pull at the fly or increase its speed, keep your head and force yourself to pay attention *until you feel the fish.*"

Easily said; a challenge to do.

Keeping the rod and line even with or downstream from the fly promotes a broadside presentation and also aids in hooking fish. By pointing the rod to the side and allowing some slack line, the angler lets the fish hook itself. The problem with the standard vertical-rod approach is that the hook will often pull free from the fish's mouth because the fly is pulled away from the fish instead of into the corner of the fish's mouth as in the side-rod angle approach.

Even with the rod held to the side, you still need to wait until you feel the fish because essentially the fish must set the

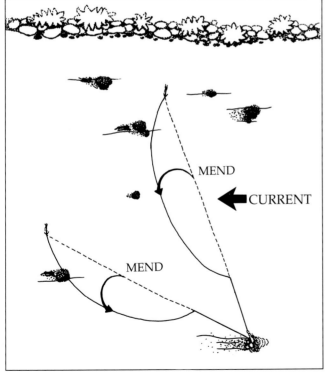

Mend as necessary to keep the fly sideways to the fish.

hook itself. If the fish takes the fly and turns towards you, by jerking the rod instead of waiting, you will probably pull the fly right out of the fish's mouth.

The surface or near surface take of a steelhead to the lightly dressed greased line fly is an exciting moment in steelheading and one of the most rewarding, but it also dares the angler with the supreme challenge to keep your cool. We are trained by years of fly fishing experience to lift the rod when the fish strikes the fly—it's tough to override that instinct.

You won't always see the fish take your greased line fly, which can be the sweet caress of good luck because you won't overreact. I remember a five-pound wild steelhead that took my greased line fly just as the sun descended over the ramparts above the Grande Ronde River. In the fading light I could see the fly line draped across the surface of the river and I could see that the drift was pretty much drag-free.

The fly transgressed through some boily areas in the throat of the run—instead of a rise, the line grew tight and the reel started peeling off line. The deer hair in the fly and the drag-free drift had kept the fly close to the surface, but I didn't have a clue that the fish had hit the fly until the steelhead was already hooked. Sometimes not seeing is fine.

One of the most radical aspects of Wood's technique was presenting a slender fly close to the surface film. He developed an elegant series of slim dressings applied to traditional Atlantic salmon patterns which Hardy Bros. sold under the name "Wood Low Water Flies". These delicate flies were designed for the greased line method, for presenting the fly in or just under the surface. His radical technique worked for Atlantic salmon over 70 years ago and it works for steelhead today.

Unknown to Wood, the greased line tactic also works as a subsurface presentation for steelhead. When Wood fished subsurface, he still mended his line, but put his fly "down on the stones" in a wet fly swing. Given the right water conditions, the modern steelheader can present a broadside, almost dead-drifting fly to steelhead at just about any depth in the river that can be covered with the classic wet fly swing or the total dead-drift nymph-like presentation.

So the term "greased line" presentation only tells part of the story: greased line surface presentation for steelhead, and greased line subsurface presentation for steelhead. Both methods hinge on Wood's mending techniques and the basic component of presenting a broadside view of the fly to the steelhead.

GREASED LINE SURFACE FLIES

Wood's greased line surface flies were sparsely tied traditional Atlantic salmon patterns such as the Blue Charm, March Brown, and Lady Caroline. Carrying the sparse Low Water theory to its limit, Wood also used a series of "Toy" flies and a Redshank and Blueshank that were little more than a sprinkle of color on a hook. These Low Water greased line flies would only sink a matter of inches when fished on a drag-free drift in moderate current.

Wood said, "As regards pattern, I do not believe that this matters at all. Blue Charm and Silver Blue are my stock, simply on the principle that one is more or less black and the other white and so give me a choice. I once fished through a whole season with a March Brown only, and got my share, and more, of the fish caught."

In that same vein of tradition, steelheaders have delighted in tying lovely Low Water steelhead flies that are variations of fully dressed steelhead flies. In his book, *The Western Angler*, Roderick Haig-Brown wrote, "For greased-line fishing, I think only two flies are necessary, the Blue Charm and the

Long time steelheader Harry Lemire is most well known for his Grease Liner, which Trey Combs wrote about in Steelhead Fly Fishing and Flies. *In 1962 Lemire designed the Grease Liner with its cinched down deer hair wing, leaving the stubble intact over the fly's head. (His wing design predated Troth's Elk Hair Caddis with its stubble wing by many years.) Photo by B. J. Meiggs*

Lady Caroline; even the Blue Charm is probably superfluous, but on a really dark day it is possibly a little more effective than the Lady Caroline. Steelhead like the Lady Caroline surprisingly well, whether she is fished as a simple wet fly or by the greased-line method."

Haig-Brown was probably one of the first steelheaders to use Wood's technique, since *The Western Angler* was published in 1939, only a few years after *Greased Line Fishing For Salmon.*

Scott/Wood's book was reprinted in 1937, 1950, 1970, and 1982, so over the years steelheaders have adapted many steelhead patterns to the Low Water Wood style. In his book, *Steelhead Fly Fishing And Flies,* 1976, Trey Combs included Harry Lemire's fly, the Grease Liner.

I had always assumed that Lemire designed the fly for Wood's greased line technique and that Lemire had named the fly in Wood's honor, but that isn't so. Lemire says, "I tied it and started fishing it in 1962 for use on the Wenatchee as well as the Green River. The Green River has a very good hatch of fall caddis; the Wenatchee where I fished it is under water now, where it dumped into the Columbia.

"The Grease Liner pattern hasn't changed, the only thing that changes is that in different rivers there are different colors of caddis so that the body color is changed to approximately match the hatch. I use black, dark brown, gray olive, burnt orange, or yellow orange.

"I notice a lot of flies picking up the stubble head now. There's a good reason for it, because the stubble on the head of the fly will cause a lot of commotion—it's the commotion that catches the fish.

"When fishing a Grease Liner you're actually imitating a caddis or an insect that is struggling in the current while trying to get to shore or perhaps laying eggs. You're doing whatever is necessary to keep the fly swimming broadside to the fish as the fly comes towards the shore.

"The name of the fly is strictly accidental. The only reason I named it the Grease Liner is because that refers to a dry line which you grease."

The fact that Lemire's Grease Liner wasn't specifically designed for the Wood greased line technique certainly doesn't preclude it from being used as an effective greased line fly. In fact, Haig-Brown's Steelhead Bee works well as a greased line fly although Haig-Brown designed the Bee as a dry fly. Being of practical minds, steelheaders also use greased line patterns as wakers and skaters for surface presentations. As is the case in most of steelheading, the pattern used for greased lining is of secondary importance to the broadside presentation of the fly—but where would we be without our beautiful steelhead flies?

Because deer hair adds buoyancy, it aids in keeping the fly close to the surface, and that makes sense in designing a greased line pattern. But considering that none of Wood's flies incorporated deer hair, it's obviously not mandatory. Wood's angling background was rooted in fly fishing for Atlantic salmon—his use of the "Toy" flies and painted hooks, the Redshank and the Blueshank, was no less heretical than some of the other aspects of his greased line revolution.

Steelheaders have their roots in fly fishing for trout, a tradition which has produced flies that can be as gaudy as any Atlantic salmon fly, but at the same time a tradition that has a more practical bent to it than just color for the sake of color. Steelheaders design flies that often look like trout patterns meant to float in the surface film and trigger a latent feeding instinct. Steelhead flies tend to incorporate more deer hair and hackle than Atlantic salmon flies, perhaps because many of the problems posed by matching a trout feeding preference involve floatation and reaction to current disturbances, similar to what surface steelhead patterns often demand.

In the book Wood remarked that "there is no universal standard for hook sizes," which is still true today, over 50 years later. He said, "As the water gets warmer and clearer I use smaller sizes down to No. 6. As weather and water become still warmer I use still smaller flies, No. 6 to No. 12; but as long as the fish will take a No. 6 I do not go any lower. I only reduce the size of the fly as the fish become shy of the larger sizes of small hooks.

"If you rise a fish to, for example, No. 6, change to a No. 8 and you should get him, for that fish has shown you No. 6 was on the large size for that pool, place or time. If you have the right size fly on it is very rarely that you get merely a rise; the fish always means business if he comes. If, however, he rises and refuses, it is a clear sign that the fly is too big and showy for him."

Those are appropriate general guidelines for the modern steelheader, though the hook size might be a bit skimpy for husky fish that might run into heavy water once hooked. The amount and type of fly dressing is also a determinant factor—a sparsely dressed size 4 fly will probably fish just as well and maybe even better than a bushy size 6 fly. A steelheader tempting 20-pound fish to the surface might go with a slim fly on a bigger hook. In one of his Cairnton fishing logs, Wood recorded catching two 21-pound Atlantic salmon on May 5th, one on a size 8 March Brown and one on a size 10 March Brown.

The hook must be light enough to allow a close-to-the-surface presentation of the fly, yet at the same time be strong enough to land the fish. Besides which, you must read the steelhead's mind to a degree, because you must fathom what size is best for any given patch of greased line water. Starting with a size 6 or 8 sparsely dressed fly will do the trick most of the time.

GREASED LINE SURFACE PRESENTATION

The type of water compatible with the greased line technique is well illustrated in the second Scientific Anglers video hosted by Lani Waller, "Advanced Fly Fishing For Pacific Steelhead." The water is of medium depth, three to six feet, moderate current, with holding and resting areas interspersed throughout. The area that Waller fishes is classic greased line water, but could also be fished with the wet fly swing or a skating fly. Even though the surface is broken with miniature wavelets, mending is easy and offers ideal line control for any of those three methods. And none of those methods is the "right" method—the angler has the option to choose the tactic most suited to the mood of the day for both fish and fisherman.

The greased line method is appropriate in any stretch of stream that has medium depth, moderate current, and resting or holding places for steelhead. In many rivers there will be areas that are ideal in one or more of those respects, and possibly borderline in relation to one component. For instance, an area may have medium depth and lots of holding water, but may have current that is too fast to allow the angler to mend the line and maintain line control to present that all-important broadside view of the fly to the fish. In that case, the angler might be wiser to present a wet fly, mending the line to slow the swing, and exploit a more prolonged "hang down" technique.

There are countless variations in water that may be compatible with the greased line strategy, but the one question that must be addressed is this: if the water holds steelhead, can I mend the line to allow a slow broadside presentation of the fly?

The most appealing aspect of the near surface presentation of the greased line fly is that you can often see the steelhead take the fly. Much is made of that visual component of the greased line method by Wood and Scott in their book. From our point of view, steelhead react well to that sideways drifting fly, probably because the fly looks very lifelike, responding to each nuance in the surface current. For the most part, steelhead prefer a fly that is presented slowly, as with the greased line technique. It's not always the case, but in the vast majority of steelhead scenarios, a slow fly will outfish a fast fly, whether it's greased line, wet fly swing, or skated.

Wood determined whether to fish the greased line tactic by comparing air and water temperatures. He said, "As to the temperature of the atmosphere affecting sport with the greased line, the answer is very simple: when the air is colder than the water sport is bad; and when the air is warmer than the water it is good." Steelheaders needn't take Wood's advice as critical; Wood fished for Atlantic salmon from February to July mostly on one section of one river, the Cairnton on the Dee—we fly fish for steelhead year round and on a tremendous variety of rivers. When water temperatures reach the vicinity of 45 degrees, surface tactics like the greased line technique are effective for steelhead.

To fish the classic greased line technique, cast crosscurrent with your floating line and lightly dressed fly, upstream, downstream, or straight across, depending on the water. As needed, mend your line in smooth folding loops, keeping light tension on the line via the rod held to the side and pointing downstream ahead of the fly. Your sparsely dressed fly will be drifting broadside just under the surface. You want your fly to drift down and across the stream at the same time, as slowly as possible, so experiment with varying mends. You can extend the drift or the mend over faster water by releasing slack line.

As you lead your fly cross current with the rod pointed ahead of the fly's trajectory, you see a steelhead rise, inhale the

There are countless variations in water that may be compatible with the greased line strategy, but the one question that must be addressed is this: if the water holds steelhead, can I mend the line to allow a slow broadside presentation of the fly? Photo by Frank W. Amato

fly, and drift down with it. Somehow you manage not to jerk the rod skyward, but maintain the side-rod posture. Remembering to breathe, you feel the pull of the fish on your rod and line. You lift the rod up and to the side, reeling in any slack. The steelhead feels the burn of the hook and explodes in a spraying leap, securely hooked in the corner of the jaw. You are jubilant, fighting a steelhead that you saw rise to your fly, which was then hooked in the classic Wood greased line surface presentation.

GREASED LINE SUBSURFACE FLIES AND PRESENTATION

The first time I remember observing the subsurface greased line presentation for steelhead was on a bright January day on the North Umpqua. The angler cast his sinking fly line with fluid grace, mending the line while the cast was in mid-air. The line landed on the water in a curve upstream from the fly. The slack line near the fly allowed it to sink, while the mend bought some time before the current caught the fly line.

Once the fly had sunk and the current straightened the fly line, the angler mended to allow the fly to drift downstream and slowly come crosscurrent. Just as with the surface greased line presentation, the fly was drifting without excessive drag—but with enough tension to present the fly broadside to the steelhead.

Wood wrote, "When fishing sunk fly, I never use a smaller hook than 4/0; if I want to use anything smaller, I change to greased line and No. 1. My experience is that no sunk fly smaller than 4/0 is worth fishing—No. 1 and greased line will beat them every time; and indeed, my sole reason for using a big fly is to get down on to the stones."

Wood's method for fishing the sunk fly for Atlantic salmon wasn't the same as the then prevalent down-and-across cast with a tight line tethered to the fly swinging crosscurrent.

He wrote: "Fishing the far side of the stream I would cast square across with all the slack line in the dead water on the far side of the stream. I would then continue lifting my line upstream the same as with a greased line; not attempting to move or pull the fly in the slack water, but letting it sink. Only when I think it has sunk enough would I let the stream gradually begin to move it; and if I could lift I would continue to do so all the time, but when I expect the fish to take the fly I would be careful not to have any slack line. To hook a fish in deep water with a big fly and the line slack is almost an impossibility; if you watch the fish (and on the Dee the water is sometimes clear enough for you to see everything) you will see he takes it into his mouth and spits it out fairly quickly, directly he feels the big, hard hook; but if you have enough tension on the line to just move the fly—a slight tension will cause the stream to move the fly—you would then have a good chance of hooking the fish at the back of the mouth as he tries to let go. I endeavour to keep in touch with a big, sunk fly all the time."

In essence, Wood practiced a greased line presentation with the sunken fly because he mended his line to allow the fly to drift downstream but imparted enough tension to bring the fly crosscurrent, presenting a broadside view of the sunken fly to the fish. The main differences with the sunken fly included the initial mending to allow the fly to sink before it started its downstream run and using the jumbo fly as the sinking component.

The principles and tactics of the sunken greased line presentation and the surface greased line presentation are the same; the surface method employs slim flies dressed to fish in or near the surface, while the sunken fly method parlays a much larger hook as a sinking agent.

I suspect that Wood may have viewed the two methods as totally different because one was fished in the surface film or a few inches below and the other just above the river's bottom—Wood didn't believe in fishing at any other depth, strongly stating, "Mid-water fishing is of no use."

The improper hook set and poor fighting angle of the usual downstream swing (left) and the proper hook set and fighting angle of the greased–line technique. Move downstream of the fish if necessary.

Grease line water on the upper Klamath River. Photo by Brad Jackson

Wood may have also felt that the necessary aspect of treating the silk fly line to float for the greased line tactic further divided his radical surface method from his modified wet fly swing with the sunk fly.

Modern steelheaders can easily execute the surface film greased line tactic, but in addition we can use the same strategy with floating, sinktip, or sinking lines to present the steelhead with the broadside view of the sunken wet fly. Because we can tailor our lines to the depth and speed of the river, by judicious mending and application of line tension techniques we can control the almost dead-drifting subsurface fly at just about any depth. Unlike Atlantic salmon, steelhead respond to the mid-depth fly, particularly if the fly is presented slowly.

Leading the fly and line downstream with the rod tip is still important for the subsurface greased line tactic because it allows the fish to hook itself in the corner of the jaw.

Wood wrote: "You can almost always hook a fish where you like by controlling your nerves and the fly. For instance, when you are fishing a streamy bit of water and a fish takes the fly, you will, if you move or strike at once, most likely pull its nose; but if you wait until it goes down (and even a little longer), you will find every time you have hooked the fish in the angle of the jaw.

"With a No. 1 hook down to say, size 4, it is necessary to tighten *fairly* quickly *when* you feel the fish; or if your line is slack, when you see that the part of the line nearest the fish begins to move. The reason of this is that the fish feels the hard iron of the larger fly and rejects it. This is not so with the smaller summer sizes, unless the line is being dragged. I have often landed a fish and found the cast through the mouth and

gills and the hook in the side of the fish. The chewed fly had been ejected through the gills; a clear proof that my line had no drag on it and was slack. The fish generally takes somewhere downstream of me.

"Regarding the reason for striking, or rather tightening sooner with a big fly than a small one: in February and March, when I use a No. 1 to No. 4 fly, in strong water or even in low water, the fish come *so slowly* at the fly near the surface, that if you allow the fly to pass over them quickly, they will not move to it. I use greased line and keep the fly as near the surface as I can, and bring it over the fish so slowly that it is only just moving. To do this, I have to fish at the same angle as one would with a big, sunk fly, but I throw (or mend) the line outwards straight above the fly and keep doing so if necessary, according to the strength of the current; but let the fly come slowly across and slightly downstream. When the fish comes to the fly it is more or less in the same position as one would be that came at a sunk fly. Owing to this position, it is impossible to get the line to drop below the fish, so therefore, as soon as the fish goes down—and not before—I have to tighten quickly. Experience soon convinced me that, in cold weather, provided that the air was warmer than the water, greased line and a No. 1 hook would pay better than sunk fly provided one could fish it really slowly. I succeeded in doing this by switching (mending) over the greased line, always keeping it above the fly; in other words, controlling the speed of the fly by the line, and I think this accounts chiefly for my success on days when others do not get any fish.

"Directly the water gets warm and on the low side and fish are more lively, I use my ordinary method of letting the fly drift down and across, invariably letting the rod lead the line. In this way the fish hook themselves, but *then* I am fishing with smaller flies and the line pulls from below. If the fish are on the take, and keen for the fly, then I fish this way with a No. 1 hook; but as the barb is bigger on the No. 1, I tighten fairly sharply, though by no means a strike, in the generally accepted sense of the word."

Wood was often asked when is the best time to use the greased line approach, and because it seems that he saw a vast difference between surface greased lining and his sunk fly approach, he addressed the problem by comparing air temperature with water temperature. I believe that the main difference between the surface greased line tactic and the subsurface greased line tactic is the depth of the drifting fly, so it doesn't matter what the air versus water temperature is; as a generality, when water temperatures reach the vicinity of 45 degrees, some steelhead will move to the surface. On any given stream on any given day, the angler must prove or disprove whether a steelhead will rise to the surface by presenting the fly in that manner.

In the "Greased Line Fishing" chapter under the subheading, "The Time to Fish with the Greased Line," Wood wrote: "Many people seem to think that surface fishing is no use, except in shallow water and during hot weather. Experience has shown me that it is equally good in icy water, as long as the *air is warmer than the water*. It is also good in all depths of pools, if the water is reasonably clear. My favorite pool in February and March is a slack water on the edge of a strong stream, and that pool is twelve to fifteen feet deep. At that time of the year I usually use a No. 1 hook. Later in the season and in warm weather, the fish lie in the strong stream of this pool, and deep as it is they often take a summer hook No. 8. Every day I fish, even in February, I start by using a greased line and only when it fails do I use a sunk line and a big fly. As a result my fishing book shows that forty-three per cent of my fish caught in February in the last ten years were taken on greased line and small fly, sixty-five per cent in March, ninety-four per cent in April, and ninety-eight in May, and so on. I used to think it was no good fishing the greased line and small fly except in warm weather; but some years ago on the opening day, the 11th February and very cold, by late afternoon my sunk line was frozen up in the rod-rings. As a last hope to end a good day's fishing, I tried a greased line and small fly No. 1 hook, as the greased line does not freeze up so quickly, and managed to get two more fish. That made six; four on big fly and two on greased line, the last two both caught after four o'clock. Since then I have always fished greased line in all weathers and under all conditions, even in snowstorms, and it rarely fails or is beaten by sunk line; but I like to know that the *air is a bit warmer than the water*. In early Spring when the temperature of the water is more often under 38 degrees Fahrenheit, that of the air is generally higher. On the other hand, the air may well be colder than the water on a May evening, when the water is as much as 60 degrees and over. This does seem to put the fish down. I use, therefore, a big fly under those conditions; and this accounts for the occasional fish caught by me on a big fly, as late as April and even May.

"In hot weather during May, June or July, when the water is really warm, it pays always to cast across and upstream and to let the fly float and drift down, as it likes, and at times to lift the line upstream to prevent drag. For three-quarters of the distance travelled the fly will float on the surface, practically dry. You will get a lot of fish to take the fly in this position, although it lies flat on the surface and not

cocked up like a dry fly riding on the tips of its hackles. When the line reaches its full extension downstream and across the fly may skim across the surface of the water, leaving a wake behind it. Never let this occur; as soon as the line tightens, give it a jerk, which will put the fly under water, you can then fish it round to your bank."

Given the grace of 50 years and the quest for a different fish, we gain much from Wood's writings, but still need to delineate some basic differences: steelhead show their trout-like heritage by nailing the waking surface fly; and we fish year round for steelhead in a tremendous variety of streams influenced by varied watersheds, stream gradients, and types of holding water. It's impossible to establish rules that hold true under all fishing circumstances, including air and water temperatures. Besides, that would take the fun out of experimenting with new methods, which is what sparked Wood in the first place—the pursuit of new answers and approaches to challenging fishing puzzles.

OTHER WRITINGS ON GREASED LINE FISHING

We are fortunate that Wood's book is still readily available; *Greased Line Fishing For Salmon* immediately inspired at least two other books, long out of print in England and difficult to obtain.

In 1937 G.P.R. Balfour-Kinnear wrote *Flying Salmon*, which included an explanatory chapter "Greased Line," a clear and concise rendition of the Wood greased line approach. Balfour-Kinnear wrote two additional chapters on fishing the greased line technique and one entitled "Greased Line Methods Applied to Sunk Fly." These take the form of a dialogue between Shepherd and Sheep, which are Balfour-Kinnear and his friend Percy Deas. Unlike the explanatory chapter, the dialogue format is difficult to read.

The Floating Line For Salmon And Sea Trout by Anthony Crossley in 1939 includes Crossley's attitudes about salmon fishing with a dry line, and some fascinating correspondence between the angling writers of the day. One of the most interesting chapters is written by John Rennie, "Dry Fly Fishing For Salmon," which is a brief account of Rennie's limited dry fly successes with Atlantic salmon. Rennie poses more questions than he answers; many of which are only now being addressed by dry fly steelheaders 50 years later.

Like steelheaders, Atlantic salmon fishermen use various strategies to take fish, and like fishermen everywhere, the "experts" disagree about most aspects of fly fishing, including rod tapers and lengths, types of lines and how to use them, single versus double hooks, effective colors of flies, how well fish see, how much flash should be in a fly, what tactics are best for any given time or place on the river, and other questions of interest to fishermen. In one section of *Greased Line Fishing For Salmon* Wood answered 55 separate questions about his methods.

In 1952 Jock Scott went to press with his book, *Fine And Far Off, Salmon Fishing Methods In Practice*, in which he described the techniques of Alexander Grant and Percy Laming: "It must be remembered that Mr. Grant was using an oiled-line system in the 1890's, long before the greased-line was known. I believe that Mr. Laming began grease-lining in 1897 on the Dee. Mr. Grant was oiling his line in 1895."

In the chapter "Fishing The Oiled Line" Scott tells how Grant lubed his fly line with "raw—not boiled—linseed oil." (Wood used Hardy's Cerolene grease on his line.) Grant used

---

Facing page: As soon as Frank Amato's grease-line touched the water's surface this long, slim 16 pound hatchery summer run steelhead attacked it. Hungry for fish and not wanting the male to spawn with wild fish, Frank took it home. Photo by Frank Amato

linseed oil because, Scott wrote: "Mr. Grant strongly objects to the line floating on the surface film; he likes to have his line below it. He argues that the floating line, as it comes across, is nearly bound to cause a riffle; indeed, if there be a downstream wind, it is almost certain to do so. A line coated with raw linseed oil does not float on the surface, it just goes under; but of even greater importance, the oil acts as a lubricant between line and water, and the line can easily be lifted for a cast, slipping sweetly out of the river when pulled by the rod."

Grant fished a lengthy line, without mending, keeping the fly from scooting crosscurrent by casting downstream at a shallow angle. He kept his rod low to the water, letting the extended length of line and water resistance help to hook the fish. Like Wood, he advised not striking the fish, merely waiting until the angler could feel the fish, already hooked, pull on the line.

In the chapter "Controlled Drag" Scott wrote, "The method described in this chapter is based upon that devised by Mr. Percy Laming in 1897, and first practised by him on the Aberdeenshire Dee." Laming greased his line but fished it differently than Grant or Wood. Scott wrote, "If you are floating a dead fly down in the Wood style, i.e., the fly is drifting down like a dead insect—the proper way to fish it—you will only see a quick swirl which hardly breaks the surface, and then your line will tighten almost instantly. If you are fishing a tight line in the Grant style you very probably will not see anything before you feel the pluck, the two being simultaneous. When fishing the dragging fly the angler is likely to see the quick swirl as in dead fly procedure. Then comes the instant's doubt, the line rips tight, and you have him.

"The fly drags, certainly, but I do not like to see it ploughing a big furrow along the surface. You can undoubtedly catch salmon in that way, because I have seen it done on the Spey, but personally I prefer to do all my dragging with the fly just not cutting, and about three or four inches under the surface.

"At times the skimming fly obtains results. One summer day I watched an angler fishing fast water, and dragging so fast that his fly was making a V-shaped wake like a tiny destroyer, and a fish fairly hurled himself on that fly—bang, smash, and the belly of the line ripped off the water and tightened with a twang.

"The *modus operandi* is simple and lends itself to the use of a long line. Put briefly, you cast more or less square across, keep the rod steady and let the line do what it likes. The line naturally bellies and pulls the fly down and across in a big arc until the whole thing straightens out across and below—say at an angle of 30 degrees to the stream.

"I have no doubt whatever that many anglers will wonder why a salmon takes a dragging fly when they have been told both by their sunk fly and greased line—Wood style—friends to avoid drag like the plague. Frankly, I do not know for certain, but, so far as I am aware, flash is the chief attraction. I have tried all kinds of tricks on every sort of water and they will all kill salmon at times. So when anyone talks to me about a 'best' method, I just smile and say nothing. The only thing to which I hold strongly is that the Wood system does give you a higher percentage of hooked fish than does any other."

Recently Mark Bachmann told how he was hooking Deschutes steelhead in deep, slow pools by letting his floating line form a long belly, which made the fly speed up as it swung across, similar to Laming's method, but contrary to the standard steelhead doctrine of presenting a slow fly.

Grant's subsurface wet fly swing could be easily accomplished with an Intermediate sinking line, but I suspect that steelhead would respond more readily if the swing was slowed by incorporating some of Wood's mending tactics. Mending also opens more water for an effective fly presentation—perfect pools are rare and perfect pools for cast after cast from different positions are even more rare.

In Scott's *Fine And Far Off, Salmon Fishing Methods In Practice,* he said, "Mr. Grant never fishes in any other way (than the Grant method); I fish in several styles; I graft his ideas on to the Wood and Laming methods so that it is difficult in my case to keep an accurate score. So that I may be fishing Grant, or Grant-Wood, or Grant-Laming, and very seldom pure Wood or Laming."

If there is a moral here for steelheaders, it may be that it pays to be flexible and to experiment with a variety of tactics for any given river—the maximum enjoyment of fly fishing for steelhead comes with the perfect union of fish, river, and method, as defined by the individual fisherman.

RUMINATIONS ON GREASED LINE FISHING

Reading *Greased Line Fishing For Salmon* often raises as many questions as it answers, leading the angler to try new tactics while afield, then to reopen the Wood/Scott book upon returning, searching for answers to greased line puzzles. It would be lovely to open a time portal back to the 1930's and see Wood in action, teasing his Cairnton fish to the fly, then to videotape his techniques and interview him in depth. Wood's salmon strategies were revolutionary; we are lucky that we have his methods available in print, but we are cursed with his tantalizingly sparse book that still challenges and haunts us after 50 years.

Whether fishing a surface greased line fly or a subsurface greased line presentation, I find them demanding techniques. Greased line strategies demand precise mending and rod work, in addition to the absolute concentration needed to detect the strike to the subsurface fly and great restraint when the steelhead takes the surface fly. I tend to start daydreaming after the first half hour or so of greased lining, watching the flow of the river downstream where an ouzel dips for caddis, or mentally marking the progress of the setting sun, or I silently speculate on the scenery of canyon walls softened by hundred year old trees. After awhile I switch to a controlled wet fly swing, content to let a steelhead surprise me out of my reveries by striking the fly. On the days I have the patience and interest to respond to a more involved scheme for catching steelhead than the wet fly swing, I often hunt for water that allows me to skate a dry fly. There is nothing inherently right or wrong about choosing the greased line tactic or the classic wet fly swing or the skated dry fly—it's the steelheader's choice, according to the time of the year, water conditions, layout of the stream, preference of the fish, and mood of the fisherman.

In his chapter "Summer Steelhead" in *The Western Angler,* Haig-Brown wrote: "Those are the good wet-fly days, when a run is fresh from the sea and conditions are right. There are others. And later in the season, with fewer and staler fish, the wise angler will not be content with the wet fly, unless it happens to do well for him. There is always the dry fly, which may take fish, and there is greased-line fishing, probably the most delicate and worthwhile method of taking dour non-feeders under difficult conditions that man has yet thought out. The essential principle of greased-line fishing is a compact, lightly dressed fly fished right up under the surface film and without drag. The normal cast, in straightforward water, is across and slightly downstream, with a slack line. As the current pulls the slack into a belly that threatens to draw the fly, the fisherman makes an upstream "mend"—lifts the belly of the line without moving the fly and places it upstream—and the fly continues to fish down and slightly across at the speed of the current, instead of being drawn against it by the pull of the line. But it is not necessary to go into the details of the method here; that has been well and fully done in Jock Scott's book, *Greased-Line Fishing For Salmon*. It is enough to say that summer steelhead will respond to the method and that the streams of the country lend themselves to it almost perfectly."

Scott wrote, "Notice the delightful variations. This is the charm of greased-line fishing; it compels you to think. Each stream and eddy presents a new problem, so that even a blank day passes with the speed of thought. Concentration is vital, and the casual and inattentive fisherman who allows his fly to drag all over the river is missing ninety per cent of the joy which successful greased-lining brings."

THE HUNTER AND THE SEEKER

The hunter is an intense fisherman, bringing the quest for daily bread to the stream, fishing with a burning intensity, with fish as the quarry. Some challenge the river, themselves, and the fish with a fervor akin to combat. They bring a mindset that demands the perfect tight-loop cast, the perfect error-free presentation, and the perfect fish, as if bending the convolutions of the river into a set of diagrams, bending the will of the fish to their own design, ambushing fish in a crunch of personal superiority over the piscatorial foe.

I find myself there sometimes, fraught with anxiety and tension from the reality of the modern world, blasting my troubles away with the intense concentration of the hunter, tightly squeezing the cork grip as I would throttle my problems. I'm like a tightly wound spring, but instead of loosely uncoiling, I cock and unwind in the quick crescendo of the graphite rod. Fortunately, the physical demands of wading, casting, and sometimes catching fish slowly mellows my charge to a more enjoyable communion with the river, the fish, and the fishing.

I prefer to be the seeker, a heron of a non-predatory sort, wading and communicating with the river, its environs, and its most delightful of critters, its fish. I embrace fishing as a balm for the inner being, a cleansing of things outside the realm of the river, a bathing in this release of tensions.

Steelhead are magnificent fish and catching one always energizes the fisherman with a stab of adrenaline. Although we desire the excitement and crave catching the gorgeous steelhead, the satisfaction of fishing a pleasing method and being as one with the river is as important as any other reason for fishing.

The Morice River in British Columbia presents the angler with an incredible amount of water for floating line fishing techniques. Unfortunately, its fish runs have suffered from commercial fishing exploitation. Photo by Frank Amato

Dry Fly Steelhead

V

Most fly fishermen have a secret desire to catch a huge trout and preferably on a dry fly. For many of us, steelhead fulfill that fantasy because these giant sea-run rainbow readily take dry flies under the proper conditions. But as most dry fly fishermen will tell you, presentation of the fly is at least as important as the fly pattern, and in most cases the appropriate presentation is critical for success.

There are some anglers who are concerned about the difference between a skated fly and a waked fly, but the distinction between them is minimal. In the strictest sense, a skater glides atop the surface, leaving little or no wake; whereas the waker is intentionally fished to produce a distinct wake behind the fly.

Historically, trout skaters skipped over the surface, barely indenting the water. As far as I know, there were no traditional trout flies designed as wakers, where the fly burrowed into the surface film, causing a wake. In recent years it's become common practice to swim mouse patterns in front of big Alaskan rainbow, and because these flies move the surface water enough to produce a wake, they might be considered waking flies. They might also be considered bass bugs, as that is the origin of the deer hair mouse.

Because most long-time dry fly steelheaders use the terms skater and waker interchangeably and because I believe that there is little tactical difference between the two, I consider the terms synonymous. However, there is merit in examining some of the crucial elements in dry fly design that

affect the amount of wake that a waker or a skater causes. These include the silhouette, denseness, and floatation of the fly, which I'll delve into later.

Some anglers construe a radical disparity between a dry steelhead fly that is fished dead-drift versus a steelhead dry fly that is skated or waked across the river. Some feel that a waking fly is actually a "damp" fly because it's in the surface film instead of on top of it and thus has crossed an arbitrary dividing line and is not a "true" dry fly.

That line of thought may have evolved from anglers wanting to draw some type of distinction between the greased line presentation of a surface film fly as opposed to a completely "dry" dry fly. Both tactics require concentration and skill; one strategy is not inherently better than the other. Others feel that imparting motion to the dry fly is not true dry fly fishing, but the history of fly fishing chronicles just the opposite—from the very beginning anglers have added judicious movement to the fly to excite a strike. Controlled drag imparted to a waking dry fly also requires patience, concentration, and skill, and is just as challenging as the dead-drift dry fly tactic. Correctly reading surface currents and altering your presentation to match existing river conditions requires an equal degree of watermanship with both tactics.

I believe that a steelhead dry fly is one that is on or in the surface film and not under water, and is "dry" enough to bring a steelhead to the top for a surface rise. It's not a contest

Haig–Brown was probably the first to design a dry fly specifically for steelhead. Like many anglers he cast no distinctions between a dead–drifted dry fly versus an active dry fly, but instead explored various top water tactics using diverse flies—with mixed success. He tied this Steelhead Bee in 1975 at the Federation of Fly Fishers 10th anniversary conclave in Eugene, Oregon.
Facing page: *The author writes, "I remember standing on a bluff overlooking the North Umpqua River, watching the jade green flow of water, almost mesmerized by the lines of bubbles and flotsam twisting this way and that, inexorably borne downstream. On the far side of the river beneath on interlocking of rock ledges, a summer steelhead eased out into the current, holding briefly under the current seam. The fish tipped up, drifted downstream a few feet while dangling just under the surface, then rose to the top, opened its mouth on an insect, and went back down under the ledge just like a jumbo trout." Photo by Joe Howell*

as to whether a steelhead will rise to a greased line presentation or to a dead-drift dry fly presentation or to a skated dry fly presentation—there is a measure of skill in all these tactics and no "right" or "wrong" approach based on method alone. Because steelheading is not a tournament, a discussion as to what constitutes a "true" dry fly presentation is not nearly as important as the tactics behind these strategies. If one method is more gratifying to the angler, so be it, but there is only one true judge, and that is the steelhead.

Roderick Haig–Brown was one of our most admired steelheading authors and although he wrote primarily of the Pacific Northwest and British Columbia, from this desk he also spun fishing tales of South America, Iceland, his home waters in England, and eastern spring creeks like the Beaverkill. Photo by David Lambroughton

THE FIRST STEELHEAD DRY FLY

Roderick Haig-Brown was one of our most admired steelheading authors and although he wrote primarily of the Pacific Northwest and British Columbia, he also spun fishing tales of South America, Iceland, his home waters in England, and eastern spring creeks like the Beaverkill.

Though he died in October of 1976, the Haig-Brown legacy of flies, fly fishing techniques, and philosophy of respect for our anadromous fish lives on. He was a pioneer in adapting Wood's greased-line strategies to steelhead and advocated dry fly fishing for steelhead years before it was generally acknowledged that steelhead would take flies, let alone on the surface.

Haig–Brown was probably the first to design a dry fly specifically for steelhead. Like many anglers he cast no distinctions between a dead–drifted dry fly versus an active dry fly, but instead explored various top water tactics using diverse flies—with mixed success.

Haig-Brown first wrote of a prototype for his Steelhead Bee in 1959 in his book, *Fisherman's Summer*. He said, "This was an early September day, still in 1951, bright and sunny and with the river in perfect shape. I started in at the lower end of the bar in the Main Island Pool with 2x gut and a new fly pattern—a variation of the McKenzie River Brown and Yellow Bug, tied Wulff fashion with fox squirrel wings and tail on a No. 6 hook."

His descriptions of rises, fish missed and hooked and fought are truly delightful. He summed up, "As nearly as I can remember the details, I had risen at least twelve good fish,

all to the dry fly, had missed six or seven, been broken by three and killed three. So far as I know they were all steelheads—not a cutthroat among them."

With a *Fisherman's Fall* in 1964, Haig-Brown presented a firm dry fly steelhead pattern. He wrote, "Most of my fish have been taken on a No. 8 hook with a dressing I now call the Steelhead Bee. There is nothing sacred or mystic about this dressing, except perhaps its general shape and coloration. Other brown hairs than fox squirrel may be used and I have used them. The body could be made of fur dubbing instead of silk, and the hackle could equally well be ginger or honey. In heavy water a No. 6 hook is not too large; in very low water No. 10 or even No. 12 may be a little better. But after using this fly in various forms for more than ten years I feel that if a steelhead can be persuaded to rise to the surface at all he will come to this pattern just as surely as any other."

In Part Four of *Fisherman's Fall*, "Steelhead and Low Water" Haig-Brown writes of raising, hooking, missing, and landing steelhead on a floating fly. Even though he was fishing a small stream on a lightly fished Vancouver Island of almost 30 years ago, his discussion of water types and tactics is still appropriate today. At one point he wrote, "In *Fisherman's Summer* I described in some detail the successful use of the floating fly for summer steelhead. Since that time I have had many opportunities to test the matter further, especially in the Heber River, and I am more than ever convinced that dry-fly fishing, under summer and fall conditions, is the most effective fly-fishing method, as well as the most attractive.

"Fishing Heber Creek I generally use an eight-foot cane rod weighing about four ounces, with an HCH or HCF fly line, a hundred yards of backing and leaders tapered to 1x—sometimes to 3x. Most of my fish have been taken on a No. 8 hook with a dressing I now call the Steelhead Bee.

The dressing for the **Steelhead Bee** is as follows:

Tail: Red fox squirrel, quite bushy. Slightly longer than hook shank
Body: Equal sections dark brown, yellow and dark brown silk
Hackle: Brown, sparse
Wings: Red fox squirrel, quite bushy and slightly longer than the hook shank, tied forward, divided and straightened back within about 10 degrees of upright."

In 1981 his daughter Valerie and wife Ann collaborated on a collection of Roderick's writings in *The Master And His Fish*. In the chapter "Evolution of a Steelhead Fly", first printed in 1976 in *Roundtable* magazine, he wrote: "Shortly after the Second World War I began to notice that floating flies commonly produced more action from summer steelhead than wet flies. I had long used the old McKenzie bucktail floaters for cutthroats in fast broken water because they floated well, and these were the first floaters that rose steelhead for me, so far as I can recall. I had a fair proportion of short rises, missed rises, swirls, lunges, tail slaps, and follow-backs, and this led me to search and experiment over several years to find something more convincing. I won't go into detail except to say that some of my worst looking flies, creatures that flopped over on their sides instead of riding upright, produced the liveliest action and the most honest rises.

"This convinced me that what I needed was a representation of a terrestrial insect, drowned or drowning. I wanted a relatively dark colour, tending to brown rather than grey, hair wings and tail, because of its floating qualities, a fairly heavy body that would settle down into the surface film, and a very sparse hackle. I preferred a brown and yellow body because it had always done well for me and it obviously suggests a number of summer creatures that may fall into the water—bees, yellow-jackets, deerflies, caddisflies, even some dragonflies. The fly that grew out of this extensive trial and error was the Steelhead Bee. It can be tied on a wide range of hook sizes from 2 to 10, depending on the state of the water, but sizes 6 or 8 are usually about right.

"This is a very effective fly, for me and many other fishermen who have tried it. Obviously there is nothing very original about it. In type it is a Wulff, and the dressing has clear echoes of the Western Bee and the McKenzie Brown and Yellow Bug. It raises summer steelhead at least as well as any fly I have tried and hooks a higher proportion of them."

DRY FLY
HOLDING WATER—STRIKE TRIGGERS

Some anglers are immediately smitten with steelheading and leap right into it, but for many of us our first steelhead comes to the trout fly. Mine was a wild female on the Santiam River in Oregon. The steelhead was feeding on western March brown mayflies as she progressed back downstream after spawning. She fell to a dead-drifted size 12 Comparadun in a smooth surfaced back eddy where I fought and landed her on trout gear. Some fly fishermen hook their first steelhead when their Elk Hair Caddis or Humpy abandons its drag free drift and skitters crosscurrent, only to be taken in a smashing rise. Few of these trout-fly-hooked steelhead are landed because of light tippets and desperate excitement. I was fortunate in that my fish was tired from spawning and elected to stay in the pool instead of rushing downstream with the current.

The best type of water for dry fly steelheading is of medium depth from 3 to 6 feet and medium current. However, these are general guidelines because steelhead will rise to the dry in water that is deeper or more shallow, and in slower or faster current. The prime factor is that the fish feels secure where it's holding and is willing to move to the dry fly.

For dry fly fishing you can also consider steelhead as large trout that tend to hold in the same types of water that trout favor. Steelhead-as-trout need rest and cover from the relentless current. Holding areas include riffles, current seams, the middle or throat of the run, tailouts, and in front or behind rocks and boulders and along ledges. Steelhead will take a dry in any of these holding areas. Because steelhead favor the same types of holding water in any given river, you can spot prime areas even on rivers new to you.

Choice dry fly water is usually prime for the classic wet fly swing, greased line presentation, or dead-drifted nymph technique. But the payoff for the surface presentation is the rise to the dry fly—that supreme moment of fly fishing exhilaration.

The best water temperatures for surface steelheading are from 45 to 65 degrees, although steelheaders take fish on top in water temperatures that exceed those parameters. Under ideal conditions winter steelhead will sometimes take topwater flies, but because of warmer water temperatures, summer run fish are more likely surface fly candidates, particularly in water with good clarity.

Your chances at raising a steelhead are better if the fish are rested and unmolested by other anglers because of the basic conflict of survival that all fish face—to run for cover or to feed. For steelhead, the prime needs are rest, cover and spawning, which includes a measure of aggressive competition for a mate and a spawning site. A rested steelhead is more likely to take a surface fly because it trips either of two strike triggers: territorial aggression or reactivated feeding instinct.

There are times when the dead-drifted dry will work better than the skated dry, but overall, the skated fly will raise more steelhead because even though you can cover lots of water with either method, the waker has a broader range of appeal to the fish—the waker taps on both strike triggers.

Generally, the dead-drifted fly elicits less strikes because it only activates one strike trigger, the feeding instinct provoked by a topwater insect. Factors that determine when steelhead will move to the dead-drifted fly instead of the skater are hard to recognize. These include the mood of the fish as affected by river variables such as shifts in barometric pressure, air or water temperature changes, heavy aquatic insect hatches, or other underwater catalysts that we can't see or specify, including the whims of individual fish. Steelhead are also affected by the movements of salmon and other steelhead, and predators such as eagles, osprey, heron, and otter. For steelhead the spawning run is an upstream progression of ever increasing tension between fish that compete for mates and a choice site for the spawning nest. At best we have a mere glimpse into the complex world of the steelhead that changes from river to river and day to day.

Water that is choice dry fly water is usually prime for the classic wet fly swing, greased line presentation, or the dead–drifted nymph technique. But the payoff for the surface presentation is the rise to the dry fly—that supreme moment of fly fishing exhilaration. Howard West of Scientific Anglers is certainly excited about his fish. Photo by Howard West

It's a field ripe with speculation; just as with the classic wet fly swing, theories vary according to the person speculating and their success with specific tactics or favorite fly patterns. There is no cast iron theory that has proven reliable for accurately determining when steelhead prefer a dead-drifted fly over a skated fly. In fact, one successful strategy is to first cover the water with a dead-drifted dry, then go back and rework the water with a skater. Another tactic is to fish upstream or straight across with a dead-drifted fly, then let it

For dry fly fishing you can also consider steelhead as large trout that tend to hold in the same types of water that trout favor. Steelhead–as–trout need rest and cover from the relentless current. Holding areas include riffles, current seams, the middle or the throat of the run, tailouts, and in front of and behind rocks and boulders and along ledges. Photo by Frank Amato

skate across the current on a tight line. Sometimes a steelhead will follow the fly as it drifts drag-free, but won't take until the fly begins waking.

One fall day I watched J.D. Love fish his way downriver on a stream on the Olympic Peninsula, scooting his fly over the watery ceiling of each steelhead holding lie. He was using a fly similar to Harry Lemire's Grease Liner, tied on a size 6 hook. It had a pale orange dubbed seal body, no tail, no front hackle, and a deer hair wing cinched down like the wing on an Elk Hair Caddis. In one spot he cast crosscurrent with a slack line so the fly would not skate, but instead drift on the top of a small pool on the other side of the current. While the fly rode the tiny currents of the backeddy, an 8-pound steelhead gleaned the fly from the surface. The rise was sweet, J.D. yelled in jubilation, and after a pleasant battle landed the fish. He took other steelhead on the same day with the same method. Because we can't read the steelhead's mind, it pays to be flexible, both in types of flies and presentations.

The skated fly ignites more strikes because it treads on both triggers. A moving fly simulates lifelike animation, causing the fly to appear to trespass on contested territory. The steelhead responds with an open mouthed attack on the intruder waking crosscurrent over its head. The dead-drifted fly is not much of a threat to the fish because the fly passively drifts downstream. Even if the angler imparts movement, such as making it hop or scoot a bit while it floats downstream, it probably isn't seen by the steelhead as an aggressive movement, but more likely as an insect struggling in the stream. The skated or waked fly also appeals to this sea-run trout's remembered feeding drives because many insects hop,

skip, and struggle as they swim crosscurrent on top of the water.

I remember standing on a bluff overlooking the North Umpqua River, watching the jade green flow of water, almost mesmerized by the lines of bubbles and flotsam twisting this way and that, inexorably borne downstream. On the far side of the river beneath an interlocking of rock ledges, a summer steelhead eased out into the current, holding briefly under the current seam. The fish tipped up, drifted downstream a few feet while dangling just under the surface, then rose to the top, opened its mouth on an insect, and went back down under the ledge just like a jumbo trout.

I've talked to anglers who have seen steelhead on the Umpqua taking size 14 cream mayflies in late August and early September; Joe Howell of the Blue Heron Fly Shop has seen a steelhead's stomach chock full of mayflies. (During prime circumstances on the Olympic Peninsula, guide J.D. Love and his clients have taken topwater steelhead on Comparaduns as small as size 16.) On the North Umpqua and on numerous other rivers of the Pacific Northwest, it's not uncommon in the fall to see steelhead chasing large adult caddis, the giant orange sedge or October caddis (*Limnephilus Dicosmoecus*).

An angler told me that one August day on the Deschutes he saw a steelhead feeding on size 14 tan caddis. The fish was holding behind a rock, making "humping feeding rises just like a trout." He later took that steelhead with a Green Butt Skunk; the fish weighed 12 pounds. He said that in retrospect he wished he had tried a dry fly, but he figured, "Hey, it's a steelhead, I should use a regular steelhead fly."

Dave McNeese has seen winter steelhead with several dozen tiny winter black stoneflies in their stomachs (these are size 16 and 18 insects): "It's got to be individual fish because not all steelhead do it, even under ideal feeding conditions. There are individual steelhead that will feed." He's also observed steelhead in the Elk River feeding on size 14 and 16 cream mayflies in the latter part of March. The Elk hosts a late run of wild winter steelhead; these 23 to 30 inch fish were fresh, caught a mile from tidewater on Light Cahills.

DEAD-DRIFT DRY FLY

One of the most straightforward ways to take steelhead on a dead-drifted dry is to use trout tactics, mending your line to achieve a good drift without lining the fish with the fly line or leader. Like trout, steelhead can be spooked in clear water by the passing shadow of the line.

Steelhead will rise to oversize trout patterns such as the Clark's Stonefly, Bucktail Caddis and Wulff flies, and to dry Atlantic salmon patterns like the Bomber, and to the Steelhead Bee. The tradeoff with a heavily hackled fly such as a Humpy or a Royal Wulff is that the hackle can impede a hookup. The same holds true for a fly with a long, stiff tail.

Flies that float lower in the water, such as the Bomber or the Steelhead Bee, attract more steelhead on a dead-drift because the fish can see the fly more clearly, which pushes their strike trigger just that much more. However, when fishing a flush floating fly, you must be sure to allow it to drift well past the fish before picking it up for the next cast, because of the surface disturbance the fly makes when you pull it out on the backcast.

Guide John Hazel says: "The Bomber has been around since the mid-1960's on the Atlantic coast; my variation, the Rusty Bomber, developed in 1979 when I was experimenting

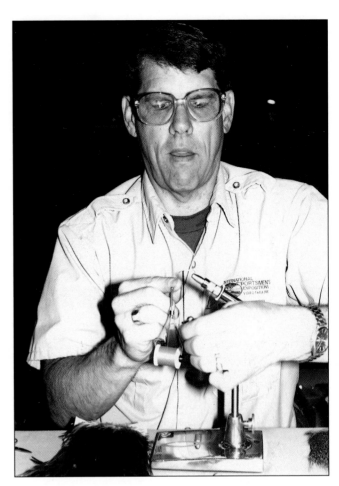

Lee Clark has developed a series of tinsel bodied dry flies that reflect the coloring in their yarn wings. The Clark Stonefly was originally designed for trout but has proven to be an effective steelhead fly as well.

with different pattern variations, trying to depict the emerging *Dicosmoecus* caddis. Although the *Dicosmoecus* typically crawls out to hatch on available structure, in larger rivers where there is less mid-river surface structure, they do indeed swim to the surface and painfully struggle to break the meniscus, and become extremely vulnerable to steelhead.

"The Rusty Bomber proved very effective, particularly in the manner in which the water resistance pushes back on the forward wing, creating a very life-like impression of the natural. The Rusty Bomber fishes very well by hanging the fly into boulder strewn pockets, letting it simply bobble and sputter, as well as the more traditional greased line technique in the riffles and tailouts.

"The Rusty Bomber has been unbelievably effective as a dead drifted dry fly in autumn's low water flows with an up-and-across technique. Originally tied to suggest the October Caddis, I now use the pattern effectively throughout the spring, summer, and fall seasons from southern Oregon to the northwestern B.C. coast and on both sides of the Cascade Mountain Range."

The Clark's Stonefly is hackled like a traditional dry fly, but with its tinsel body and no tail, it sits low in the water on its rear end. The design factor that sets it apart is its body/yarn/wing reflection component. The body is flat gold tinsel. The wing is two layers: the bottom is strands of yarn in yellow, brown, or rust; the top layer is deer or elk hair, which adds to floatation and gives the appearance of large dark

John Randolph, editor of Fly Fisherman *magazine, with his first British Columbia steelhead. Photo by Lani Waller*

wings as found in big western stoneflies or the equally large October caddis.

Looking at the deer hair wing from below, as a fish would do, the fly also gives the impression of having buzzing wings, as exhibited by the natural stonefly or caddis when trying to get airborne. In effect, fish can clearly see the tinsel body and yarn/body/wing reflection from the tinsel, while the hackle and hair keeps the fly afloat. The Clark's Stonefly makes an excellent dead-drifted dry fly for steelhead because of that twinkling of light reflected by the tinsel, and because it has good floatation and a buggy appearance. (The Clark's Stonefly can also be skated, but not as effectively as other patterns.)

John Randolph, editor of *Fly Fisherman* magazine, fished the Dean in August, 1989: "A steelhead boiled my Bomber twice, so I tied on a Clark's Stonefly. On the next cast the fish took the dead-drifted fly hard, and after about ten minutes I landed a 12-pound steelhead. It was the first time I used the Clark's Stonefly and it performed well for me throughout the trip."

The Bucktail Caddis is an excellent fly for running a combination of strategies while using only one fly. For example, you can dead-drift the fly without motion, recast and give the fly little hopping and scooting movements, recast and skate the fly in front of the fish, then recast and align the fly sideways just under the surface, fine tuning the drift with the light pressure of the greased line presentation, or you can pull the fly under and let it swing crosscurrent in the classic wet fly swing.

One crisp autumn morning J.D. Love and I were relaxing under a tree on the Calawah River on the Olympic Peninsula, watching October caddis flitting about in streamside foliage. Every so often one of the lumbering insects would fly over the river and dip down to lay eggs. We had each taken nice fish with wet flies and were content with the day, resting the fish and ourselves.

A man walked up and asked if he could fish the water. His first choice of fly was the Bucktail Caddis, fished on a dead-drift. After he fished it awhile, he said, "I think they'll move to the top, but this Caddis is too big for them."

He tied on a size 10 Blue Dun with deer hair wings and tail and shot his cast to the head of the pool. About halfway through the drift a steelhead took the fly in a flawless head-and-tail rise, just like an overgrown trout. I can still see that hooked fish leap clear of the river, scattering light amid the spray of water droplets set afire by the autumn sun.

SKATED DRY FLY—THE WALLER WAKER

The video showing Lani Waller raising and then hooking a steelhead on his Waller Waker is some of the most exciting fly fishing footage on film. Cinematographer John Fabion told me his crew shot 850 feet of film (almost the length of three football fields) to record that steelhead taking the fly off the top of the water. That footage has started a minor revolution in steelheading—dry fly steelheaders are commonplace on many rivers that previously only hosted anglers using wet fly strategies.

Lani Waller tells how it came about: "The fly was designed at the request of John Fabion because Scientific Anglers/3M had insisted that we get footage of a steelhead taking a dry fly.

"While on the Dean we found that traditional dry flies floated too low in the water for John to really see them through the camera lens. So one night after a frustrating day, John said, 'Lani, why don't you design a true dry fly—one that

really floats high and dry, and one that is really visible to both the camera and the fish. Call it the Waller Waker.'

"When we got back from that particular shooting session I went to work designing a new fly. I knew from past experience that all of the traditional steelhead dries had design weaknesses that allowed the current to push them under. As a result, they usually fished damp or submerged in the surface film. I wanted a true dry fly—one that floated *on* the surface.

"I began to think of a dragging, or waking dry fly as a tiny speed boat that had to skim, wake, or—key word— *plane* across the surface, just like a ski–boat.

"So I designed the fly with materials that were very buoyant, and with a high wing so the camera and the angler could see it easily. I used two wings instead of one, which is a design flaw in the Bomber, because two wings balance the fly. Having only one wing tends to flop the fly on its side when it gets wet, thus making the fly sink.

"The other secret is that the front of the fly is trimmed so that the entire front surface slants forward at about a 45 degree angle. This reinforces the tendency of the pushing current to run *under* the fly, instead of pushing and rolling *over* it, which makes a fly sink.

"I added a very stiff throat or beard on the fly of untanned moose. This acts as a miniature hydrofoil and when the current hits this hydrofoil the fly is lifted and it begins to plane like a ski-boat.

Lani Waller says, "I use the Waller Waker as both a locator and a taking fly. It is very effective in rough and deep water, and my friends and I have actually raised steelhead on it in water that was over six feet deep." Photo by Lani Waller

"I use the Waller Waker as both a locator and a taking fly. It is very effective in rough and deep water, and my friends and I have actually raised steelhead on it in water that was over six feet deep. I have seen Howard West of Scientific Anglers use it on the Babine and get steelhead up in seven feet of rough water. The beard also makes the fly look very buggy in the water, and the Waller Waker takes steelhead dead-drifted, too."

Waller has designed three different Waller Wakers. All three have black tails and beards. The Standard Waker has a gray and black body with white wings. The "Bee" has a black and orange body with tan elk hair wings. The "High Visibility Moth" has a white and gray body and fluorescent yellow wings. Since their introduction, Waller has made minor modifications of the original design in that he stiffens the wings with super glue and slants them slightly more forward. He says, "That provides a stiff lip or face that accentuates the fly's tendency to rise to the top under any water conditions."

He continues, "I say with complete confidence that I've distilled the essence of a downstream waking pattern and I know what the design features are that you need to keep that thing skating and waking under tension. The single most important thing is the angle of the forward wings and their stiffness. If those two things are correct you can float anything. In fact there has been a generation of British Columbia dry flies that have emerged over the last two seasons and all they are is a stiff slanted forward dish of deer hair that has been impregnated with either super glue or silicone and they have a tail. As long as the fly is fished under tension, the water hydraulics force the fly to the top. There's no doubt in my mind if a pattern isn't designed with a stiff slanted forward wing it will not consistently make the fly skate on the surface, not under all conditions."

Of course, not everyone is convinced the Waller Waker will work. One of the guides in British Columbia told him, "That thing is not a fly, it's a lure, a bass bug. That thing sends shivers down my spine." When Waller and the guide were fishing the Copper River, the guide said, "Put that thing right over there. Now watch, ain't nothing going to hit that thing and I know there's fish there."

Waller says, "Boy, I threw it over there and the guide no sooner got the words out of his mouth when a 15-pound hen comes up and just snarfs it. He shut up after that."

"You know," Waller says, "I still get guys who come up to me at sports shows and say, come on Waller, what's the truth. Those steelhead in that video didn't really take that fly. That was something like a Skunk fished just underneath the surface."

When looking at the videos, no doubt remains because the attentive viewer can see the wake still coming from the surface fly when the fish inhales it.

SKATED DRY FLY—WAG'S WAKER

In 1973 Bob Wagoner of Lewiston, Idaho was in California watching one of the best fly tyers in the world conduct a fly tying class. Bob says, "The instructor rambled on about the floatation of elk hair wings. I thought to myself that if elk hair wings float so well, why not turn them upside down where it will do some good. That stuck in my mind for 14 years, then one day that idea came back to me and I pushed everything aside and started working on a design.

"I worked on it for two days, only I was trying to make size 14 trout flies with it. I poked a lot of holes in my fingers. Keith Stonebraker stopped by one afternoon and said, 'That looks fantastic, why don't we put that on a steelhead pattern?'"

Wagoner says Stonebraker did so well on steelhead with Wag's Skater that they kept it secret for three years. Lani Waller and Howard West also had success with Wag's Waker. The fly went public in an article in the fall 1989 *Fly Fishing Quarterly*.

The most unique feature of Wag's Waker is its ski-like downrigger wings that are slightly splayed out on the bottom like the legs on a water strider. LeRoy Hyatt of Lewiston has added perhaps the final touch by substituting spun deer hair for the original body of peacock or pearlescent Flashabou. The deer hair body is tied in tan, orange, black, yellow, or olive deer hair.

Wag's Waker is palmered with brown, grizzly, or grizzly hackle dyed brown, with additional hackle wrapped in front.

Wagoner says, "The hackle on a size 6 fly is size 8, to keep the hackle inside those wings. You want the fly to float on the wings, not the hackle. The hackle is not a critical thing; it's really for decoration, to make it look nice."

The wings on the original Wag's Waker were tied with elk, but Wagoner has now switched to moose. He says, "We switched to moose because it floats better and it's stiffer. The only elk hair you can use that's stiff enough is off the back or the flank of the rear legs and I happen to have access to a lot of black moose. You can use either one but I prefer moose because it's tougher, doesn't break off as easy, and floats better."

To fish the Wag's Waker, Wagoner casts quartering downstream 30 to 40 feet and lets it drift across water that is 3 or 4 feet deep. On his home waters in the Lewiston area, he hooks most of his steelhead 20 feet from shore. Wagoner lets his fly wake or he will "jerk the leader to make the fly dart a couple of inches." If a fish boils without taking, he says, "I usually change flies and go right back after him with something else."

Wagoner says, "Most of the fish I've caught in this area have been right after daylight. I go out at dawn and I'm back home working by 8 or 9 o'clock. I enjoy being on the river at daylight when there's nobody else around and it's quiet and peaceful. I'm usually headed home when other people are heading out."

LeRoy Hyatt of Lewiston has developed Hyatt's Steelhead Caddis, designed around the principle of separate stacked deer hair wings. Hyatt created this unique approach in 1985 when he came up with the idea of tying in several individual deer hair wings along the top of the fly. Separated by dubbing, each wing extends to the rear. The Hyatt's Steelhead Caddis is a design type that can be adapted to any tyer's whim, not only for steelhead, but for trout and bass as well. You can dub the body in a variety of colors, finishing the fly with hackle or a spun deer hair head ala the Muddler. Instead of dubbing you can use yarn, especially the sparkly acrylic yarns with Antron. You can also add a bit of fluorescent wing material to the top of the most forward stack of deer hair to better see it when fishing. Bright wing locators include fluorescent strands of calf tail, bucktail, floss, or yarn.

SKATED DRY FLY TACTICS

You will be most successful with skated tactics for summer run steelhead with river temperatures from 45 to 65 degrees in water of medium depth and good clarity. These are generalities, though, and experienced steelheaders catch fish on top during extreme conditions. For example, on a trip to British Columbia in the fall of 1989, Lani Waller fished with guide Bob Clay on the Bulkley and Kispiox rivers and raised and hooked fish every day of their trip in 36 degree water.

You will be most effective fishing from 30 to 60 feet out, covering water that offers the steelhead a measure of rest from the current, such as along current seams, behind rocks and other sunken structure, and around ledges.

The technique is simple: cast down at a 45 degree angle, tighten the line enough to put tension on the fly so it resists the current without sinking, then guide it with the rod tip so the fly skates crosscurrent. You can employ mending tactics to either speed or slow the fly's crosscurrent progress.

Besides the steady crosscurrent arc, you can excite steelhead into striking by skating the fly back and forth across a tongue of current. You need to be almost directly upstream from the fish's lie and far enough away not to scare the fish. For this example we'll suppose you are standing upstream from a riffle and just a little to the left side, looking downstream. Cast across the current, to your right, then guide the

skating fly back through the current, ending on the left side. At the completion of the skater's swing across the riffle, your rod will be pointing straight downstream or slightly to the left.

While moving the fly as little as possible, roll cast your line across the current, thrusting your rod to the right. The line will then tighten in the flow, pulling the skater back across the current in the opposite direction, from left to right. In this case the roll cast might also be described as an overhand-flip in which you roll your wrist over, flipping the line across the current.

Another option is to reach to the first guide and pull down one strip of line, then make the flip cast while releasing the retrieved line. Initially, your fly will coast a bit back upstream, but then it will skim crosscurrent in about the same track (if you don't pull additional line from the reel).

Your goal is to scoot the skater back and forth in approximately the same path, continually tugging at the steelhead's strike trigger. By using this back and forth tactic, you can cover a riffle or current tongue very thoroughly. Because summer steelhead love to hover in the cover and oxygen richness of riffles, you'll pick up fish others have overlooked.

Waller's "Hang Down" technique for wet flies also works for dries: when the skater has come to rest below you and is just "hanging" there, leave it alone for a few moments. Steelhead will often follow the fly into shallow water and nail it after it stops its crosscurrent slide.

Hooking a steelhead with a dry fly is easy to envision but can be difficult to execute: when a steelhead takes your fly, let the fish go down with it and don't tighten up until you feel the fish pull.

Waller says, "A common problem when using surface presentations is to strike when you see the fish take your fly. Wait until the fish pulls on your line, then pull the rod to the side."

COLD WATER SKATERS

British Columbia guide Bob Clay says, "As water temperatures drop in late fall, steelhead tend to slow their reactions to the skated fly. The fly must be presented more slowly because the longer the steelhead looks at the fly, the better our chances are of getting the fish to rise. The best attribute about coldwater surface steelhead is the rise. Like the speed of the fly coming crosscurrent, the rise is also very slow and deliberate. You often get the 'alligator rise', the top of the steelhead's head comes out of the water, the jaws open, then snap down on your fly. Now it's your turn to be slow. When the fish rises and the fly disappears, raise the rod tip slowly, and when you feel the weight of the fish, set the hook.

"If the fish should miss the fly or you miss the fish, wait a minute and recast. Should you not get him up in the next two or three casts, drop your fly down a size. In general, I start with a size 4 Purple Moose Bomber as a searching fly. The fly is tied with dyed purple moose hair and has a larger forward wing for better visibility. For the body I flair and clip the moose hair on top of the hook, rather than spinning it around the hook, to give the hook more gape. The bottom of the body and the head area is glued so the fly won't twist on the hook. I use a regular length wet fly hook in standard wire for more hook gape than the same size Atlantic salmon style wet hook or a 3xlong hook. I am also experimenting with the Tiemco 8089 bass stinger hook in size 10, which looks more like a size 6 to me. When fishing the fly I almost always riffle hitch it.

"If the size 4 Purple Moose Bomber is refused, I size down to 6 or 8. If I still have no luck I change the silhouette of the fly to a hackled bivisible type. Failing this, I try a slimly dressed wet fly, riffle hitched. This fly will often save the day. If you've thrown the lot and still have no luck, mark the position of the fish and return after you've finished fishing the rest of the run. Fishing the surface fly to coldwater steelhead is the most challenging way to take steelhead. It is also the most rewarding, watching those slow motion 'alligator rises'."

CHANGE-UP DRIES

The Waller Waker design offers the advantages of a top-water fly that can handle rough currents, while imparting lots of surface commotion that brings steelhead to the top.

Waller says, "Most of the time they'll take a Waller Waker because it pushes a lot of water, stays high and dry longer, is highly visible under all conditions—dirty water, low light—and is easy for fish to see at great distances. Most of the time steelhead will take it, but if they don't, I then use a smaller version. If they don't take that, then I prefer to follow with a dry that rides higher on the water and has a slimmer silhouette. So not only is the fly different in terms of its silhouette, but also in terms of the way it skates. Almost always, if they've rolled on that large fly of mine, but haven't taken it, they will take Wag's Waker."

The only disadvantage to the Waller Waker is that it's wind resistant to cast because of its bulk, and the flat face of the fly creates drag in the air. Waller says he has experimented with 6 and 7-weight rods, but recommends at least an 8-weight.

The advantage of Wag's Waker and Hyatt's Steelhead Caddis is that both offer steelhead an alternate profile and waking indentation on the surface of the water compared to the Bomber or Waller Waker. They are lighter and easier to cast, but they do require fairly smooth water to skate properly. The disadvantage of Wag's Waker is that it will sometimes flip upside down, putting the wings in the air so the fly won't skate, or it will flip up and ride on its head. The disadvantage of Hyatt's Caddis is that the butt end of the fly will sometimes sink too far under the surface to wake properly. But both fly designs offer intriguing possibilities as followup flies or as dead-drifted or skated dry flies.

In the future we may see more innovative dry fly designs for steelhead, such as using Evasote closed cell foam material for the body or incorporating rubber legs for dry flies such as the Steelhead Madam X.

Traditionally, if the dead-drifted or skated dry fly doesn't work, steelheaders go with a riffled hitched wet fly to bring steelhead to the top.

RIFFLE HITCH

The riffle hitch originated on Atlantic salmon waters, and is still an effective tactic: On August 23, 1988 Mike Crosby caught a five-foot long salmon estimated at over 60 pounds on New Brunswick's Restigouche River—on a dry fly. The massive fish was caught on "a No. 2 long shank brown bug with orange hackle," according to an article in *Eastern Woods & Waters* magazine.

The fish was released but color photos of the fish laying in the water next to the fisherman's canoe allowed fisheries biologists to closely estimate its weight. By measuring the distance between the thwarts in the canoe and comparing it to the distance between the nose of the fish and its dorsal fin,

---

Facing page: For steelhead the spawning run is an upstream progression of ever increasing tension between fish that compete for mates and a choice site for the spawning nest. At best we have a mere glimpse into the complex world of the steelhead that changes from river to river and from day to day. Photo by Scott Ripley

Lee Wulff first introduced the riffle hitch to the fly fishing world in an article in Outdoor Life. *On September 11, 1988 Wulff took a 9–pound steelhead on the Copper River in British Columbia on a size 28 hook. Photo by Joan Wulff*

which was 31 inches, the fish was estimated at between 60 and 62 inches long. A 55-inch salmon of average girth would weigh 60 pounds. Since this leviathan had a 5-inch hook nose, that length was subtracted, but it was still estimated to weigh over 60 pounds.

"I thought the guide was going to have a heart attack," Crosby reported, "the first time the fish raised for the fly it was just like a big shadow. The second and third times he came I just knew he had the fly and I pulled, but I didn't connect. I found out why later on when I saw that big hooked jaw.

"The fourth time he came he just showed deep under the fly and I started to get worried. So I changed the fly.

"It took me two or three minutes to find him again and I was starting to panic. But the fifth time he came for the fly it didn't travel three feet and he had it.

"The only way I can describe what happened when he took off downstream was that he churned the river up so much it was like looking inside a washing machine. The 250 yards of backing was gone in one run so we had to pull the anchor and start up the motor and go after him.

"I would gather my line back and we would go downriver after him. Then he would strip the reel again and we would go upriver. We did that for an hour. I only had 8-pound test leader so I couldn't do much with him. He was taking line so fast I couldn't go ashore and play him."

"When we got him to the boat all I could think about was getting him loose before we hurt him so we didn't get any scale samples or measurements. But I don't really care whether he was a North American record or not. I know I caught a salmon that no one else will probably ever top again and I'm happy with that."

According to statistics from the International Game Fish Association, the current world record fly rod Atlantic salmon on 8-pound test weighed 31-pounds, 8-ounces, caught by Darryl G. Behrman on the Alta River, Norway, on June 25, 1983. At twice the breaking strength, in the 16-pound tippet class the record is 44-pounds, 12-ounces from the Moisie River in Quebec. Both fish are well short of Crosby's immense male. The all-tackle record was just shy of 80 pounds, caught in the Tana River in Norway in 1928.

Lee Wulff first introduced the riffle hitch to the fly fishing world in an article in *Outdoor Life*. Just before his 85th birthday in February 1990, he told me: "In 1946 I wrote about the Newfoundland hitch, the riffling hitch, and that has been very successful with steelhead. It means you take a wet fly and put two hitches behind the head and the fly skims along on the surface. And that skimming fly is the most successful type of surface fly, so most of the dry flies are fished skimming instead of free drift. I think the steelhead react more surely to a skimming fly than a free drift.

"The riffle hitch was originated on one particular stream, because the British officers were giving their guides salmon flies as tips. These were old gut eye flies, not snelled, just gut eyes, and the flies were old and the eyes would pull out when you hooked a fish. So someone in this particular group of fishermen on this river took a couple of half hitches behind the gut eye and secured the fly that way, and they found they caught more fish.

"On that particular river in Newfoundland, which was called Portland Creek, where I had a fishing camp, it's about a 20 to 1 ratio in catching salmon with a hitched fly as against a standard wet fly. I'm not sure why, but it was a short, flat, wide river with deep pockets made by ice piling up against the big rocks. And it may have been that the fish, lying deep as they were, with shallow water around them, were more interested in something coming across the surface. It's hard to say;

The riffle hitch originated on Atlantic salmon waters, and is still an effective tactic: On August 23, 1988 Mike Crosby caught this five–foot long salmon estimated at over 60 pounds on New Brunswick's Restigouche River—on a dry fly. The massive fish was caught on "a No. 2 long shank brown bug with orange hackle."

I have no serious theories as to why it happened. On the next river down, The River of Ponds, it's about a 50:50 ratio; the same with the next river the other way, Western Brook; all the rivers on the coast were about the same except that one.

"Some friends of mine who read that article used the riffle hitch as a secret weapon and caught a lot of steelhead without telling people how they were doing it.

Wulff had a fishing camp on Portland Creek from 1946 to 1956, where he tested his strategies on mint fresh Atlantic salmon—Portland Creek flows only one mile from the lake to the sea. When Wulff first arrived on Portland Creek, things were very different than they are now: "There were only two or three people that fished. That was really wild country, and if anybody wanted a salmon they went out with a net."

On September 11, 1988 Wulff took a 9-pound steelhead on the Copper River in British Columbia on a size 28 hook. The skated fly had two parts. The Mustad size 28 hook was tied in separately, ahead of the fly. The hackle on the fly just barely touched the hook, to allow for the maximum bite with the tiny hook. The size 10, 3xlong fly consisted of the body, wing, and parachute hackle of the topwater fly Wulff developed in 1950, the Surface Stonefly, which he calls his "best, deadliest fly to skitter for steelhead."

Wulff says, "The fish made six or eight rushes at the fly. It was very interesting. She came again and again, as they often do for surface flies—it's sort of a challenging thing for a fish. But all predators can be challenged. I've also caught a 9-pound Arctic char on an egg imitation and free drift with a size 28 and a 12-pound Atlantic salmon on a 28.

"I've experimented with free drifting flies for steelhead and it works, but not as well as skating the fly. Steelhead are not as willing to take a dead drift as well as ordinary trout or as well as Atlantic salmon. The most successful pattern of fishing is to have the fly cross in front of a fish's nose and head upstream just beyond him. I fish the Surface Stonefly skidded for steelhead."

RIFFLE HITCH TACTICS

There are two main factors that make the riffle hitch effective: first, because the tippet comes off the fly at a slant, the fly tends to fight the current at an oblique angle; and second, the fish sees the fly in a broadside perspective instead of the butt-first orientation of the standard wet fly presentation. Because of this, the riffle hitch is effective for steelhead by swimming the fly in both the surface film and under the surface. (This departs from Atlantic salmon tradition where the riffle hitch is used strictly as a surface waking technique. In fact, Atlantic salmon tradition says that salmon will not strike a sunken riffle hitched wet fly or one that throws spray—however, steelhead will take either.)

The technical aspect of the riffle hitch technique is to put two half hitches around the head of the fly just behind the eye of the hook. You need two hitches or overhand knots because one hitch won't hold—the monofilament is too springy and the hitch will slip off the hook and form a wind knot in your tippet. (Even with two hitches, you should check to be sure the hitch doesn't slip off the eye of the hook, forming a wind knot that will weaken the tippet by 50 percent.)

The other consideration with the riffle hitch is to have the tippet coming off the fly so the fly pulls against the current. If you have the tippet coming off the fly on the wrong side, the fly will not fight the current and will swim like a normal wet fly. There's nothing really wrong with that, except that the riffle hitch is ineffective.

To determine which side of the fly the tippet must exit, just remember that it's the same: if you face downstream with the eye of the hook towards you and with the current to your

Helgie Byman lived in Houston, British Columbia most of his life and was one of the earliest proponents of the dry or damp surface fly in the Morice and Bulkley rivers. Photo by Frank Amato

right, the tippet must come off the right side of the fly; if you face downstream with the current to your left, the tippet must come off the left side. (See illustration on next page.)

After you've tied two overhand knots to form the riffle hitch, to fish opposite sides of the river you can slide the knot from one side to the other without retying.

There is disagreement among Atlantic salmon fishermen as to the best angle for the tippet to exit the fly. In his book *The Atlantic Salmon*, Lee Wulff wrote:

"The making of the hitch is important. Arthur Perry, in common with most Portland Creek guides, makes his so the monofilament pulls away from under the turned-up eye at the throat. This will make both the single- and double-hooked flies ride correctly (hook down) on the retrieve. Such a retrieve is effective on standard salmon-fly hooks with turned-up eyes but awkward if the eyes are turned down."

"I use the same throat hitch for double-hooked flies, but with my favorite—the single barbed iron—regardless of whether the eye turns up or down, I shift the hitch 45 degrees to one side or the other, depending upon which side of the current I cast from, so that on a crosscurrent retrieve the fly will always ride with the point on the downstream side. This position seems to give it much better hooking and riding qualities."

In *Eastern Woods & Waters* magazine, editor Jim Gourlay wrote an article entitled "The Portland Hitch: The correct application of a technique pioneered by enterprising New-foundlanders," about the Atlantic salmon guides on Labrador's Pinware River: "But on the Pinware the local guides insist the hitch should be tied so as to fish the fly on its side with the hook turned outward towards the centre of the

The Snake River fishes well for summer steelhead which usually arrive in fishable numbers by mid–October. Photo by Frank Amato

stream. In this way, they suggest, when the fish rises, takes the fly, and turns to return to its lie, it will be hooked squarely and securely in the scissors of the jaw."

That presentation would require the monofilament to come off directly under the fly, at a 90 degree angle, to make the hook point ride parallel to the water's surface. The disadvantage of this approach is that you lose some of the broadside effect because the fish see the top of the fly instead of its side.

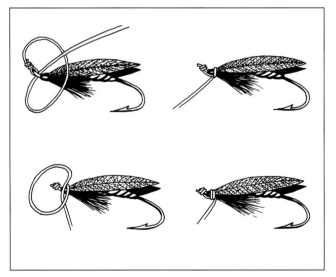

The riffle hitch is two overhand knots near the head of the fly. To determine which side of the fly the tippet must exit, just remember this: if you face downstream with the eye of the hook towards you and with the current to your right, the tippet must come off the right side of the fly; if you face downstream with the current to your left, the tippet must come off the left side of the fly.

I don't believe that the angle of the tippet coming from the fly is nearly as important as the speed at which the fly crosses the current. As long as the tippet is coming from the correct side of the fly, then you should concentrate on monitoring the fly's crosscurrent speed. For steelhead, slow is usually better, but that is not always the case—go ahead and experiment by increasing the speed of the presentation—sometimes steelhead like it fast.

For a topwater presentation with the riffle hitch, make the wet fly skim in the surface film, forming a "V" in the water, which makes it a type of waker. Effective flies for this tactic include the Muddler or standard steelhead wet flies like the Skunk.

I believe there are two reasons the riffle hitched surface wet fly is sometimes more effective than the waking dry fly: first, the riffle hitched wet rides lower in the water and fish can see more of it; secondly, it comes across almost broadside to steelhead holding downstream. That broadside aspect is why some steelheaders riffle hitch dry wakers. The riffle hitch also causes the dry skater to resist the river's flow, making the waker bobble and sputter in the current, as guide John Hazel so aptly describes it.

For steelhead, the riffle hitched wet fly is also effective under the surface, in a standard wet fly presentation. The fish clearly see the fly struggling against the flow of the current because it's totally submerged. Just as with a surface ploy, the speed of the crosscurrent arc is a crucial component—vary your presentation from slow to fast before moving downstream or changing flies.

Whether the riffle hitch is used with a wet fly on the surface or subsurface or with a dry fly, it adds a potent option to steelheading tactics.

As more fly rodders are finding out, nailing a steelhead "on top" is one of the most exciting moments in fly fishing. Like most steelheading, all it takes is an effective fly, a well planned strategy, willing steelhead, and a fly fisher with patience.

Row 1: **Steelhead General Hairwing, Steelhead General Simplified Spey**

Row 2: **Steelhead General Skater, Steelhead General Simplified Spey**—reduced

Row 3: **Steelhead General Soft Hackle, Steelhead General Matuka,** *Tied by author*

All flies in the color plates are tied by the pattern originator unless otherwise noted.

FLY DESIGN AND THE STEELHEAD GENERAL

Rather than a rearrangement of colors and materials, steelhead fly design has more to do with how the fly acts in the water and how we present the fly to the fish.

The Del Cooper and the Surgeon General Hairwing patterns both include a red tail, purple body, and red hackle. You could conceivably call a hairwing steelhead by your own name if you tied it with a purple tail, red body, and purple hackle. But would it be that much different? Wouldn't the steelhead see it as a red and purple hairwing? This series of flies illustrates that color is only one aspect of fly design. Hence, the idea of Steelhead General—you can change the general overall color scheme to suit your own whims.

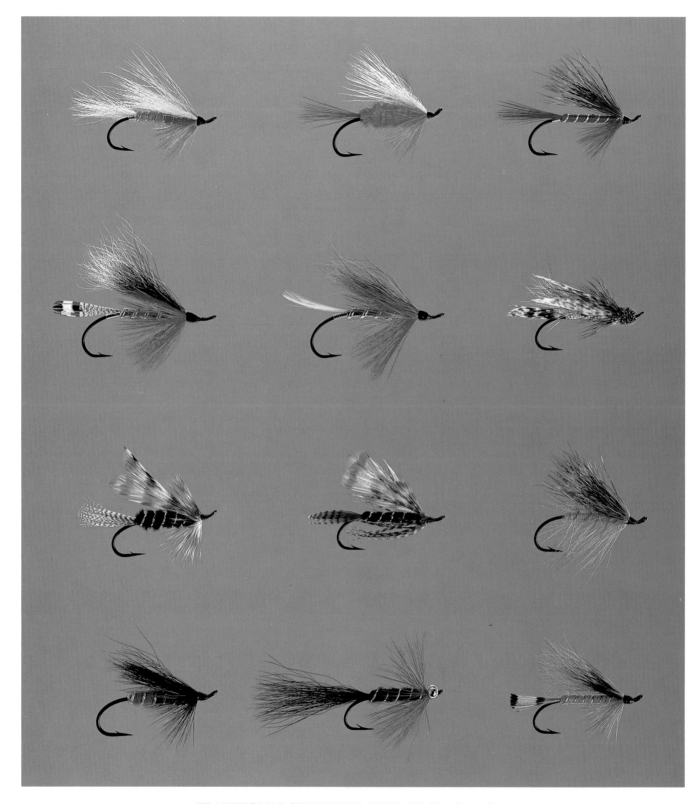

TRADITIONAL STEELHEAD FLIES *(Tied by the author)*

Row 1: **Brad's Brat,** *Enos Bradner;* **Polar Shrimp,** *Clarence Shoff;* **Purple Peril,** *Ken McLeod*

Row 2: **Silver Demon,** *C. Jim Pray, (Tied by Jim Stovall);* **Golden Demon** *(Tied by Jim Stovall);* **Muddler,** *Don Gapen*

Row 3: **Silver Hilton; Gold Hilton Spider** (non-traditional); **Bucktail Caddis**

Row 4: **Black Gordon,** *Clarence Gordon;* **Boss; Dark Caddis,** *Mike Kennedy*

TRADITIONAL AND NON–TRADITIONAL STEELHEAD WET FLIES

Row 1: **Skunk,** *Clarence Gordon (tied by Deke Meyer);* **Skunk** *(tied by author);*

Green Butt Skunk, *Dan Callaghan*

Row 2: **Deschutes Skunk,** *Forrest Maxwell;* **Coastal Skunk,** *Alec Jackson;* **Inland Skunk,** *Alec Jackson*

Row 3: **Peacock Woolly Bugger,** *Mark Bachmann;* **Umpqua Red Brat,** *Polly Rosborough;*

Steelhead Sculpin, *Harry Lemire*

Row 4: **Copper Top,** *Brian Silvey;* **Blue Max,** *Mark Melody;* **Prizm,** *Mark Bachmann;* **Stewart,** *Marty Sherman*

NON–TRADITIONAL STEELHEAD FLIES

Row 1: **Flashdancer, Dahlberg Diver** — *Larry Dahlberg*

Row 2: **Black's Buster Leech,** *Bill Black;* **Black Woolly Bugger,** *Mark Bachmann*

Row 3: — **Pink Puff; Red & White Puff; Eyed Shrimp** —*Mark Bachmann*

Row 4: — **Marabou Streamer; Steelhead Shrimp; Leggo–My–Eggo** (two versions) —*Deke Meyer*

NON–TRADITIONAL STEELHEAD FLIES

Row 1: **Popsicle,** *George Cook;* **Winter's Hope,** *Bill McMillan*

Row 2: **Spawning Purple; Bi-color Hairwing** —*Dave McNeese*

Row 3: **Black Marabou,** *Deke Meyer;* **Sauk River Shrimp,** *Alec Jackson*

STEELHEAD DRY FLIES

Row 1: **Clark's Stonefly,** *Lee Clark;* **Telkwa Stone,** *Mike Maxwell;* **Grease Liner,** *Harry Lemire*

Row 2: **Steelhead Caddis,** *Bill McMillan;* **Lemire's Fall Caddis,** *Harry Lemire;* **Purple Muddler,** *John Hazel*

Row 3: **Wag's Wakers,** *Bob Wagoner* (two versions)

Row 4: **Hyatt's Caddis,** *LeRoy Hyatt* (two versions); **Steelhead Bee,** *Roderick Haig–Brown* (tied by author)

STEELHEAD DRY FLIES

Row 1: **Waller Wakers** — *Lani Waller,* (top row) **Standard, Hi-Visibility Moth ,** (2nd row) **Bee**

Row 3: **Bomber** *(tied by Vic Brockett);* **Rusty Bomber,** *John Hazel*

Row 4: **Purple Moose Bomber,** *Bob Clay*

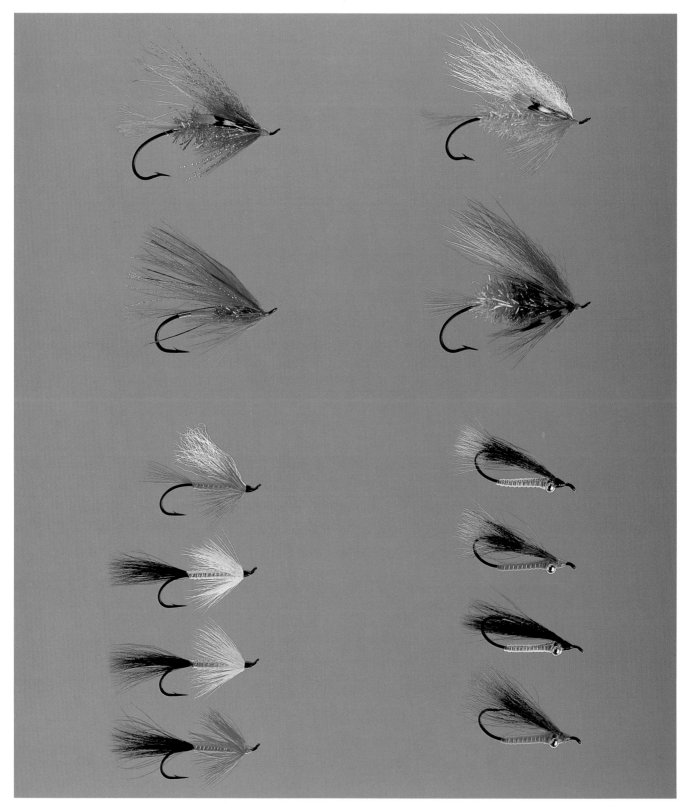

"PLASTIC" FLIES

Row 1: **Deschutes Madness; Plastic Polar Shrimp** — *Dave McNeese*

Row 2: **Marabou Madness; Summer Fling** — *John Shewey*

Lower Left Vertical: **Edge Bright Polar Shrimp; Dean River Lanterns** (three versions) — *Bob Wagoner*

Lower Right Vertical: **Steelhead Charlies** (four versions) — *Bob Wagoner*

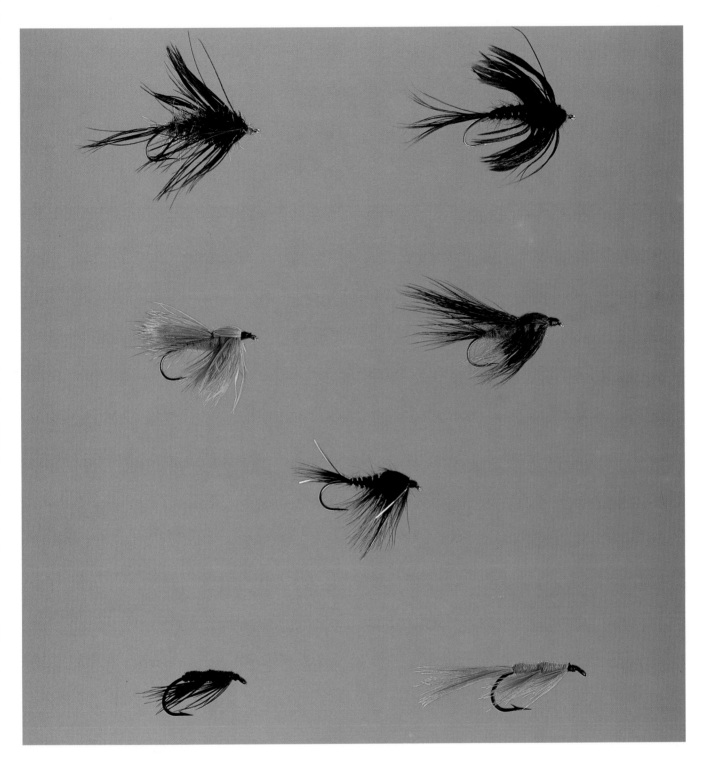

STEELHEAD NYMPHS

Dave Hall Steelhead Nymphs

Row 1: **Natural Crawler; Black Crawler**

Row 2: **Golden Stone Tie–Down; October Caddis Tie–Down**

Row 3: **A.P. Flash Black Nymph**

Jim Teeny Steelhead Nymphs

Row 4: **Teeny Nymph; Teeny Leech**

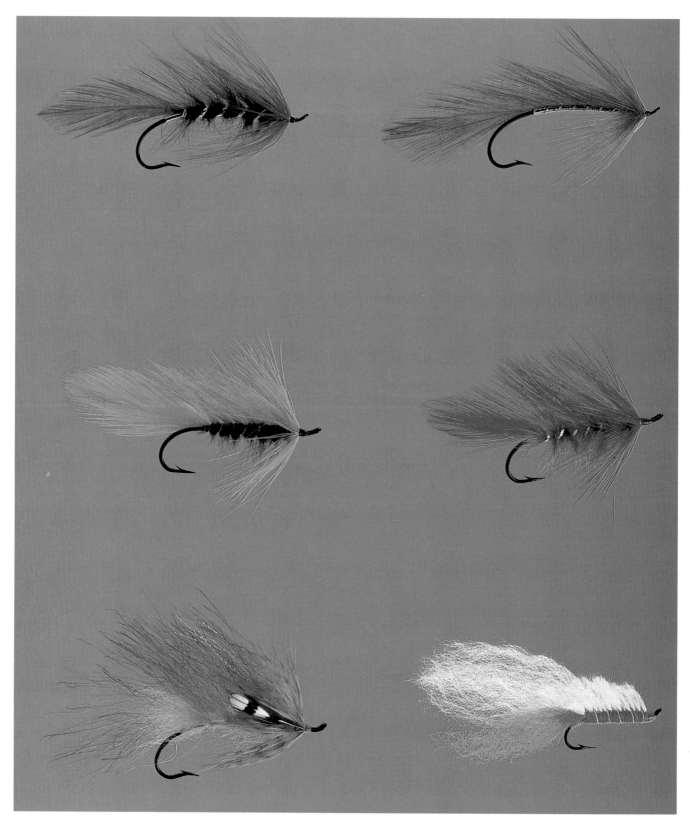

STEELHEAD MATUKAS

Row 1: **Purple Matuka**, *Forrest Maxwell;* **Purple Matuka** (tinsel body) , *Forrest Maxwell*

Row 2: **Holloween Matuka,** *Deke Meyer;* **Steelhead General Matuka,** *Deke Meyer*

Row 3: **Bi–color Polar Bear Matuka,** *Dave McNeese;* **Aztec,** *Dick Nelson*

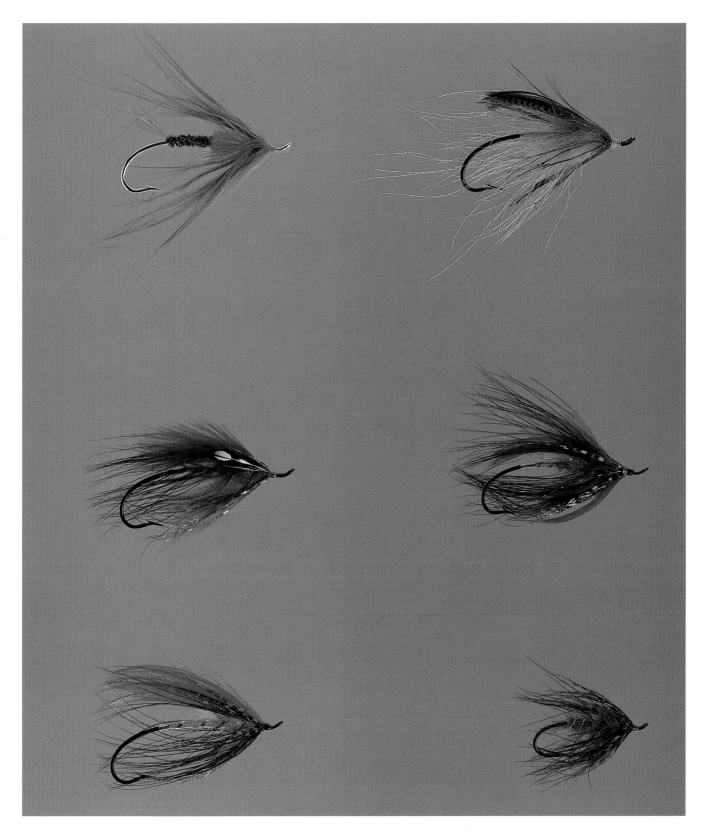

SPEYS

Row 1: **Pseudo Spey,** *Alec Jackson;* **Polar Bear Spey,** *Dave McNeese*

Row 2: **Purple Spey,** *Originated by Keith Mootry (tied by Dave McNeese);* **Purple Spey,** *Dave McNeese version*

Row 3: **Mr. Glasso,** *Originated by Dick Wentworth (tied by Dave McNeese);* **Soft Hackle Spey,** *Deke Meyer*

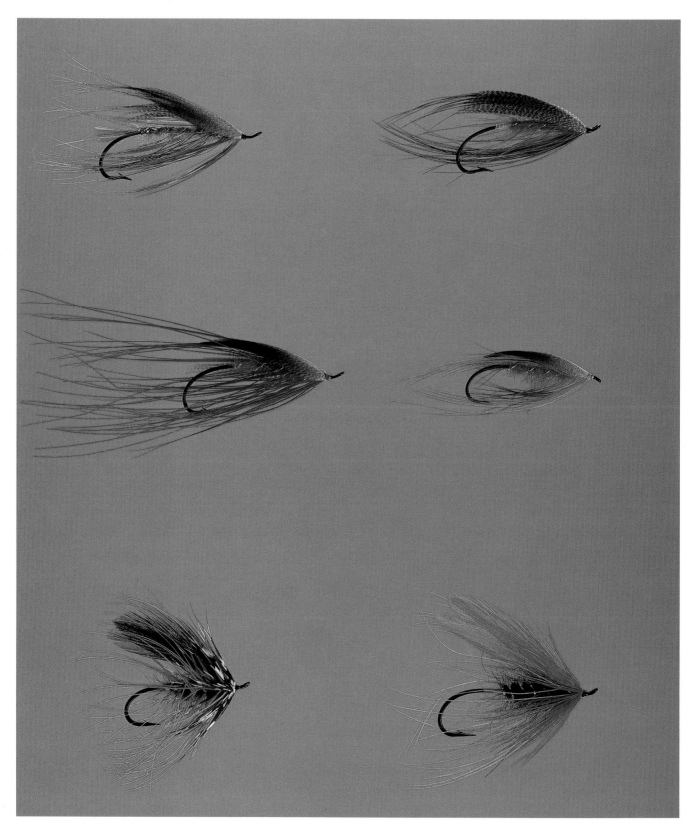

SPEYS

Row 1: **Lady Caroline** – traditional *(tied by Bill Chinn);* **Steelhead Spey,** *Bill Chinn*

Row 2: **Pink Shrimp Spey – dark; Pink Shrimp Spey – light** — *Bill Chinn*

Row 3: **Halloween Spey; Purple Goose Spey** — *Deke Meyer*

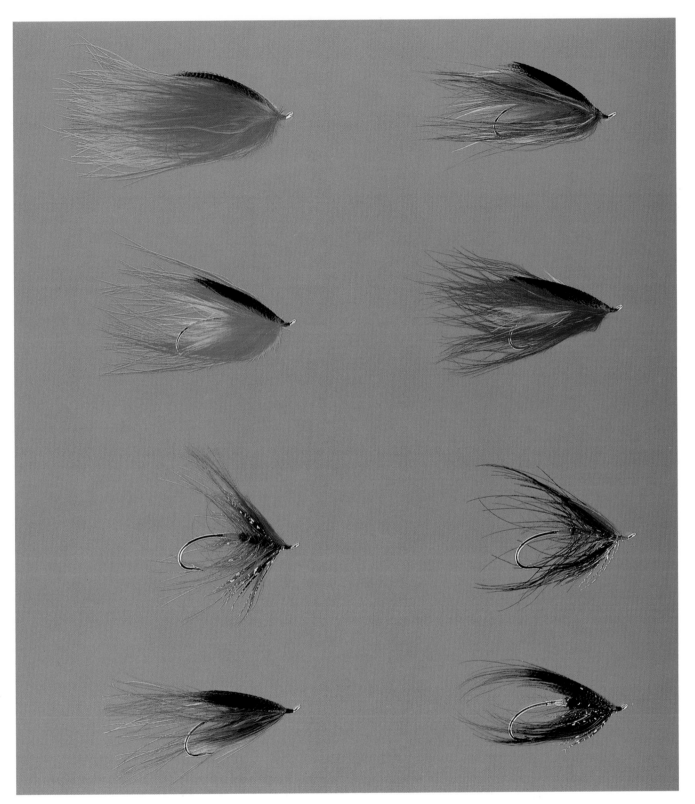

GARY ALGER SPEYS

Row 1: **Flame; Marabou Paintbrush**

Row 2: **Pink Prancer; Purple Deceiver;**

Row 3: **Trophy Hunter; Golden Purple Spey**

Row 4: **October Caddis Spey; Green Butt Spey**

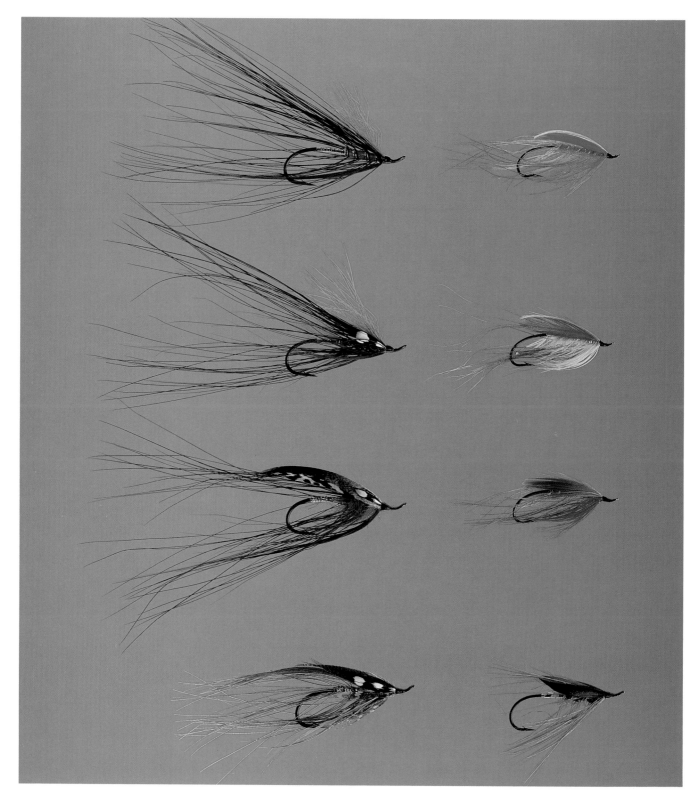

SPEYS

Row 1: (Left Vertical) **Red Phase Spey; Black Phase Spey; Feather Strip Wing Spey;**

Silver Streak Spey — *Joe Howell*

Row 2: (Right Vertical) **Red Shrimp; Golden Spey; Deep Purple Spey** — *Walter Johnson*

Row 2: (Lower Right Vertical) **Rooster Spey** — *Richard Bunse*

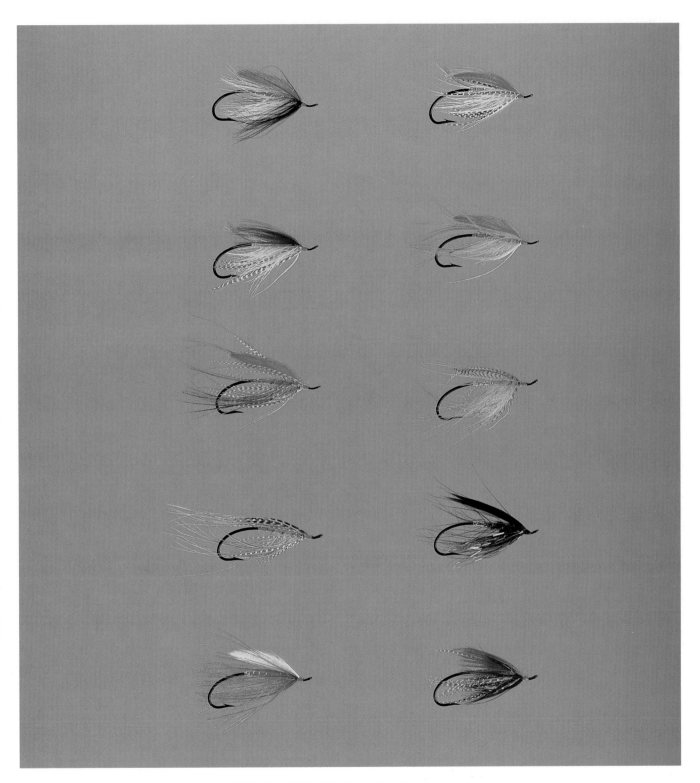

SYD GLASSO SPEYS *(tied by Bob Ververka)*

Row 1: **Sol Duc Spey; Sol Duc**

Row 2: **Sol Duc Dark; Courtesan**

Row 3: **Orange Heron; Gold Heron**

Row 4: **Brown Heron; Silver Heron**

Row 5: **Polar Shrimp; Quillayute** *(originated by Dick Wentworth)*

Stalking Small Streams

VI

Small stream steelheading has a totally different feel to it than most steelheading. That feeling is one of intimacy with the stream and its fish. The world is compressed into one creek, its width, depth, intimate little pools and riffles, and steelhead hidey holes. You are plunged into the fishing world of the moment—no deep wading or long searching casts on the far-flung river—just intimate puzzles that demand precise presentation in a scaled down biosphere of man, fish, and stream.

The small stream is a study into the nature of steelhead. In many respects the fly fishing arena is contained, like the scene-in-a-jar that you got when you were a kid: tip the jar upside down, then right side up, and the scene sparkled with falling snow.

If you can slow down and look closely, you can treat yourself to a unique porthole, a kind of steelhead microscope. You can glimpse the evolution of steelhead as a species, the steelhead as survivor, dodging predators and pitfalls like logjams and low water. You can observe steelhead navigating the aquatic paths that traverse underwater snags and ledges, and watch these giant trout seeking rest and cover amid the camouflage of those same rocks and sunken logs. You can hear the murmur of current where the creek edges along the cliff or the mumblings of the stream as it etches its force against a rock strewn rapid. You can see your streamside fishing compatriot, the water ouzel, dipping for cased caddis. But in a small stream, life flows in limited quantities; you get a peek into the steelhead's world, a scant slice of what the aquatic byways are like for steelhead migrating in the bigger rivers.

That is probably the most valuable lesson in small stream steelheading—you get an intense vision into the world of the fish, the holding water, and possibly your mistakes as stalking predator. In a large river, steelhead appear as gray ghosts holding near the bottom—by contrast, if you merely amble up to the small stream without plotting a concealed approach to hide from your quarry, you may be lucky to spot any fish at all. However, because of the limited number of escape routes available to the steelhead, you might still see fish you have already spooked.

That intimacy with the stream and the steelhead and your own cloaked approach into casting range makes stream fishing an intriguing challenge.

The very nature of small stream steelheading eliminates many fishermen, partly because many are not interested in the stream arena and partly because many are secretly convinced that fishing such creeks is a waste of time because honking big steelhead wouldn't bother with such piddly little waters.

I know one guide who fishes streamlets that are home to returning native steelhead for several weeks every winter. He never takes clients; he saves his special little streams, storing them for their unique mixture of tranquility and thrill. In them he has caught fresh steelhead to 42 inches.

For most small streams your gear is scaled down. Essentially, you are making short casts with heavy trout gear for the biggest trout that swim the creek. A trout that will run five to eight pounds as a summer run and up to 10 pounds as a winter fish. These steelhead have grown fat in the ocean, not in this brook that is a spawning site for adult fish and a nursery for juvenile steelhead.

Some tributaries of large rivers host spawning native fish that weigh into the teens, fish that are safe from all predators but man, sometimes the least appreciative and the most deadly to the future of the steelhead.

Small stream steelheading has a totally different feel to it than most steelheading. That feeling is one of intimacy with the stream and with the fish. The whole world is compressed into one creek, its width, depth, and intimate little pools and riffles and steelhead hidey holes. Photo by Carolyn Z. Shelton

Facing page: *The essence of the small stream puzzle: how to plan your approach so the fish will not see you or any fish–alarming movement, how to cast so the line or leader won't spook the fish, and how to present your fly without "lining" the steelhead with the movement–shadow of your fly line or leader. The small stream steelheader invariably has the water to himself or herself. Photo by Bill McMillan*

We must have a conscience when fishing these limited runs of native fish. State hatchery biologists won't dump their expensive smolts into creeks because the angling public wouldn't see the benefit of their angling license dollars. In the hatchery system, numbers of steelhead caught only really count in big rivers where hatchery steelhead are efficiently harvested. Those punched steelhead cards are what keep hatcheries in business. Conservation of the resource is what keeps wild steelhead from disappearing from small streams.

I do know one small tributary creek that receives intermittent loads of hatchery winter runs when the hatchery on the main river fills its quota of adult fish for egg-taking. Unfortunately, some of the hatchery fish spawn in the creek, further mixing the gene pool, watering down a wild stock specifically tailored for that river over the eons by the winnowing of evolution. That illustrates one of the dangers of the hatchery system: excess adult fish, that is, fish that arrive at the hatchery after the quota is reached, are perceived as a viable fishing commodity, so why not let anglers harvest the excess fish. Locals soon find out about the 30 to 40 fish laying in a hundred yard stretch of stream and mayhem breaks out, with lures and bait flying, transforming that portion of the creek into a bizarre angling carnival. But that is the exception to the rule when it comes to stalking small streams.

TACTICS

Brightly colored shirts look great in snapshots but have no place here. Natural earth tones in muted colors that blend into the dappling effect of streamside trees and vegetation are the way to go. It is even more crucial in the brilliant light of summer. The fisherman must blend into the background of alder and vine maple, not unlike any of the wild creatures of the forest. Some stream aficionados go so far as to put bow hunter's camouflage paint on their faces to break up the light reflection.

But the most important facet of strategy lies in your approach to the stream. You must plan every step that finally puts you into casting position. Graphite rods are an absolute boon when casting the long hours and long distances required on most steelhead rivers. Their importance is minimal on small streams. The disadvantage of using a graphite rod on a creek is the way the rod will flash with brilliance when sunlight reflects from the waving rod. A muted fiberglass or bamboo rod might be a better choice. But since everyone is fishing graphite these days, knowing that your rod will flash with reflected sunlight will help you plan your sneak on the fish.

The moving shadow of the backcast and forward cast of the fly line will often spook wary steelhead. That line shadow isn't much different from the shadow of the kingfisher or great blue heron hunting for fish. It alerts steelhead to dangers that the fish outlived as a fry and during its smolthood. That dangerous combination of movement and shadow was imprinted on the fish that survived; it now triggers fear, prompting the fish to flee and hide.

While drifting in the current, the leader can spook fish when it passes over the steelhead because the monofilament can cause a similar moving-shadow effect. Because you need to use a tippet strong enough to handle a jumbo fish in tight quarters, the challenge is to make the fly pass in front of the fish before the leader or tippet.

A sidearm or roll cast will often keep the fly line and rod low enough to conceal the casting movement and rod flash from the steelhead, but each holding spot presents a unique challenge. In creeks each pocket of water is set in its own macrame of rocks and logs and has its own canopy of brush to snatch your backcast.

In Oregon, Washington and British Columbia there are hundreds of small winter streams like this one with modest to substantial runs of winter steelhead. They only need to be walked and tenderly observed before presenting the fly. Photo by Frank Amato

That is the essence of the puzzle—how to plan your approach so the fish will not see you or any fish-alarming movement, how to cast so the line or leader won't spook the fish, and how to present your fly without "lining" the steelhead with the movement-shadow of your fly line or leader.

FLIES AND PRESENTATION STRATEGIES

For small stream steelheading I subscribe to a modification of an oft repeated motto of my friend George Cronk who works as an engineering officer in the merchant navy. While on his ship, he's in charge of the maintenance and repair of all shipboard mechanics, from air conditioning to diesel engines weighing hundreds of tons. The motto: KISS, or Keep It Simple, Steelheader.

So I use two types of wet flies, a small dark fly for clear water conditions and a small to medium sized bright fly for colored water. Favored sizes are 4 to 10 on a sharp hook with a well closed eye and steel strong enough to hold a steelhead, such as the Tiemco 7999. As a general rule, the clearer the water, the smaller the fly pattern. Hook size is also governed by the size and strength of the fish. For example, huge steelhead or fresh fish that might be spooked by a big fly in clear water will often strike a low-water style fly tied on a hook that is larger in proportion to the fly.

Pattern preference is determined more by color tones than by specific recipes. For instance, the Silver Hilton is a good dark fly and the Polar Shrimp a good bright fly. The Purple Peril is effective when the water is clear but with lots of shadows on the surface. Purple shows up well in low light conditions without spooking fish and is a color I often use when fishing small streams.

The most deadly stream fly for me is a Black Soft Hackle. The fly has no tail; the body is black yarn, chenille, or dubbing; and the hackle is saddle hackle, pheasant rump, guinea, or grouse dyed black. Another equally effective variation is a Black Marabou, with black marabou tail, black body, and black marabou wing. The wing is tied about as thick as the body and not longer than the shank so the wing won't foul the hook by wrapping around the bend of the hook. A black Woolly Bugger is very effective on steelhead in small streams or wide rivers. You can also add a dab of lead in the front half of the fly or tie on lead eyes so you can impart a jigging action.

In the spirit of keeping it simple, the familiar wet fly swing in front of suspected or known steelhead holding spots will catch many steelhead for you. Just control your line by mending so that the fly eases in front of the fish—a fast moving fly is more likely to spook steelhead than decoy them into striking. One of the attractions of the wet fly method is that you can explore lots of cover with less concentration than with some of the more demanding tactics. It's a relaxing way to fish and an effective strategy for hooking steelhead.

Another efficient method for stream steelheading is dead-drift nymphing. Keep your fly sliding downstream with the current, watching intently for any break in its downstream progress. If the line pauses, you tighten it because your fly might be residing in a steelhead's mouth. Some prefer fishing this method without a strike indicator, others prefer using a bit of yarn or a Corkie with a toothpick to broadcast the fish's take. I find it much easier to watch a "bobber" that I can easily see, rather than watch the end of the fly line for that telltale hesitation in the fly's drift.

If you encounter steelhead that aren't spooky you can sometimes incite them to rise to the dry or damp fly. You can dead-drift a size 8 Bucktail Caddis over a steelhead's lie or let the fly get just in front of the fish and twitch it like a struggling insect, then continue the dead-drift. Another ploy is to dead-drift the fly just under the surface of the water. Or you can grease-line the fly by drifting it either on the surface or just under, but with enough tension on the line to present the fly sideways to the fish. If the dead-drift tactic doesn't work, you can run a combination: as the dead-drifted fly approaches the fish, tighten your line to sink the Bucktail Caddis under the surface, then swing it crosscurrent wet-fly style, in front of the steelhead.

Instead of taking the fly, sometimes a steelhead will merely swat at it or just bump it with its mouth. A steelhead that sucks in your fly with an open-mouth take is probably reacting to remembered feeding instincts imprinted as a juvenile fish. Swatting or bumping the fly is probably an expression of steelhead territorial aggression.

There are various tactics that work for catching "swatting" or "bumping" fish. These include changing to a smaller fly, or to a more somber hued fly, or to a fly with a different silhouette. Another choice is to present the fly more slowly, giving the fish more time to react. If these strategies don't work, give the fish a good rest and then try again.

In the late Roderick Haig-Brown's book, *Fisherman's Summer*, 1959, he wrote of raising a number of steelhead in September 1951 to a "new fly pattern—a variation of the Mackenzie River Brown and Yellow Bug, tied Wulff fashion with fox squirrel wings and tail on a size 6 hook.

"The majority of steelheads I catch of three pounds and up either have nothing at all in their stomachs or signs of very casual activity—a bee or two, a yellow jacket, a deer fly, occasionally a large sedge, sometimes a winged dragonfly. They also have been attracted from the quiet business of absorbing oxygen and resting by the chance drift or float of something too tempting and conveniently placed to resist. These chance feeders seem to me to hint pretty plainly at the sort of fly dressing most likely to be effective. Bee, yellow jacket and deer fly are all somewhat similar in color and all seem to be taken with surprising frequency. So I prefer a fly with a dark-brown and yellow body, tied with light-brown hair wings and tail and a brown hackle."

Later, Haig-Brown named his fly the Steelhead Bee, which is an ideal fly for situations like those found in many streams. The Steelhead Bee can be fished dead-drift just like the Bucktail Caddis, but the Steelhead Bee is also designed to be a "waker" fly. Haig-Brown canted the wings slightly forward, so the fly would resist the pull of the water when swung crosscurrent. When fished on a tight line the fly produces a flopping wake as the wings work in the surface film current. A siliconed Bucktail Caddis tied with stiff hackle can also be made to wake in the current, but the Bee is more effective.

Never is the line between steelhead fishing and trout fishing more blurred than when a steelhead takes a dead-drifted Steelhead Bee or Bucktail Caddis in a classic head-and-then-tail rise.

Steelhead often hold in riffles because the bubbly water is highly oxygenated and the roiled water ceiling gives the fish cover. Although winter fish hide there, it is a particularly attractive spot for summer steelhead. That boily water also helps mask the angler's approach.

One of the best ways to probe a riffle for summer steelhead is with a Muddler, because the fish can see the bulk of the Muddler head in the foamy water. The head also causes a certain amount of wake, convincing the steelhead an intruder is invading its territory. You can either swing the fly crosscurrent ala wet fly style or tease it back and forth in the riffle pocket by holding your rod first off to one side, then flipping it over to the other side, forcing the fly to follow the rod tip's path.

Another variation is to let the fly drift down under tension, so the fly works in the current, then pull back on the rod so the fly is lifted off the water to land upstream a few feet, then drift it back to the fish. Suspending the Muddler in the prime water for a minute or longer will sometimes ignite a steelhead into striking the intruder. You can also station a Bucktail Caddis in the current in the same manner, but whichever fly you use, be sure and mount a stout tippet on your leader—the strikes can be powerful.

There is something primal about fighting a steelhead hooked in a small stream because the arena is tight and no quarter can be given to the fish. A hooked steelhead will stitch your line through all the brush-riddled snags, riffles and log jams that it swam through to get to the spot where you hooked it.

Some creeks empty directly into the Mother Ocean and can provide the angler with a unique thrill. A fish hooked in the first few good holes will often force its way back into the surf. There you are, standing in the sand, your rod bent, fighting a fresh, sea-strong steelhead swimming back to the ocean.

You have to search out those precious little streams for yourself. They will have limited pressure, if any, which is a great attraction, but a limited run of wild fish. You can wrest the secret of the location of these streamlets and the timing of the run from Mother Nature by putting forth a little effort, because that's what it requires, some investigative effort and time. That is the coin of the realm of the small stream.

The small stream steelheader invariably has the water to himself. Even if you don't hook a fish you might find yourself hooked on the fishing, the exploring for fish—for their hiding spots that go undiscovered year after year, while the steelhead migrate up the creek in the endless procession of the seasons...

Shooting Heads For Steelhead

VII

The lower Deschutes is a rough and brawling desert river that has a fine run of native and hatchery summer steelhead that return to her waters July through October. The Deschutes plows her way through canyons gouged from ancient volcanic flows and upthrust weathered rimrock tinged with burnt gold lichen.

In the early evening chukkar calls bounce from one rock face to another before the flock makes a quick flight across the river. Mule deer leave their beds and browse in the spring fed patches of greenery high on the crumbling escarpment. The hot desert wind funnels down the canyon, fitfully tugging at sagebrush and streamside trees.

In the last few miles above her junction with the Columbia, the Deschutes is a broad river with whitecap rapids counterpointed by long, deep runs and sweeping tailouts. There are some riffles in close, but most of the best steelhead water is a lengthy cast from wading depth, even in ideal conditions.

Two fishermen casting in the pool below me are competent casters but can only manage 70 feet because of the strong wind. Using a standard weight forward line is an exercise in frustration.

Usually the cooling temperatures of early evening will cause the wind to cease, but a low pressure front moving through has brought changeable high winds to the Deschutes country. One of the pair below me quit casting, beaten by the wind.

I noticed that the wind was gusty and didn't always go straight downstream, but sometimes swirled in a clockwise direction before merging with the downcanyon funnel of air.

My 10 1/2-foot graphite rod was matched to a 30-foot No. 10 floating shooting head and flat monofilament shooting line. I pulled 75 feet of the shooting line and the head from the reel, pinched the mono in big loops in my mouth and roll cast the first 20 feet of the shooting head into the river. When I felt the irregular gusts of wind changing direction I waited while its clockwise force changed to a head-on direction, then an upstream heading, and then finally straight out over the river.

At that moment I roll cast the rest of the head and 2 feet of mono out of the fly rod guides, made a crisp backcast, then fired the head out in a high overhead cast, giving the wind a chance to boost the shooting head up and out. The head and running line snapped out in a one hundred foot cast that used less casting arm effort than a 60-foot cast with a regular line.

The shooting head setup was ideal because the wind was quartered in the proper direction for only a brief moment; there wasn't enough time for the backcasting necessary with a standard fly line. The monofilament running line causes little resistance as it goes through rod guides; once in the air and headed in the right direction the cast practically made itself.

I was pleased to have the wind as an ally instead of an adversary, particularly since I was intent on swimming my fly through some choice steelhead water out about 90 feet. Once I determined the wind direction-changing, I concentrated on timing and presenting the fly to the best advantage.

At first I was startled to hear clapping after one of my casts. But when I looked over and saw the two fishermen from the pool below sitting under a tree not far away, my surprise

---

Since Standard shooting heads are only 30 feet long, one–third the length of a regular fly line, they are easy to change when streamside, without carrying extra spools. The fisherman has the option of matching the head to the holding water at any specific depth, from full floating, to sinktip, to full sinking heads with various sinking rates. This flexibility is an advantage when traveling to unknown waters, when fishing varied rivers or when the angler is limited to a particular stretch of river with diverse holding lies. Photo by Scott Ripley
Facing page: *For wide rivers where the average cast is over 70 feet the shooting head is a natural. With a shooting head, casts of 90 to 100 feet or better are well within the reach of an average caster, and require about the same effort as a 60–foot cast with a conventional fly line.*

Making A Shooting Head Loop

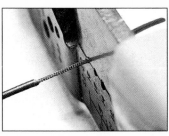

1. To install a loop to make a shooting head, first soak the last three inches of line in a solvent such as lacquer thinner or nail polish remover for several minutes. This allows you to easily remove the plastic coating from the dacron core of the fly line. You can peel the coating off with your fingernails, a wire stripper, or a knife. If the plastic stubbornly sticks to the core, soak it longer.

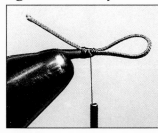

2. Place the line in your vise so that a bit of the coated fly line and core sticks out. Fold the core back on itself so it forms a loop about one inch long. Wrap tying thread around the fold of core material from where the loop begins back to the coated fly line. Wrap thread over the folded core twice. Whip finish the thread, cut off the excess thread and line core.

3. Put a drop of super glue on the thread. Don't put on a gob of glue—too much super glue works less effectively than one or two drops at the most. Work the glue around the thread with a toothpick.

4. Slip a piece of heat shrink tubing over the thread area. The 1/8 or 1/16 inch sizes fit best and are available at auto supply stores, hobby shops, or electrical supply stores. The tubing should be long enough to cover the thread area and extend over the fly line. Collapse the heat shrink tubing with a hair dryer or heat gun. If you use a lighter, you'll only succeed in burning the dacron core, frying your loop.

5. With a system of interlocking loops, you can attach the thin diameter fly line used as running/shooting line or attach a floating head to a sinking head to make a sinktip head or interlock Deep Water Express mini-heads. Photos by Gene Trump

changed to embarrassment. I'm a proficient caster but certainly not a great caster. It was done with mirrors—a properly rigged shooting head launched at the optimum moment.

Unfortunately, even though I steered several proven patterns through some succulent holding water, the steelhead were not impressed and I didn't hang a fish. On the plus side I was getting the fly to the fish instead of being defeated by the wind.

If there is a cardinal rule in steelheading, it's matching the fly line to the water. And sometimes that's best accomplished with a shooting head system because of its two major advantages: efficient distance casting and convenient line interchangeability.

A standard shooting head is usually 30 feet of fly line connected to 150 feet of "shooting" or "running" line, which are synonymous terms. The 30-foot head loads the fly rod and pulls the thinner diameter running line out much faster and more efficiently than a regular fly line because the shooting line generates less friction as it passes through the rod guides.

For wide rivers where the average cast is over 70 feet the shooting head is a natural. With a shooting head, casts of 90 to 100 feet or better are well within the reach of an average caster, and require about the same effort as a 60-foot cast with a conventional fly line. The steelheader using a shooting head can consistently cover water that only the very best casters can reach with a full weight forward fly line.

Since standard shooting heads are only 30 feet long, one-third the length of a regular fly line, they are easy to change when streamside, without carrying extra spools. The heads can be coiled and secured with a twist-on. Three or four heads take up as much room as a spare spool and are lighter.

The fisherman has the option of matching the head to the holding water at any specific depth, from full floating, to sinktip, to full sinking heads with various sinking rates. This high degree of flexibility is an advantage when traveling to unknown waters, when fishing varied rivers or when the angler is limited to a particular stretch of river with diverse holding lies.

For example, a full floating head is appropriate for most summer and fall steelheading, and is readily complemented with a sinktip head for swinging the fly a little deeper in the current. If the fish are holding off a deep ledge or in a deep shady run, they are more apt to strike a fly tracking close to the bottom via a full sinking head. For late fall and winter steelheading the fastest sinking heads are valuable for fishing the heavier river flows.

Shooting heads offer the steelheader a great deal of versatility on any river. For instance, a fisherman can start with a floater for the head of the run, use a sinktip for the throat, then switch to a sinking head for the deepest part of the pool, and finish with a floater for the tailout. By modifying tackle to match the river, the angler increases his or her chances of hooking fish.

Fly rods are rated for a specific fly line, although most graphite rods will handle two or even three adjacent line weights. Fly lines are rated by their weight in grains in the first 30 feet. For example, a 9-weight line is rated at 240 grains, but the ratings were calibrated for casting a full fly line. As a general guideline, most rods will cast a standard shooting head rated a line weight or two heavier than a full fly line. For instance, a 9-weight rod will handle 10 or 11-weight heads, depending on the stiffness and taper of the rod.

Some factory shooting heads from Scientific Anglers and Cortland come with a small loop at the end for attaching the shooting line. Factory heads are available in floating or sinking, and Cortland has a sinktip head. Full sinking heads run the gamut from slow to fast sinking to extra fast to sink-like-lead.

MAKING YOUR OWN SHOOTING HEADS

You can adapt standard fly lines into shooting heads, such as floaters, full sinking or sinktip heads. (Fly shops will sometimes offer lines at discounted prices at the end of the regular season, allowing you to make inexpensive heads.) Here is an example: a 90-foot double taper line can make three shooting heads, such as two 30-foot floating heads, and by adding a section of Deep Water Express to the middle 30-foot section, you can make a sinktip shooting head.

You can modify any standard fly line into a shooting head by shortening it to 30 feet and adding a loop at the end for attaching the shooting or running line. Traditional length for a standard shooting head is 30 feet, but don't be afraid to shorten or lengthen your shooting heads to conform to your casting style or to the tapers of a favorite rod or to specific fishing circumstances.

To install a loop on the head, first soak the last three inches of line in a solvent such as lacquer thinner or nail polish remover for several minutes. This allows you to easily remove the plastic coating from the dacron core of the fly line. You can peel the coating off with your fingernails, a wire stripper, or a knife. If the plastic stubbornly sticks to the core, soak it longer.

Place the line in your vise so that a bit of the coated fly line and core sticks out, as illustrated in the photos. Fold the core back on itself so it forms a loop about one inch long. Wrap tying thread around the fold of core material, from where the loop begins back to the coated fly line. Wrap thread over the

Label the line weight of the head on the heat shrink tubing with model enamel paint or automotive touch up paint, using a modified Roman numeral system: one long mark for five; one short mark for each weight above five. The Deep Water Express mini–heads in the photo are labeled according to length: three shorts for three feet; one long and one short for six feet.

folded core twice. Whip finish the thread, cut off the excess thread and line core.

Put a drop of super glue on the thread. Don't put on a gob of glue—too much super glue works less effectively than one or two drops at the most. Work the glue around the thread with a toothpick.

Slip a piece of heat shrink tubing over the thread area. The 1/8 or 1/16 inch sizes fit best and are available at auto supply stores, hobby shops, or electrical supply stores such as Radio Shack. The tubing should be long enough to cover the thread area and extend over the fly line.

Collapse the heat shrink tubing with a hair dryer or heat gun. If you use a lighter, candle, or match you'll only succeed in burning the dacron core, frying your loop.

Label the line weight of the head with model enamel paint or automotive touch-up paint on the heat shrink tubing, using a modified Roman numeral system: one long mark for five; one short mark for each weight above five. For instance, a nine-weight head would have one long mark and four short ones on the tubing; a ten would have two longs. Use bright paint so you can read the marks easily in low light conditions. If the fly line is a luminous fluorescent color, you can label the

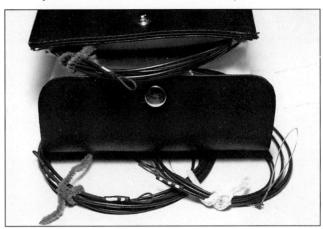

A leader wallet is handy for storing shooting heads, keeping them coiled with twist–ons and stashed in ziploc bags labeled with black magic marker.

line itself with black permanent Magic Marker. (Magic Marker doesn't work well on dark fly line.)

Instead of heat shrink tubing you can apply several layers of Pliobond or Shoe Goo or Sportsman's Goop, then label the fly line itself. These adhesives don't protect the loop knot as well as heat shrink tubing.

A leader wallet is handy for storing shooting heads, keeping them coiled with twist-ons and stashed in ziploc bags labeled with black magic marker.

You can make a custom sinktip shooting head by using the front 30 feet of a standard sinktip line with a loop added as described above. Or you can add sections of Deep Water Express to a floating shooting head. (Remember to match your rod with a shooting head at least one weight heavier than what you would use in a standard line.)

If you add Deep Water Express to a floater, you need to make loops on both. As described in the "Winter Steelheading" chapter, a series of mini-heads made from the 550, 700, or 850 grain Deep Water Express accords the angler a tremendous degree of variability in sinking rates, whether as sinktips or full sinking heads. For example, you can start with a 2-foot mini-head Deep Water Express looped to the floating head, then go to a 4-foot mini-head when you want your fly to get deeper.

You can also permanently mate a section of Deep Water Express with a floater to make a super-fast sinktip shooting head or even a full line with a super-fast sinktip. Cut off the skinny front taper of the floater so that the diameter of the Deep Water Express approximately matches the diameter of the floating line. Heavier line weights, No. 9 or bigger, work best because they are thicker and better match the Deep Water Express. The combination of a floating line and a section of Deep Water Express will result in a very heavy, super-fast sinktip; be careful not to overload your rod and break it.

To make a super-fast sinktip, the last 3 inches of the floater and the Express are soaked in lacquer thinner for a few minutes. The 3-inch sections are stripped until just the cores of

Shooting heads offer the steelheader a great deal of versatility on any river. For instance, a fisherman can start with a floater for the head of the run, use a sinktip for the throat, then switch to a sinking head for the deepest part of the pool, and finish with a floater for the tailout.

the fly lines remain. The cores are bloodknotted together and the knot is daubed with one drop of super glue that is worked around the knot with a toothpick. Then the knot is covered with Shoe Goo or Sportsmans Goop so the knot will slide through the rod guides easily. (When working on heads, you can support the lines between a fly tying vise and a stack of books.)

THIN FLY LINE AS
A SHOOTING/RUNNING LINE

Both Cortland and Scientific Anglers make shooting lines that are 100 feet of slim diameter fly line, available with or without factory installed loops. Cortland offers its 444SL .031 inch diameter (about 25-pound test) in floating in fluorescent green and Intermediate in ice blue at 1.06 inches per second sinking rate. Scientific Anglers offers its Air Cel Ultra 2 floating in sunrise or buckskin .029 inch diameter (20-pound test); Wet Cel Intermediate in kelly green in .025 diameter (20-pound test) or .035 diameter (30-pound test); and Wet Cel II in dark green at .029 diameter (20-pound test).

The advantages of floating running lines are that they are easy to see, particularly in brilliant colors, and they are easier to handle than other types of shooting line made from flat or oval monofilament. When fishing sinking heads, bright running line acts like a giant strike indicator, allowing you to track the line and fly's progress downstream. Floating running lines are easier to handle in cold weather and are easier to mend, they don't tangle as frequently as monofilament and aren't as slippery, so they are the best bet for a person new to shooting heads.

Intermediate running lines were originally designed for saltwater use, but offer the advantage of a running line that sinks with the sinking head. A floating running line retards the sinking effect of a sinking head; the tradeoff with the Intermediate running lines is that it's more difficult to see the running line than the brightly colored floating running lines. Some favor drably colored lines because either they don't like the luminous colors or are afraid of spooking fish.

This brings us to one of the great pitfalls of using shooting heads for distance casting: it's only natural to want to boom out a long cast with your shooting head—that's what you made it for. The most common tactical error committed by shooting headers is casting over or wading through prime steelhead lies in search of fish out in the middle of the river. It's very tempting; you have a spiffy high-tech graphite rod and a slick head setup that whispers through the guides in route to its touchdown 130 feet out in the run where you previously only wished you could fish.

Don't overlook that close-in water. Steelhead love to glide in close to shore to rest behind cover that breaks the current, which is usually less relentless in shallow water. Another favorite resting place is under the ceiling of bubbles in riffles, where steelhead hold in well oxygenated water in the current baffles behind rocks. Even on a grand and rowdy river like the Deschutes, steelhead will coast into shallow waters near shore, particularly in the morning and evening, and during their nighttime migrations. Many a time I've seen fishermen cast over these fish or wade right into their safety areas, causing the steelhead to scurry for the security of deeper water.

When I worked for the Oregon Department of Fish and Wildlife on the Deschutes River in 1978/1979, we ran fish traps above Sherar Falls, tagging and measuring fish as an ongoing fish population census-taking study. The biologists attempted to gather enough data to accurately determine when the fish would move at night, according to variables such as moon phase, barometric change, cloud cover, weather fronts, and other factors. They couldn't determine any such trend in advance or determine what had caused nighttime migration after they had documented it. Sometimes only a fish or two would move, sometimes none, and sometimes dozens of steelhead would start moving upstream at twilight and continue migrating on into the wee hours of night. It was fascinating and probably has some biological triggering device that we simply aren't aware of as yet. For now it remains a tantalizing steelhead mystery. No matter what steelhead river you're fishing, some fish will be close to shore in the early morning.

To attach the shooting head to the running line, you slip the loop on the shooting head over the loop on the running line, then pull the shooting head through the loop on the running line. That makes a loop-to-loop interlock.

Because of the high speed turnover on the backcast (at something over a hundred miles per hour) the end of the running line nearest the shooting head will eventually wear out. (You can extend the life of your fly lines by cleaning them often.) When the shooting line begins to show cracks from line-stress and starts to stick in the guides, turn it around, attaching the "head" end to the backing. After the shooting line has been turned and the "new" end begins to show cracks, it's time to replace the line. You can prolong the life of the running line by cutting off 5 or 10 feet from the end and

making a loop, but by the time both ends are showing wear, the line is usually sticking in the guides and not operating efficiently. Don't throw the worn out shooting line away when you replace it; store it on a plastic line spool in your field kit as a spare.

You can attach the thin diameter fly line running line to the backing with a nail knot. Even better, if you install a loop on the "backing" end of the running line, it's quick and easy to attach the backing by using an improved clinch knot. Then when it comes time to reverse the shooting line, it's a simple matter of turning the line around because you have already installed the loop.

MONOFILAMENT AS SHOOTING/RUNNING LINE

Monofilament running line has some advantages over thin diameter fly line. Monofilament is inexpensive, and it casts farther with less effort than fly line shooting line because it causes less friction in the rod guides. Cortland offers 150-foot spools of Cobra flat monofilament in red or mist blue in 20- and 30-pound test. They also make my favorite, Plion running line in fluorescent yellow/green in 20-, 25-, and 30-pound test. Some anglers I know use 25-pound gold Stren. It's important to use monofilament that is strong enough to withstand the rigors of shooting head casting, stiff enough to be abrasion resistant, yet limp enough so that it doesn't hold a "memory". When cast it should lay flat.

When fishing with monofilament with shooting heads it's crucial to stretch the monofilament before you cast the

If there is a cardinal rule in steelheading, it's matching the fly line to the water. Sometimes that's best accomplished with a shooting head system because of its two major advantages: efficient distance casting and convenient line interchangeability. A standard shooting head is usually 30 feet of fly line connected to 150 feet of "shooting" or "running" line, which are synonymous terms.

For wide rivers like the North Umpqua where the average cast is over 80 feet or better the shooting head is ideal. The steelheader using a shooting head can consistently cover water that only the very best casters can reach with a full weight forward fly line. Photo by Dave Hall

head. The advantage of using brightly colored monofilament shooting line is that you can see it and track the head and fly as it swims into the steelhead strike zone. You can mend the floating head with mono as the running line, but not as well as with thin fly line. When used with sinking heads, monofilament doesn't impede the sink rate of the head.

You can attach monofilament to the shooting head with an improved clinch knot, and use a blood knot when attaching the monofilament running line to the backing. If the blood knot won't hold, then make a loop knot or double overhand knot in the monofilament (as illustrated on page 132) and use an improved clinch knot to attach the backing. For steelheading, if your reel has the capacity to hold the fly line or the shooting head and running line and a hundred yards of backing, I highly recommend using 30-pound test backing because it holds knots better than the lighter line, is more abrasion resistant, and you are less likely to lose your fly lines with 30-pound backing.

Monofilament wears out first in the area where it's knotted to the shooting head because that section takes the most abuse in the quick-snap turnover of the cast. When using mono shooting line I snip off the first 5 feet when I begin a new day's fishing. With 150 feet of monofilament shooting line you have about 50 feet of extra line to snip off, or approximately 10 days of hard fishing. Even better is to reverse the monofilament line after 5 days, leaving you with 125 feet of running line. If you are using a two-handed rod or are casting more than 150 feet you are better off loading your reel with 200 feet of running line. One of the advantages of a shooting head system is that you can put more backing on the reel or use heavier backing or use a smaller reel than with regular fly line.

CASTING AND FISHING SHOOTING HEADS

One July day Forrest Maxwell and I watched as a fly fisherman worked one of the many submerged ledgerock runs on the North Umpqua River. The fisherman was certainly a graceful caster, his casts stroking out 85 to 90 feet in the classic unrolling loop that looks so easy when well done.

The North Umpqua is a demanding river; the problem lay in distance—the steelhead was holding in the lee of a ledge a little over a hundred feet from the caster.

After the steelheader had played through, Forrest moved into position to cast to the fish. His 12-foot graphite rod powered the shooting head the needed distance. With each succeeding sweep of the wet fly, his presentation was coming closer to the strike zone.

I had a great vantage point on a rock overlooking the river and even though I wasn't the one fishing, I felt a twinge of excitement and anticipation as I watched Forrest's 1/0 Purple Matuka drawing nearer to the steelhead. Although the river was as translucent as a glass jar, I would momentarily lose sight of the fish in the coils of the current, then regain it by looking downstream from the tip of the floating shooting head.

The steelhead was holding her position, but I noticed that the last fly swing had caused her to shift laterally two feet and then slip back to her previous lie. I debated about releasing some of my pent-up tautness by yelling to Forrest that the next cast was it, but I knew that Forrest's whole being was centered on the river, the fish, and his next cast, and I didn't want to crack his concentration.

Forrest laid the cast out perfectly; the fly sank to the proper depth and began its measured crosscurrent swim.

There was no wild lunge for the fly—the steelhead drifted up a foot and a half in the water column, matched the fly's swing for a brief moment, opened her mouth and clamped down on the Matuka.

The graphite simultaneously transmitted the take to Forrest's rod hand—his retaliating strike was instantaneous and put a deep bend in his fly rod. The steelhead answered with violent head shakes, a split-second slashing turn, and a wild 50 yard run to the shrill tune of whirling pawls and gears in Forrest's reel. The steelhead capped her rush with a glimmering silver leap that took her four feet out of the water.

The battle was measured in silver flashes, boiling swirls, powerful runs, a bending and throbbing fly rod, line squirting from the reel, and a fierce winding back of line. Eventually Forrest brought in 8 pounds of prime summer run steelhead. After confirming that she was born of the river, Forrest backed the Matuka out of her mouth and turned the wild steelhead free to spawn future generations of Umpqua sea-run rainbow.

The main drawback when using shooting heads is that they don't cast with the same fluid grace as a regular fly line because of the hinging effect at the junction of the shooting head and running line. The hinging effect is caused by the abrupt dropoff between the relatively thick shooting head and the thin running line at one specific spot, without the gradual taper of a regular line.

Learning to cast a shooting head and how to handle 80 to 100 feet of loose line can take a bit of practice. It's easier to learn in the calm setting of a nearby lake, spacious lawn, or football field than in the excitement of tossing a steelhead fly out into a wide river while up to your waist in current.

Once rod and reel are rigged, the caster should start by pulling the head and about 40 feet of running line from the reel, and letting it lay on the ground. Stretch the head and running line as you pull it from the reel to help it lay out straight on the cast. Thread the rod, pulling the head and about three feet of shooting line past the tip guide. To save the tippet and leader and to protect yourself and the rod tip, use a piece of yarn as a fly or a fly with the bend and point of the hook removed.

Pinch the running line between your fingers to prevent more line from going out, then gently flex the rod back and forth through the complete backcast and forward cast cycle several times to get the feel of the weight of the shooting head. It will feel like twirling a pregnant armadillo by the tail; casting a shooting head isn't as pleasant as using a standard weight forward fly line, but it's not unpleasant either. (Especially when your one hundred foot cast hooks a steelhead you couldn't reach with a regular line.)

After you've tested the "feel" of casting the head several times, just release the running line at the apex of the forward cast. With a moderate forward stroke, the weight of the head should shoot out the 40 feet of running line with ease. Expert casters execute tight loops when casting shooting heads, but until you have polished your delivery, an oval casting stroke works best for keeping the fly and the shooting head from hitting you or your rod. Peel off more shooting line as you become more comfortable casting the head. (Remember to stretch the running line before you cast it.) A single haul on the forward cast will increase your distance by increasing the line speed, and a double haul will increase it even farther.

Handling all that loose line is one of the challenges of fishing with shooting heads, particularly when the caster is out in the river current. Some anglers use stripping baskets made from nylon mesh. I prefer to lightly hold large loops of shooting line between my lips while casting, letting the force of the forward cast pull the line free from their light grip. (I'm hoping someone will market chocolate flavored shooting line.)

Shooting head systems are certainly not the only way to fly fish for steelhead or even the best method for all situations. But a shooting head system does offer easier distance casting with less angler fatigue, particularly for big water steelheading. Heads are easily interchanged to match the prevalent fishing conditions, which can result in more hooked fish.

Shooting head systems are certainly not the only way to fly fish for steelhead or even the best method for all situations. But a shooting head system does offer easier distance casting with less angler fatigue, particularly for big water steelheading.

Winter Steelheading With A Fly

VIII

To refine our focus, we will consider winter steelhead as fish that enter fresh water with the first heavy rains of late fall and early winter, with more fish arriving during the winter and on into spring. These are fish that arrive from November on through the winter months and early spring; winter steelhead spawn in late winter or early spring months. The term "winter steelhead" is somewhat arbitrary. For example, in Oregon the Siletz River has a fall run of native steelhead that could be considered late summer runs, but they often arrive when the river exhibits winter conditions; the Nestucca and Santiam rivers host a late run of native winter fish in March and April when these rivers can be low and clear.

The arrival of any particular race of steelhead varies from watershed to watershed and can vary among rivers within the same watershed. Hatchery fish tend to clump up in their arrival time, whereas native fish arrive over a longer period of time. That makes sense from an evolutionary standpoint, because a run that is spread out over time will have a better chance of perpetuating itself by overcoming any temporary blockage to spawning, such as a flood. Native fish spawn over a long period of time for the same reason, and that is one of the reasons why fish native to any rivershed are specifically adapted to that river. Their genetic blueprint is irreplaceable—we need those fish.

Winter steelhead encounter water conditions that vary from low, clear water to high, brown, muddy water, with water temperatures that range from the low 50's to freezing. We will consider winter steelheading tactics as those relating to water temperatures below 45 degrees. When water temperatures rise above 45 degrees, you can incorporate surface tactics because even winter steelhead often become more active and surface oriented in warmer water. In the same vein, even if you don't pursue surface tactics, fishing a light rod with a floating line/wet fly swing with a slimly dressed fly can be effective and is a pleasant respite from more demanding winter tactics.

In fact, when rivers get low and clear, water temperatures sometimes rise, and it can often be ideal for fly fishing because there are fewer fishermen on the river and conditions favor fly fishing. It can be a mistake on the fly fisher's part to view the river as a "winter steelheading" river. Because of the warmer water conditions winter steelhead become more active and summer tactics are often more appropriate than traditional winter strategies.

The key to much of the enjoyment of steelheading is to modify your tactics and presentation strategies to what you hope the fish will respond to, and not have a preconceived mind set that eliminates other tactical possibilities.

Many fly fishermen quest to hook fish with Olympian zeal, but perhaps fly fishing for winter steelhead should be judged under a different criterion. A fly fisherman is at a disadvantage because of high, cold water, line control problems, built-in limitations of using a fly, and the fact that most of our winter steelhead waters are flogged by an army of drift fishermen armed with bait and deadly wobbling, flashing lures. It boils down to a preference of method. In *Fisherman's Spring,*

To be effective, the winter steelhead fly must explore at the steelhead's depth in a slow, provocative manner. The fly must investigate prime steelhead territory close to the bottom, in resting places of lessened current and protective cover. Some of the author's non–traditional winter flies: Marabou Streamer on Gamakatsu Octopus hook, Marabou Streamer on Tiemco 7999 hook, Winter's Hope Marabou Streamer on Tiemco 800 hook, Steelhead Shrimp on Tiemco 207BL hook and Leggo–My–Eggo on Gamakatsu Octopus hook.

Facing page: *The North Umpqua is an exceptionally beautiful river that has a magical quality to it, with its moss shouldered canyon walls, deep flowing opalescent green currents, and strong, silver winter steelhead that are native to the river. The river is known for its summer run fly fishing, with a legacy passed on through the writings of Zane Grey and Ray Bergman.*

It is most important in winter steelhead fly fishing to select your water carefully and fish it slowly.
Photo by Bill McMillan

1951, Roderick Haig-Brown wrote, "In sport, method is everything. The more skill the method calls for, the higher its yield of emotional stir and satisfaction, the higher its place must be in a sportsman's scale of values."

Every year more winter fish are caught on flies by fishermen using new techniques coupled with specialized lines and flies tailored to specific strategies.

Because of low water temperatures, most winter fly rod steelheading can be encapsulated into "low and slow." The fly must be presented to the fish close to the bottom (within 18 inches) and moved across the fish's vision as slowly as possible, giving the steelhead the maximum amount of time to react. A selection of dark and bright flies from 6 to 6/0 will catch steelhead anywhere, but it's the fly line and its manipulation that controls the presentation of the fly, and that is the keystone to successful winter steelheading.

The whole winter steelhead stream is not for the fly fisherman; you must choose specific types of water to stack the odds in your favor. Leave heavy water and extra deep pools alone. Concentrate on water that allows you to fish the fly both close to the bottom and slow. Covering fish that you've spotted is a deadly technique, but much of the time you'll be fishing blind, probing holding water without actually seeing fish. Look for resting areas that offer some type of current deflection for the fish, like behind boulders, rock ledges, and fallen logs. Other choice spots are along the edges of the main current and in flat tailouts just above rapids.

One of the most overlooked spots for winter steelhead is at the head of a riffle, in the bubbly water of moderate depth

and speed. Winter steelhead rest there because the riffle contains lots of oxygen and the broken ceiling of riffled water provides cover while the steelhead gathers strength to ascend into the next run. Steelheaders overlook the top of the riffle because at first sight the water looks too shallow and swift.

On one early April trip on the lower Bogachiel River on the Olympic Peninsula with J.D. Love, he rolled a husky red-striped buck steelhead. The fish moved to his fly about half way down the riffle, in a patch of perfect fly water. But after that initial boil, the steelhead wouldn't come to that fly or any of the other patterns he tried.

When we returned to that spot the next day, J.D. was pumped to try that fish again. He started working his fly about a third of the way down the riffle. After thoroughly working the rest of the riffle, the throat of the run, and the tailout, he said, "It looks like that buck either moved out or doesn't want my fly. Why don't you give it a try."

Having noticed that J.D. hadn't fished the very top of the run, I started probing the head of the riffle with a 1/0 Halloween Matuka tied with a black body and orange wing and fished on a 9-weight sinktip. The second or third swing through the fly stopped in a fish's mouth. She shook her head angrily, then burned downstream to the very end of the tailout, about 100 yards. After catching up with her, she made a strong run upstream about 50 yards.

J.D. said, "Looks like you've got a real slab-side there, Deke."

Before long the fish tired and we got her in. She measured 36 inches and was estimated at 16 pounds. She wasn't far from the ocean in either time or space, still glowing in her silvery ocean colors, with several sea lice clinging to her belly just aft of her ventral fins.

We speculated that she had moved up during the previous evening or early morning and was resting at the head of the riffle. I always probe the top of the riffle for winter fish, even though it's more like summer run water.

The two most efficient methods for presenting the fly to winter steelhead are with a dead-drift or controlled swing. The dead-drift technique is simple to describe but can be difficult to execute. The fly is allowed to freely drift downstream without drag and at the same level as the fish. The controlled wet fly swing brings the fly in front of the steelhead in a slow crosscurrent arc. For both methods, mending and manipulating the fly line are of the utmost importance in presenting the fly "low and slow."

No matter what technique you employ to search the winter river, when the fly is straight below you, be sure to pause before you retrieve it for another cast. As described in the wet fly chapter, you will catch fish by executing the hang down strategy because steelhead often follow the fly without striking, then nail it while it hangs suspended in front of them. I find the hang down strains my patience, but it does catch fish. How long you should let your fly dangle in the current depends on scientific data such as water temperature, amount of current, depth, and cover where the fly hangs, amount of fishing pressure, and the whims of individual steelhead. (The time you actually spend on the hang down will depend on unscientific factors such as your store of patience and the amount of confidence you have in the hang down, but the colder the water, the longer you let the fly hang.)

The fly rodder can use a floating line, a long leader, and a large fly or a weighted fly; a fast sinking sinktip line with a short leader; a Teeny Nymphline with a short leader; or a shooting head system with a variety of sinking shooting heads.

But the crux is to be able to get that fly down fast and keep it there, while maintaining contact with the fly to detect a strike. While it's not always the case, winter fish tend to take the fly lightly. The challenge is knowing when a fish has the fly in its mouth. It can be a serious error in tactics to fish too far out. Cover water closer in. Don't overcast—you can't read the strike.

FLOATING LINE TACTICS

The advantage of using a floating line is that you can concentrate on mending and line position, coupled with specific fly density, size, and brightness to entice a strike. The floating line is compatible with the classic wet fly swing and the hang down technique as described in the wet fly chapter, particularly when done "low and slow." When the fly is dead-drifted, it's much like nymphing, which I cover in the nymphing techniques chapter. The main disadvantage in using the floating line and extended leader is that the casting rhythm is more like fly lobbing than fly casting, whether the fly is tied on a big hook or weighted or accompanied by split shot.

When using a floating line for winter steelhead, a longer rod is an advantage, particularly when roll casting and using the more open-loop cast required by the weight of the fly. The added mass of heavier weight fly lines is needed to propel the fly on its long leader.

The two variables with the floating line setup are the length of the leader and the weight of the fly. The leader must be long enough so that the fly is close to the bottom and in the strike zone. The tippet must be stiff enough to handle the fly.

The fly can also be a sinking component. A faster sink rate is accomplished by using a large hook or by weighting the

fly. A selection of flies incorporating different sink rates through variation in hook sizes or weighting the flies allows the angler to cover a variety of water. Some tyers whip finish the head of a weighted fly with a different colored thread to denote that it is weighted. Another option is to add lead to the leader, via split shot, Twist-ons or lead sleeves.

The business end of the fly line acts as a strike indicator, especially when using brightly colored lines. Another effective approach is to use the fly fisherman's bobber—the strike indicator. Some examples are fluorescent foam pads with peel-off backing; the drift fisherman's Corkie held in place on the leader with a bit of toothpick or matchstick; an inch or two of fluorescent fly line with the core removed; or a tuft of lustrous yarn tied onto the leader.

The floating line is particularly effective for fish you've spotted in less than six feet of water in moderate current or similar slots that you suspect might hold fish and where you can control the line and the presentation of the fly.

SINKING LINE TACTICS

Sea-strong winter steelhead swim into fresh water on the incoming tide because the push of the spawning urge is accelerated by ocean water surging up the natal river. If you can find a steelhead stream with a deep pool and a riffle just above the junction of salt and fresh water, you have located the initial resting place of most winter steelhead that come in on the high tide.

I was fishing such a river on a calm, cool, overcast January day speckled with intermittent rain. In some areas snow lay unmelted on the banks of the river. Cool as the winter ocean, steelhead with pale green backs and grayish silver sides had ascended on the morning tide. Spin fishermen had nailed a fish or two; in several spots fresh blood and fish remains decorated the brown and gray rocks along the bank.

I found a spot to fish right at the apex of the tailout above the beginning of the first riffle. I cast the sinktip line upstream and mended quickly, allowing the size 1 Polar Shrimp to plumb the depths of the current.

I cast again and again. My attention wandered to the seagulls floating on air currents above the ocean's breakers, about 100 yards downstream.

While fishing another cast my inattentive gaze noticed that the bright floating section of my line was curling upstream. I pulled back on the rod, half expecting a snagged fly. The fly was tight to something, so I pulled back a little farther. The line transmitted that most glorious of feelings up the rod to my hand—the throbbing of a fish. With all my being tuned into that rod and line, I let out a surprised yelp.

Feeling the sting of the hook and the downstream pressure of the rod and line, the steelhead plunged upriver, peeling line and then backing from the reel.

With 20 yards of backing in the river, the line shuddered and went limp. Totally deflated, I reeled in the line and found the leader severed. I'll never know for sure, but I suspect the fish sheared it off when the leader and fish intersected stout monofilament snagged on the bottom. I can't really complain, though, because that fish was really a gift—the downstream pull of the current on the fly had actually hooked the fish.

The rub with sinking lines is twofold: the sinking line sinks, putting the fly in the strike zone but at the same time drifting the fly into rocks, wedged branches, and other snags; and the angler needs a way to know when a fish has the fly in its mouth. It's a tough proposition with a sinking line dead-drifting the fly downstream, even with a brightly colored sinktip line.

The trick is to use a line that sinks quickly enough to get the fly down close to the bottom, but not one that constantly snags because it sinks too fast. You want your fly to drift freely, within two feet of the bottom. Ideally, the fly should occasionally tick the bottom without snagging, but if your fly is down where it should be for most winter steelheading, you will lose flies. Anyway, it's better to lose a few flies than miss a chance at a nice fish.

No matter what type of sinking line is used, here is a warm-up strategy that will help you catch more fish. Pick a small area of river where you can watch your fly line and fly. Cast out and see how deep the fly line sinks the fly before the current sweeps it downstream. You can then make a mental note of how many mends it takes to allow the fly to get to the bottom in that current. It will show you if you need to cast upstream to allow the line more time to sink to achieve an optimum drift.

An optimum drift occurs when the fly coasts downstream either at the same speed as the current or a bit slower, but at the same depth as the fish. Whether using the classic crosscurrent wet fly swing or a nymph-like dead-drift presentation, mending tactics slow the fly's drift. In either case the two most important factors are depth and speed of the drift. Even if the fly is at the right depth, if it's moving too fast the chances of hooking a steelhead are greatly diminished.

Using this warm-up strategy gives you a comparison gauge to use on other parts of the river that hold fish but are such that you can't see the drifting fly. Many fly fishermen don't realize how quickly fast water will take a fly downstream. The most common mistake winter fishermen make is underestimating the current speed and resultant depth of the drifting fly.

The key to successful winter steelheading with sinking lines is matching the correct sinking fly line to the water for both depth and current speed. Carrying lines of varying sink rates is a basic part of winter steelheading with sinking lines, bearing in mind that because they weigh more, heavier line weights sink faster; for example, a 9-weight sinks about a third faster than a 6-weight of the same type. And when dealing with fast currents there is no substitute for density—faster currents demand more density to get the fly down. Deep holding water also requires density.

Choosing the most effective sinking line depends on current speed, water depth, and distance cast. As long as the sinking line is drifting downstream at the same speed as the current it will sink at its maximum rate. Drag will cause the line to plane upwards, reducing the sinking rate. Excessive drag makes the line rise to the surface.

The length of the sinking line also relates to the water depth, whether it's a Sink Tip with a 10, 13, 20, or 30-foot sink-tip, the 24-foot tip of a Teeny Nymphline, a full sinking line, or a shooting head. Once you conquer the speed of the current, the properly matched fly line will drift the fly downstream or swing it crosscurrent at the desired depth. If the sinking portion is too light or too short you can add split shot to the leader or crimp it to the fly line to make it sink faster, but lead impairs casting fluidity.

Line control is crucial. The floating portion of the sinktip can be mended to increase the depth and distance of the fly's drift, while at the same time acting as a strike indicator. When the floating section curls back upstream it's signalling that the fly is either hung in a fish's mouth or on a snag. I know one fly fisherman who puts a Corkie and toothpick strike indicator on his Teeny Nymphline at the junction of the floating/sinking sections, just as you would on the leader of a floating line. It helps him detect the strike from soft-biting winter steelhead. For that matter, you can place a strike detector on any sinktip line. It's a good idea if it helps you catch fish because your

J.D. Love has hooked a winter fish on the Elwha an the Olympic Peninsula. Because of low water temperatures, most winter fly rod steelheading can be encapsulated into "low and slow." The fly must be presented to the fish close to the bottom (within 18 inches) and moved across the fish's vision as slowly as possible, giving the steelhead the maximum amount of time to react to the fly.

concentration is fixed on one specific spot instead of the junction of the floating with the sinking line, which can be hard to see in low light conditions. If the holding water is too deep or too far away to be effectively fished with a sinktip, then a Teeny Nymphline, a full sinking line, or a shooting head may be the only way to cover the fish. The disadvantage of the full sinking line is that line control is lost when fishing most rivers—you can't tell when a fish has taken the fly and you also snag up fairly often because the line is draped over the river bottom.

SHOOTING HEAD SYSTEMS FOR WINTER STEELHEADING

A shooting head system allows for a high degree of versatility because shooting heads take up little space in your vest and can be interchanged quickly on the river to match prevailing river conditions. They are handy if you are traveling to an unknown river because heads take up less room than a selection of spare spools and an assortment of heads allows you to cover almost any contingency.

Cortland and Scientific Anglers factory heads are available in 30-foot floating, sinktip, and fast sinking. A floating or sinktip head is an effective tool for summer fishing where distance casting or casting for long hours is important. But for winter fishing, the full sinking factory heads or heads you construct for your own fishing are most useful.

I remember one January trip to the North Umpqua when I lolled around on the river, enjoying brief spells of winter sunshine while I pitched out a fast sinking shooting head.

The North Umpqua is an exceptionally beautiful river that has a magical quality to it, with its moss shouldered canyon walls, deep flowing opalescent green currents, and strong, silver winter steelhead that are native to the river. The river is known for its summer run fly fishing, with a legacy passed on through the writings of Zane Grey and Ray Bergman. But compared to the sunny months, the winter run of wild fish receives scant pressure from fly fishermen, even though there is over 30 miles of fly-only water.

One of the joys of fishing such a magnificent river is the enjoyment of the riverine cathedral of rock canyon and flowing water, both of which soothe the winter soul. My eyes panned up and down the canyon, only turning to the fishing business at hand to direct the recasting of the shooting head.

I let the head swing broad arcs under the surface of the green water, with the 3/0 Halloween Matuka cutting cross current in bold sweeps. A steelhead intercepted the fly in midswing, sending a sharp thump up the line and rod. Jolted from daydreaming I focused on the pumping rod and the reel spinning line downstream. I had hooked the fish in the expansive tailout above Wright's Creek, and helped by increased current speed, the steelhead wouldn't surrender an inch of line.

I scrambled over the rocks and headed downstream until I was 20 yards from Wright Creek rapids and the end of the tailout. It was the fish's decision—go downstream through the rapids or fight it out here in the tailout. Fortunately for me,

J.D. Love playing his fish on the Elwha. A selection of dark and bright flies from 6 to 6/0 will catch steelhead anywhere, but it's the fly line and its manipulation that controls the presentation of the fly, and that is the keystone to successful winter steelheading.

the steelhead chose to remain in the run. I pulled sideways on the fish by lowering my rod and pulling towards shore. Reluctantly the fish gave ground, and even though the steelhead made several crisp runs, I soon tailed it in the shallows. It was a native buck of about nine pounds with a bold red stripe and dark coloration, so he was probably a late summer run fish. I didn't care—he was a gorgeous fish on a gorgeous river.

One of the most versatile heads for winter steelheading is the Deep Water Express in 550, 700, and 850 grains, although the whole 30-foot head is seldom used as one shooting head because it weighs too much. The Deep Water Express offers density within a short length of line, which means you can make a selection of Express mini–heads, tailoring your shooting head system for specific segments of any river. Another advantage is that the Express remains flexible because it's made with powdered tungsten, as opposed to less efficient lead core heads. For instance, when fishing a lead core line, when it drifts into a rock it bends around the rock and then stays bent in the water, making it hard to get a proper drift and to detect strikes to the fly.

Factory shooting heads come with a loop installed, but for fishing the Deep Water Express, you need to install a loop for attaching the shooting or running line. There are various methods for making the loop needed to attach the shooting or running line; Gene Trump showed me an excellent one, as illustrated in the chapter on shooting heads.

One of the most efficient ways to cover winter steelhead water is with a selection of Deep Water Express mini-heads. Fill your reel with backing and running line, then add an Express mini-head of a specific length, depending on the current speed and depth of the water. In one area of the river you might use a 3-foot head, whereas just downstream you might need a 4-foot head. With loops already installed on Express mini-heads of varying lengths, you can approach the winter river with a high degree of versatility. If you put loops on both ends of your Express mini-heads, you can interlock heads; for instance, you can add a 2-foot section to a 4-foot section making a 6-foot Express mini-head. (As an example, from a 30-foot Express you can make two heads each of 2, 3, 4, and 5-foot lengths, with 2 feet left over, for a total of 8 mini-heads.)

Traditionally, one of the factors to determine when building your own shooting head is to match the weight of the head with the specified line weight of your rod. As discussed in the chapter on shooting heads, a rod will usually cast a head of one or two line weights heavier than a standard fly line because of the way a 30-foot shooting head loads the rod.

However, when building and fishing Express mini-heads for winter steelhead, it's more important to match the sinking rate of the head to the water fished than to the rod. With Express mini-heads, and particularly those built from the 850 grain Express, most of your shooting head lengths will be drastically shorter than standard heads. Most will be less than 10 feet because of the density and weight of Deep Water Express and because longer heads may sink very fast but they also snag quickly and offer the angler less control over the drifting fly. Even though you may be using a more powerful rod for winter steelheading, you can still cast these mini-heads by opening up your casting stroke, pausing at the end of the stroke and giving the head a little flip at the end of the backward and forward strokes. One of the tradeoffs with a shooting head system is that they are not as much fun to cast as a standard fly line.

There are two types of shooting or running line, and both have advantages for winter steelheading. Thin diameter fly line used as shooting line offers the advantage of being readily visible on the water. The best fly line shooting lines for winter steelhead are those in luminous fluorescent colors because you can track your shooting head and your fly as it fishes the river. Brightly colored running line is particularly important when fishing a length of Deep Water Express because the running line is a strike indicator; you can see that bright line curl back upstream when something has your fly. Fly line shooting line offers some mending capability and it's fairly easy to handle in the cold when your fingers are stiff. The disadvantage when using thin fly line as shooting line for winter steelheading is that the sinking rate of the sinking head is slowed by the buoyancy of the floating shooting line.

Monofilament running line is best for allowing Deep Water Express to sink at its quickest. Fluorescent monofilament offers the same advantages as fluorescent fly line for tracking the head and the fly and it's less expensive. This isn't a complete list, but some options include Cortland's fluorescent green Plion shooting line, Cortland Cobra red flat monofilament, and High-Visibility gold Stren in 25 or 30-pound test. Beware of monofilament that is too stiff because it will kink and drive you crazy with tangles. Monofilament doesn't mend as well as thin fly line, and is slippery and more difficult to handle when fingers are cold.

MATCH YOUR GEAR TO THE WATER OR FIND WATER TO MATCH YOUR GEAR

As I discussed before, the object of winter steelheading is to get your fly down to the fish and then work it so it undulates as slowly as possible in front of the fish. Whether you use a floating line, sinktip, or shooting head system, the two most effective tactics are the controlled wet fly swing and the dead-drift nymph-type presentation.

You can also work in variations such as a jigging or slow stripped retrieve, particularly for steelhead you've already spotted. Joe Howell likes to strip jumbo Spey flies in front of winter steelhead he's spotted on the North Umpqua, coaxing the fish with the long trailing hackles of the Spey design. He says that at times the fish will charge as far as 20 feet to take the fly.

On one winter trip to the same river, my fishing partner kept referring to a secret spot on the river where he claimed he caught mint February winter fish when no one else had caught anything. After fishing various areas that morning with no success, we went to his spot. It was hardly a secret, though; the pullout is on the main road and I had fished the run many times myself.

After completing a wet fly swing, part of his strategy was to jig the fly upstream past some ledgerock, quickly lifting the rod tip to make the fly jerk upstream and then allowing it to flutter back, pulling in a bit of line each time. The jerking, fluttering fly undulates in front of the fish, stirring aggression and triggering latent feeding instincts that demand the fish attack the wounded prey. Not getting any strikes from the steelhead he hoped were holding along the ledge, my partner gradually worked his way downstream and around the bend.

I decided to follow with a variation of the jigging method. I figured that the fish had already seen a fairly standard wet fly (I can't remember what he was using) so I followed with something that might be a bit more outrageous and stir the steelhead to strike—a full dressed 3/0 Brad's Brat. My variation of the jigging approach was a slow strip retrieve, a retrieve that is smoother than a jigging tactic and possibly appeals to the steelhead's predatory instincts in that the fly-prey "is getting away." I would cast out, mend to slow the wet fly swing, then strip the fly back in easy six-inch strips. That tactic nailed a six-pound fish and brought my partner charging back upstream with mixed emotions because I had caught

Joe Howell with a winter run North Umpqua steelhead. Joe caught this fish in February, 1970, just after he got out of the Air Force. He now owns the Blue Heron Fly Shop on the North Umpqua.

a fish in his "secret" spot with a variation of his specialized strategy. By the time we had finished the drive home, he had reduced my six-pound steelhead to three pounds and was trying to convince me that the fish had spawned! That was in 1980 and we still get a chuckle out of it.

When you find your enthusiasm glazing over from the repeated presentations that winter steelheading requires, throw caution to the steelheading winds and experiment with something that is exotic—a change of flies, more radical in color, brightness, or design—or better yet, employ a radical change in tactics. Try a different presentation, or present the fly from a different angle, or string up a different line and explore a whole different strategy, such as changing from a wet fly swing with a sinktip to a very slow greased line presentation with a floating line.

The two ways to gear up for covering winter steelhead in a variety of water are with a shooting head system or with lines on extra spools. Extra spools or reels loaded with full fly lines are more bulky to carry, but standard fly lines are more pleasant to cast than shooting heads. When fishing a small stream, full fly lines are more efficient because you aren't casting very far and the shooting head knot isn't constantly sliding in and out of the rod guides. And a full fly line will load the rod better in the often cramped quarters of the smaller stream. However, shooting head systems are more compact and offer a higher degree of versatility than standard lines. I usually carry an assortment of Express mini-heads and factory and custom made heads, a spool rigged for shooting heads, a spool with a full floating line, and several spools with different sinktips—my winter steelheading vest tends to be heavy.

The basic option for the winter steelheader is that the fly fisherman can either find water that is matched to the line the angler prefers to use or the fisherman can carry various lines or shooting heads to match the water that is available. For example, if the river is uncrowded you may choose to fish a 10-foot fast sinking tip, covering riffles and tailouts with a favorite fly in the classic wet fly swing, moving from spot to spot. If you only have one stretch of water to yourself, you will probably start out with your favorite tactic, but after you've gone through the run several times with different flies, you have the option of changing tactics, which usually involves changing lines as well. For instance, you might go from that sinktip approach to an Express mini-head and search deeper portions of the run, or you might change to a floater and fish dead-drift nymph-style or combine it with a wet fly swing and a hang down. By expanding your techniques and developing new approaches to winter fishing you will not only enjoy steelheading more fully, you will catch more fish.

WINTER STEELHEAD FLIES

Winter steelhead hook sizes vary from the wee to the heaviest irons, but usually range from 6 to 2/0. Winter steelhead are caught on flies tied on extra strong 8's and 10's and on fully dressed 3/0's and 6/0's. Almost any wet fly steelhead pattern will catch winter steelhead, but the presentation of the fly is crucial, coupled with the two most important aspects of the winter fly—size and brightness.

Think of the size of your winter steelhead fly as a package. It's the overall size of the fly that's important. For instance, you can tie a size 4 dressing on a size 2 hook, resulting in a compact fly on a good-sized hook for husky winter run steelhead. If you tie your fly on a short shank hook, you can approximate a size 4 fly on a 1/0 short shank hook, which

results in a reduced fly on a hook with a wide gap for fish with tough, bony mouths, while the short shank reduces the number of snags.

Ask yourself these questions: do you want a small bright offering, a large luminous attractor, or just a dab of subtle color designed to provoke a strike without causing the fish to flee from a too-bright intruder? Flies tied with fluorescent or phosphorescent materials further excite steelhead into striking, particularly in low light or turbid water conditions.

I've seen steelhead hit incandescent flies in low, clear water and black flies in high water, which is just the opposite of the traditional high water—bright fly, low water—dark fly rule.

The "rules" for winter steelheading are not bound in cement. That can be frustrating, but it is also one of the attractions of winter steelheading—there are no fixed answers. In many respects the winter steelheader is exploring unknown fly fishing territory, proceeding without the benediction or the binding fetters of tradition because there is little written about winter fly fishing for steelhead. The general attitude among many anglers is that winter fly fishers are merely flogging the water with no chance of catching a fish, but that isn't true. Every season more fly anglers are catching winter steelhead. It's become quite common to see fly fishermen on winter rivers.

HOOK AND FLY OPTIONS
FOR WINTER STEELHEADING

The black Mustad 36890 has been the standard winter steelhead fly hook for many years. It's readily obtainable in sizes 12 to 6/0, is strong enough to land steelhead and defeat

Ask yourself these questions: do you want a small bright offering, a large luminous attractor, or just a dab of subtle color designed to provoke a strike without causing the fish to flee from a too-bright intruder? Photo by David Lambroughton

snags, but it should be sharpened before fishing. It's available in Accu-Point in sizes 6 to 2/0, a chemically sharpened version that Mustad claims is tempered to 20% more hardness. Accu-Point hooks are much sharper than Mustad's standard hooks and feature a smaller microbarb. The 36890 has a turned up loop eye but the taper is very blunt, resulting in an unnecessary tying hassle.

In recent years Partridge hooks have been difficult to obtain because Partridge's deliveries to American fly shops are unpredictable. Daiichi, which used to be Kamasan, makes a beautiful winter steelheading hook, the 2421, but Daiichi hooks can be hard to find.

The Tiemco 7999 is the best made hook for winter steelheading because of its heavy wire and consistently high quality—it's extremely sharp, has a small barb that is easily bent down and a nicely tapered turned up loop eye. The 7999 is available in sizes 8 to 2/0 in a black finish. The main drawback to these gorgeous hooks is that the wire is heat treated and they tend to be brittle and can't be bounced off rocks, either on the backcast or underwater. The tradeoff is a hook made of softer wire, which won't stay sharp and might bend under the pressure of fighting a big fish. For those who prefer a standard down eye hook, the Tiemco 700 is similar to the 7999, available in sizes 8 to 1/0.

The best thing about the Eagle Claw 1197 series is that they are American made. It's a down eye hook, bronze or nickel plated, available in sizes 8 to 1. The 64B is the same hook, offered as a barbless version in bronze only. The "Lazer Sharp" chemical sharpening process has resulted in a sharper hook, but the closure on the down-eye is still rough enough to cut the tippet if the hook closure area isn't filled with thread when the fly is tied. The wire is soft enough to bend instead of breaking when snagged or bounced off rocks, but can be marginal when trying to hold a jumbo fish. Eagle Claw's new cryogenic treatment called "Diamond Point" immerses hooks in a sub-freezing bath of liquid nitrogen for several hours before returning the metal to room temperature. This cold tempering process stiffens the metal so the hooks don't bend as readily. Eagle Claw claims the hook will also stay sharp longer. The Diamond Point 1197 and 64 are still soft when compared to Mustad or Tiemco, but are about 50% stiffer than previous versions.

There are other hook designs which address the problem of losing flies when bottom-scratching for winter fish. If you visualize the ideal shape for an anchor, it would have a curved, pointed claw for digging into the river bottom and a shaft running from the claw to the eye for attaching the anchor rope. That description also sketches the shape of the traditional steelhead hook, with its eye, shank, and hook point all functioning to attach the hook to the river bottom.

Even though still in the shape of an anchor, you can lessen the number of snags by tying your flies on short shank hooks such as the Tiemco 800B, which is black and has a straight eye, in sizes 8 to 1/0. These are an O'Shaughnessy style, as is also the Daiichi 2451, Gamakatsu O'Shaughnessy, Eagle Claw L254N, and Mustad 9174, 9175, and 3407. By adding lead eyes to the top front of flies tied on these short shank hooks you can decrease snags by about half because the lead causes the fly to flip over when under light tension or dead-drifting in the current, so the fly tends to ride with the point up, away from most snags. Examples of flies that readily lend themselves to a lead eye design include a compressed Steelhead Woolly Bugger, Pink Puff, Red-And-White Puff, and Black's Buster Leech.

Tying lead eyes on the top side at the head of the fly is also effective on standard steelhead hooks. Lead eyes won't eliminate snagging, but they reduce the number of lost flies. That's probably why the Boss and Comet series with their bead eyes have been so popular over the years as deeply sunk flies. (Bead eyes whistle in the air when cast, however, while lead eyes are silent.) Lead eyes are available in various sizes in plain or nickel plated and are more dense for their size than bead eyes.

A particularly effective lead eye fly for steelhead is the Steelhead Woolly Bugger because the marabou tail and palmered hackle move well in the water; best colors are black, purple, orange, and pink. I suppose you could tender the theory that the Steelhead Woolly Bugger is shrimp-like in orange or pink and resembles fresh water prey in black and that purple may excite territorial aggression in steelhead. (Who knows, all of the above may be true.)

The 207BL is Tiemco's heavy wire barbless version of the Mustad Wide Gap hook and the Eagle Claw Kahle hook. The 207BL works well for a dead-drift presentation of flies such as a Black Stonefly Nymph or Steelhead Shrimp or any number of marabou soft hackle patterns. The greatest advantage of the 207BL is that it's curved shape causes it to ride upside down, which lessens the chance of snagging. You can accentuate that effect by adding lead to the hook shank.

Another approach is to use the Mustad 79666, a forged keel hook. In sizes 10 to 1/0 this fairly light wire hook is strong enough for steelhead if you leave the barb on, but the hook needs to be sharpened for fishing. The keel hook is overly large for its size designation; for example, a size 6 keel hook is equivalent to a size 2 standard steelhead hook. A keel fly is not as elegant as the traditional steelhead streamer, but there isn't anything elegant about being constantly hung up on the bottom, either. The keel hook isn't totally snagless, but is an improvement over the traditional hook. Wrapping lead wire around the center of the hook shank helps reinforce the "keel" of this hook design, keeping the hook riding point up. (I've taken fish to 15 pounds with keel hooks.)

I've experimented with jig hooks and offset hooks that bassmasters use with plastic worms because they too are trying to get to the fish while defeating a host of snags. For steelhead, jig hooks must have extra strong wire; they perform much like the short shank hooks mentioned before, particularly when tied with lead eyes. At some point however, you cross over an arbitrary line and are no longer fly fishing but fly lobbing because you have destroyed the enjoyment and grace of fly casting and fly fishing. (I discuss this more thoroughly in the "Nymphing" techniques chapter.) Offset worm hooks work in heavier wire, but most are either too light and/or too big for most steelheading; for example, the smallest heavy wire Owner worm hook is 1/0, equivalent to a 2/0 standard steelhead hook. Although available in smaller sizes, the wire in Eagle Claw's L95 and Gamakatsu's offset worm hook is too light; the weedless Mustad features a wire weed guard, which reduces snags but might make your fly fish-proof as well, particularly for soft-biting winter steelhead. (I've pretty much given up on these types of hooks for steelhead, opting for the keel hook instead.)

Another effective approach is to use a short shank drift fishing hook, such as the Eagle Claw L183 in bronze or L182 nickel plated, or the nickel plated Mustad 92553 Accu-Point. The Eagle Claw L182B and the Mustad 92553X are barbless. My favorite is Gamakatsu Octopus hooks which have small barbs that are easily bent flat, needle sharp points, and are made of tougher steel than Eagle Claw or Mustad. Gamakatsu Octopus hooks are available in sizes 6 to 4/0 in nickel, bronze, green, blue, black, red, and gold. Drift hooks don't snag as readily as standard fly hooks because of their extra short shank and curved point configuration. Reduced soft hackles,

There are two basic options for the winter steelhead fly angler: he can find water that is matched to the line he prefers to use or carry various lines or shooting heads to match the water that is available. Photo by Ted Richter

marabou streamers, or trimmed-hackle shrimp imitations work well on these hooks.

Egg imitations tied with lustrous yarn trimmed to a round shape on these hooks is as simple as it gets. Of course, whether steelhead take these flies because of their egg shape or coloration or because they are biting at a bit of life-like color is debatable. It raises the question of how many winter steelhead have ever seen a fish egg or fed on them, even as juvenile fish. By drifting egg patterns, friends of mine regularly catch sea-run cutthroat feeding on dislodged eggs of spawning salmon on the Alsea and Siletz rivers, and have occasionally hooked steelhead, too. A friend told me that he has observed steelhead on the Rogue River repeatedly swim through beds of spawning salmon, presumably feeding on their eggs.

Acrylic "pom-poms" found in the yarn or craft section of department stores make effective egg flies. These decorative puffs of yarn are dyed various luminous colors and are already trimmed to a round egg shape. These yarn puff balls have a loop of wire or thread in the center that holds the yarn together, allowing you to simply insert the hook through the center of the wire. To keep the yarn ball from slipping down to the bend of the hook when fishing, you can either tie a mound of thread behind the yarn or wrap several turns of thread through the puff ball. Or you can put a drop of super glue on the shank of the hook before sliding the puff ball on.

To be effective, the winter steelhead fly must explore the steelhead's depths in a slow, provocative manner. The fly must investigate prime steelhead territory close to the bottom, in resting places of lessened current and protective cover. Steelhead holding slots invariably harbor fly-plucking snags, particularly for the standard steelhead streamer. By experimenting with new fly designs and different hooks, you can defeat many of those snags, the result of which will be more time spent actually fishing—the longer your fly stays in the strike zone in front of the steelhead, the better your chances will be for hooking that fish and ultimately, you'll catch more steelhead.

A WINTER STEELHEAD FLY SAMPLER

This is an arbitrary sampling of fly types that have proven effective for winter steelhead. They are considered different types because they are not just a rearrangement of colors and materials; these flies actually look different in the water, appealing to steelhead because of varied factors, including feeding instinct and territorial aggression.

This isn't a complete list of winter flies, but hopefully will offer you new ideas or approaches in the ever-changing fields of fly tying and fishing. If you want to pare down to the minimum number of fly types and want to tie quick, inexpensive flies because of the frequency of snags while winter steelheading, I would recommend the Leggo-My-Eggo yarn puff fly and the Marabou Streamer tied in a range of colors from dark to bright, with speckles of Flashabou or Krystal Flash, in sizes 6 to 2/0. I would tie the egg pattern on a Gamakatsu Octopus hook and the Marabou Streamer on standard, short shank, and keel hooks, to cover varied water conditions.

Polar Shrimp—Clarence Shoff

Tail: Red or hot orange hackle fibers
Body: Orange or fluorescent orange chenille
Wing: White polar bear, bucktail, or kip tail
Hackle: Orange or fluorescent orange chenille
  (Hot pink or fluorescent red also work well for the
  body and hackle in this fly and the body can be
  ribbed with silver tinsel.)

In the summer 1983 *Fly Tyer* Les Johnson wrote, "Clarence Shoff opened his small Kent, Washington, fly shop in 1922. Hitting the roads for weeks at a time he sold flies and hand-tied gut leaders at fishing camps on the banks of rivers from Washington to California. Being a totally gifted and smitten angler, it was not uncommon for Clarence to set up his vise at a fishing lodge and tie custom orders well into the night, then, rise early to fish a few hours on a noted pool before heading out to the next stop along his route. The Polar Shrimp, first tied by Shoff in 1936, caught on quickly with the California angling gentry on the Eel River."

Retired salt water guide Woody Sexton (whom Thomas McGuane wrote about in his story "The Longest Silence"), fished the Eel in the 1950's with a Polar Shrimp tied with a body of plastic wire insulation obtained from the telephone company. The plastic was a pale pink and added a denseness to the fly which helped get it deep.

Bob Wagoner's version of the Polar Shrimp as shown in the color plates is tied with a body of Edge Bright, a translucent plastic wrap that radiates the color of the Edge Bright, illuminated by the light reflected from the silver tinsel beneath. (See the Dean Lantern and Crazy Charlie series on pages 117 and 118.)

The Polar Shrimp is still an effective bright winter fly that also represents the traditional hairwing steelhead fly.

Brad's Brat—Enos Bradner

Tail: Orange and white bucktail
Body: Rear half orange chenille or yarn; front half red
Rib: Gold tinsel
Wing: One-third orange over two-thirds white bucktail
Hackle: Brown

In the May 1980 *Fly Tyer* Ralph Wahl related the story about how the Brad's Brat came about: "Enos Bradner told me a wild tale of an opening day's fishing in 1939 on the North Fork of the Stillaguamish River in Washington, when, for the first time in history, the river was designated 'fly only' for summer steelhead. On his mad dash to the river he was arrested for speeding, paid his fine, and was the first angler on the river. He took two bright summer fish, dashed back to Seattle and dumped them on the floor of Dawn Holbrook's fly shop. 'That's some brat of a fly you have there' was what Dawn was alleged to have said. From then on it was a Brad's Brat."

Although originated over 50 years ago for summer run steelhead, the Brad's Brat has since proven an effective winter fly as well. To fish a Brad's Brat dusts yourself with steelhead tradition, an omen of good luck.

The Polar Shrimp and Brad's Brat hairwing steelhead flies are fairly luminous and colorful; sometimes they are too visible and spook fish. A deadly alternative is to present the steelhead with a dark hairwing pattern, using black and purple instead of radiant colors. One effective traditional somber hairwing pattern is the Purple Peril listed in the Fly Index. For winter fishing with traditional hairwings tied with deer hair or bucktail you might want to substitute non-buoyant materials, such as kip or calf tail, red fox squirrel tail, or black bear hair.

Marabou Streamer

Tail: Tuft of marabou
Body: Chenille or yarn
Wing: Marabou

Ribbing on the body, hackle, and Flashabou or Crystal Flash added to the tail and wing are optional. Color schemes include black, orange, red, pink, purple, and white.

This is a pattern prototype for winter steelhead designed to be quick and easy to tie with inexpensive materials, which is a factor if you lose many flies. Fly tyers and fly fishermen are picky about fly patterns, not steelhead. Traditional winter fly patterns are bright, but steelhead can be put off by glowing colors or flies that are too bulky, so it's wise to carry an assortment of bright and drab flies, in sizes 6 through 1/0. Your flies will then be effective in low, clear water or high, off-color rivers.

Popsicle—George Cook

Body: None
Hackle: Marabou in several color schemes

In 1985 when George Cook first tied this fly he was asked what he was going to call it. He said, "It's got orange, cherry, and purple in it—I'm going to call it a Popsicle."

The Popsicle in the color plates has the original color combination, starting from the rear with orange, then cherry, then purple, highlighted with gold and purple Flashabou and orange Crystal Flash. The fly has no body; the marabou is wrapped as a hackle on the front third of the hook shank. The color combinations are unlimited; some favorites are orange, red, and then black, with gold and red Flashabou; white, then two segments of salmon egg color; or red with purple in front.

Cook's favorite method for fishing the Popsicle for winter steelhead is to cast either straight across or slightly downstream, mending so "the fly is slowed down enough so that the fish gets quite a long look at it as the fly swings broadside towards the fish, fluttering in front of the steelhead. I want to slow it down as much as possible because typical winter water conditions can be fairly cold.

Marabou Streamer

1. Attach thread, tie in tail then chenille or yarn, wrap forward, tie off and trim.

2. Tie in marabou wing, but not longer than hook shank to prevent tangling with the hook. You can successfully fish this fly as is, or add hackle.

Whether the steelhead is irritated or attracted to the fly, the longer it's in front of the fish, the longer the steelhead views it, the more apt the fish is to take."

Halloween Matuka—Deke Meyer
Body: Black chenille, yarn, or dubbing
Rib: Gold or silver round tinsel
Tail/Wing: Orange hackle
Hackle: Orange

The Matuka style offers steelhead a fly with a wide silhouette, besides imitating the dorsal and caudal fins of prey fish. There are various effective color schemes for winter steelhead, including the Purple Matuka with a black body and purple hackle and the Surgeon General Matuka with a purple body and red hackle. (It can also be called the Del Cooper Matuka as the two original hairwing patterns are very similar.) The reverse, with a red body and purple hackle, is also deadly on summer and winter steelhead.

Leggo-My-Eggo
Hook: Short shank reversed drift hook or short shank streamer hook
Body: Glow yarn of various colors tied on and trimmed to a round shape or an acrylic puff ball of yarn slipped on the hook. Effective colors include white, orange, red, pink, and pearl in "regular" and dyed fluorescent.

Pink Puff
Hook: Eagle Claw L254N size 2
Thread: White
Body: Pink Super Fly Flash tubing wrapped around the hook
Wing: Pull up the end of the Fly Flash tubing and tie it back for the wing, fraying it out with a dubbing needle.
Eyes: Nickel plated bead chain
Head: Cross wrap around the eyes with fine fluorescent pink chenille.

Tying Instructions

3. Tie in hackle. Fold wet–fly style by moistening and stroking hackle to the rear.

4. Wrap hackle, tie down and trim. Whip finish and cement head.

Red and White Puff
Same as Pink Puff except body and wing are white everglow tubing and the head is fluorescent red chenille.

Mark Bachmann says, "The Puff series was originally tied for Caribbean bonefish and permit. We wondered if they might be effective for steelhead; we've used them on winter steelhead for the past three winters with great success."

Eyed Shrimp—Mark Bachmann
Hook: Eagle Claw L1197N size 4 or 6
Tail: Thick, short, bright red marabou
Rib: 16/18 or fine oval gold tinsel
Body: Lead wire .035 covered with flat flame yarn
Wing: Fluorescent white calf tail, body length
Head: No. 503 Danville flat waxed thread (flame orange, matches body color; head is tied large enough to accommodate the eyes
Eyes: Painted enamel; yellow iris, black pupil

Mark Bachmann says, "As far as I know, I was the first to tie the Eyed Shrimp. The fly was first used in the fall of 1981. As with most weighted flies tied on turned down eye hooks, the fly rides hook up and is less prone to snag on the bottom. The Eyed Shrimp is one of the most consistent flies we have found for both summer and winter steelhead west of the Cascades when water temperatures are below 50 degrees. It is usually fished deep with a sinking tip fly line and short leader."

The Puff flies and Eyed Shrimp are reminiscent of other winter steelhead flies with either bead eyes or prominent eyes, such as the Boss or Comet series, and the C. Jim Pray Optic. *In Steelhead Fly Fishing and Flies,* Trey Combs wrote: "Any fly with an extra-large head sporting 'eyes' qualifies as an optic. This was not an original idea with C. Jim Pray, but its use on steelhead patterns is strictly a Pray innovation. Whereas optics were the result of heads built up with fly-tying thread, the original Pray optics were optics because of split brass beads—1/4 inch for size 2 and larger, 3/16 inch for size 4 and smaller.

"Jim Pray of Eureka, California, was one of the fly-tying greats of our steelhead west. His optics were for the late season Eel River when a bright, fast-sinking fly was correctly felt to be a real advantage. Though many other patterns had preceded them to the winter steelheading grounds, they must be considered the first of a new breed, flies designed especially for those cold weather dreadnaughts.

"He first tied up his optics in the fall of 1940, and a confusing optic vernacular soon followed. Because the flies were originally peculiar to the Eel, they became known as 'Eel River Optics.' Because they had huge eyes painted on their heads, they were commonly referred to as 'Owl Eyed Optics.' And because Jim Pray invented and sold them, they were called 'Pray's Optics.'"

Steelhead Charlie—Bob Wagoner
Underbody: Flat silver tinsel
Body: Edge Bright dyed fluorescent red, orange, green, yellow, or chartreuse
Wing: Squirrel tail dyed black or to match body
Bead Eyes: Nickel plated, on top of the fly

Fly fishermen have used Crazy Charlie bonefish flies for steelhead for some time now; no matter what the body is tied with, the main design principle of an inverted fly with a stiffish wing to hide the hook is effective for winter steelhead as well as bonefish.

Dean River Lantern
> *Tail:* Squirrel tail dyed black, as long as the body
> *Body:* Edge Bright dyed fluorescent green, orange, red, yellow, or chartreuse
> *Hackle:* Matches body material

The Dean River Lantern series is similar to Boss or Comet flies but without bead eyes. In fact, to tie a Boss or a Comet you merely add bead eyes to the top front of the fly. Originally devised for summer and fall fishing on the Dean, the Lantern series is effective on other rivers and for winter fish as well .

Steelhead Woolly Bugger
> *Tail:* Marabou
> *Body:* Chenille or yarn
> *Body Hackle:* Palmered saddle hackle

Lead eyes are optional, but if used should be tied on top of the fly so it will flip over when fished, reducing snags. Color schemes are varied; one of the most effective is an all black version with the lead eyes painted black. This is an inexpensive fly to tie and entices the fish with lots of underwater movement. It's a fly overlooked by steelheaders. You can tie a Steelhead Leech version by using a short shank hook and tying in a rabbit fur strip as the tail.

Black's Buster Leech—Bill Black
> *Tail:* Black or purple marabou; Flashabou or Krystal Flash optional
> *Body:* Black or purple chenille
> *Legs:* Two sets of gray medium sized rubber legs about hook shank length
> *Eyes:* Nickel plated lead eyes

Black's Buster Leech is tied on short shank Tiemco 800B hooks, although the basic design works almost as well on a standard Tiemco 7999 steelhead hook. The darker colors are set off by the shiny glint of nickel plated lead eyes, with excellent "action" provided by marabou and rubber legs, an excellent combination for winter water. Bill Black says these flies work for summer run steelhead and jumbo trout as well, whether dead-drifted or jigged.

Winter's Hope—Bill McMillan
> *Hook:* 3/0 to 6/0
> *Thread:* Burgundy 6/0
> *Body:* Flat silver tinsel
> *Wing:* Hackle tips, orange enclosing yellow (can substitute pale orange for yellow)
> *Overwing:* Sparse pale olive calf tail
> *Hackle:* Deep blue, then purple

In his book *Dry Line Steelhead*, Bill McMillan wrote, "I began developing the pattern in 1971 as a variation to a Silver Doctor and settled on the final design in 1972. It has remained a most effective pattern ever since.

"In cold water fishing one must have absolute faith in the chosen fly pattern to keep it fishing the 10 to 30 hours often required between strikes. The Winter's Hope has a wide enough color spectrum to stir faith under a broad range of difficult water and light conditions, and it adapts well to the big salmon hooks required for successful floating line fishing. Even on the darkest winter days the purple-blue hackles give off a neon glow. While much of this attraction is in the angler's eye, in chill flows that's an absolute necessity. If the pattern isn't attractive enough to the eye it won't stay in the water long enough to provoke that eventual and well earned strike."

The Winter's Hope is a beautiful winter fly designed to appeal to steelhead by presenting a fly that incorporates the full spectrum of colors. McMillan is a proponent of floating line strategies for winter as well as summer run steelhead and fishes this fly in that manner, using hook size and mending tactics to control the depth and swimming rate of the fly.

An alternative dressing is the Winter's Hope Marabou, which substitutes marabou for the hackle tip wing and eliminates the calf tail. The marabou wing is tied with yellow or pale orange marabou on the bottom and orange marabou on top, with the marabou the same length as the hook shank so it won't wrap around the bend of the hook. The Winter's Hope Marabou is quicker and easier to tie, and offers the same wing colors but with marabou's easy movement in the water. Of course, the most carefully crafted marabou wing will never match the beauty of the matched hackle tips wing.

Steelhead Soft Hackle
> *Tail:* Optional, soft hackle fibers as listed below
> *Body:* Dubbing, yarn, or chenille
> *Rib:* Tinsel is optional
> *Hackle:* Natural grouse, pheasant rump, guinea, duck flank feathers or saddle hackle; or dyed bright colors

Advantages to the Soft Hackle style of steelhead fly are that it's quick and easy to tie with inexpensive materials and you can vary the color scheme to suit your whims. For example, tied with a pink body and hackle it could be a Shrimp Soft Hackle; tied with a black body and hackle it could be a Stonefly Soft Hackle.

In *The Practical Angler*, 1857, author W.C. Stewart wrote of fishing soft hackle flies he called "Spider" flies for trout. Stewart recommended using soft hackles from various birds. He wrote, "We, however, think the cock-hackle by no means deserving of so much attention as is bestowed upon it, being too stiff and wiry." As such, the Steelhead Soft Hackle is an excellent fly for slower waters that allow the maximum underwater movement of the soft hackles. (I go into more detail about soft hackles in the "Fly Design" chapter.) Steelhead Soft Hackles are but one example of types of flies that fish in a tremendous variety of water conditions for winter and summer steelhead; these include the Steelhead Woolly Bugger, Matuka, Marabou flies, traditional hairwings, and others.

A GLIMPSE OF
WINTER STEELHEADING PAST

Woody Sexton first walked into C. Jim Pray's fly shop in Eureka, California in 1948. The sign over the door read: "There's no place like this place so this must be the place." Armed with Pray's advice and that of regulars who hung out at Pray's shop, Woody started fishing the Eel River and caught his first steelhead in the fall of that same year.

Woody says, "On the Eel we used Comets, the Fall Favorite, and the one I used the most, the Polar Shrimp. For the Eel it seemed like the fly needed to be bright and dressed large. I used 2's and 4's and some 6's. If there was a hot fly for the river then everybody used that same fly.

"In those days we had to make our own shooting lines. The sinking lines didn't sink very fast so we would coat them with powdered lead. The Dickerson cane rod that I used was a 9-footer that handled a 300 or 330 grain head. I put a 38 to 40-foot head on my Hardy St. George. The Dickerson was an amazing rod—it was the stiffest cane rod I've ever cast for its

Retired saltwater guide Woody Sexton with an Eel River steelhead he caught in the winter of 1951.

great big "U" and went back into shallow water. There was a lot of yelling and excitement going on but we landed the fish.

"The Eel winter steelhead were all wild fish averaging 29 or 30-inches and about 10 pounds. By Thanksgiving you were seeing a steady show of fish. You could fish from then on into the winter as far as you cared to take it. There would be fresh fish coming in all winter long. The watershed has stabilized now, but there was a period that lasted for a number of years when the river was high and muddy because of continuous logging; there was no fishing in the deep part of the winter at all. You could fish before Thanksgiving and that was it. Now, the river will still rise with heavy rains, but it will clear rapidly and it never gets as high because most of the old timber has already been logged or is on private property and is not being logged."

Woody had his best day on the Eel in the middle 1950's, when he caught his biggest fish of 18 pounds: "It was deep in the winter, after six to seven weeks of freezing conditions, with ice on the banks and no rain, the river had dropped, and the fish were pooled. There was ice on the rod guides, fires on the banks, and a lot of people weren't in the water. We didn't have winter gear on our bottom ends in those days so it was a freezeout. In those years I was fishing with extra large, black, all-rubber bootfoot commercial waders and I would wear everything I could get on. I got an 18-pound fish, a 15-pound plus, a 12, and an 11 all on the same day."

weight. Dickerson did it with his tapers because he didn't use a lot of heat when building his rods, and he made them with reinforced ferrules; he made that model of rod specifically at Pray's request for the Eel River. Even after fishing that Dickerson for almost 20 years, it never took a set."

Woody caught the fish in the accompanying photo in the winter of 1951; the steelhead weighed 15-pounds, 2-ounces and gave Woody quite a fight: "We would cast out, then retrieve the fly in slow strips or with a hand twist or a combination of both. As I retrieved the fly, I would put the monofilament shooting line in my mouth.

"I was wading deep, pitching cast after cast, fishing the right hand side of the river looking downstream; there were people fishing the other side of the river, probably 75 to 100 yards away, but the river was too deep to wade across. It was in the afternoon, so there was a right hand wind blowing, which means we were on the wrong side of the river. So some of the fishermen on my side of the river quit fishing and drove around to the other side.

"I hooked a fish about half way in on the cast. It was a going-away strike—the fish was going in the opposite direction as the retrieve. The steelhead was hooked instantly and made a straight run right across the river, out about 100 yards. The fish ran between two men on the other side of the Eel and then turned left. The fish then ran up on some gravel; the fish was not in very much water—I could see it digging in the sand and gravel. Then the steelhead hooked a left, swam 15 or 20 yards out towards the center of the river—one guy had to step over the line—then the fish turned around, making a

THE JOYS OF WINTER STEELHEADING

I love the bright sparkley flies, the powerful rod that makes light work of steelheading, and the exotic reel that has the feel of a well-tuned race car. I like eating lunch under the arms of a hundred year old cedar, swapping fishing talk with a friend while leaning against the bark of a tree that has sucked rain from a thousand winter storms. Sure I like to hook steelhead, but that's only part of it. The success of a trip can't be adequately measured in pounds or inches, so why reduce the sensual pleasures of fly fishing to a sheet of statistics?

Fly fishing for winter steelhead is a potent pretext to be out among the trees while listening to the river, watching it cascade its path to the sea, smelling the scents of the river laden forest. Fly fishing is a great relaxant, a way to painlessly cauterize jangled nerves. To the home-bound, winter steelheading is a sacramental re-initiation into the rites of fly fishing and sometimes, fish.

Two-Handed Rods For Steelhead In Evolution

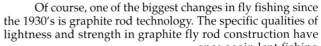

IX

In *Salmon Fishing*, by Eric Taverner, 1931, he quotes one of the earliest works written about Atlantic salmon fishing. The *Driffield Angler* was published in 1808 by Alexander Mackintosh, who wrote: "I caught one (Atlantic salmon) when angling with the fly at Castle-Menzies in the year 1765, that weighed fifty-four pounds and a half." Taverner mentions that Mackintosh recommended a four piece 18-foot rod with a tip that incorporated six to nine inches of whalebone to better absorb the fish's strike.

Fishing rods were first built from the materials at hand: hickory, lancewood, and greenheart. The earliest split and glued bamboo rods appeared around 1800. One of the first American split bamboo rod builders was Samuel Phillippe of Easton, Pennsylvania, who in 1845 built three and four strip bamboo rods constructed with ash butts. Charles F. Murphy of Newark, New Jersey built the first rod shaft made entirely of split bamboo in 1862. These early rods ranged from 11 to 18 feet. (More information is available in *Classic Rods and Rodmakers*, Martin Keane, 1976.)

Two-handed rods are not new to fly fishing, nor or they new to fly fishing for steelhead.

In *The Western Angler*, 1939, Roderick Haig-Brown wrote: "The summer steelhead, like the winter steelhead, is probably an easier fish to catch than the Atlantic salmon, though one may well go about trying to catch him with almost exactly the same methods that are used for Atlantic salmon. ...As to the rod—well, the streams are of a fair size, particularly early in the year, and Spey or roll casting is the only way of getting out line in many places; so a double-handed thirteen or fourteen-foot split-cane is not out of place for fishing an honest wet fly."

Of course, one of the biggest changes in fly fishing since the 1930's is graphite rod technology. The specific qualities of lightness and strength in graphite fly rod construction have once again lent fishing credibility to two-handed rods. Graphite two-handers are light enough to be fishable without requiring a body builder physique, and these rods are potent fishing tools in certain fishing situations.

George Cook of Sage says, "A two-hand rod is ideal for fishing big rivers like the Skagit, not only for distance casting and line control when presenting the fly, but for areas where your backcast is limited by trees, brush or cliffs. You can roll cast or Spey cast with a two-hand rod and cover the fish.

"One day I was fishing the Stillaguamish for steelhead and I was covering 90 to 100% of the water but I was working pretty hard to do it. A fellow using a two-handed rod was fishing down behind me and it was easy for him to cover the same water with only a flick of the extra long rod.

"If you go out and just watch a fly rodder in a steelhead drift, you can watch the amount of time he spends picking line up off the water, making a false cast, a secondary false cast, a third, and then finally laying it down. When you add up the amount of time he spends on each cast when he picks it up, makes the cast, fishes the drift, then starts again, you have to ask—how much time is that fly actually in the water? When you watch an angler with a double handed rod, he's wasting a lot less time in terms of that pickup and getting the fly back into the drink. What that adds up to for a steelhead fisherman or an Atlantic salmon fisherman is that he may spend 30 percent or more time with his fly in the drink then he ever did

---

Two–handed rods are certainly not going to replace the more common 9, 9 1/2, and 10 footers, but they do have a place in steelheading, and it's a niche that many steelheaders will enjoy exploring. Photo by Frank Amato
Facing page: *Flyfishing magazine Editor, Marty Sherman with a native summer run steelhead from the Deschutes River landed with his two-handed rod.*

before. And in steelheading, as anybody knows, volume counts," says Cook.

Guide J.D. Love once told me that he estimates that given the same amount of effort and skill and equal possibilities for catching a fish, a winter steelheader using conventional gear will catch seven steelhead for every one caught on fly gear. Part of that lopsided ratio stems from the fact that after fishing a drift, the conventional fisherman reels in and then merely lobs his slinky or lure back out in the stream, essentially taking only a few seconds to get his lure back in front of the fish.

Hot shotting steelheaders constantly poise their lures in front of fish, only pulling them out of the water to negotiate shallow water or rapids. By contrast, a fly fisherman works diligently to get his fly down to the fish, putting that fly in front of the fish for only a fraction of the time that he's actually fishing because of prolonged casting strokes, the time it takes for the line to sink, and the time required to retrieve the line by hand.

For summer steelheading the ratio is more even, and in some circumstances shifts to the fly rodder's favor. The point is, with a two-hand rod you can keep your fly in the water up to twice as long by reducing the number of backcasts, greatly increasing your chances at summer steelhead and dropping that winter fish ratio to maybe four or five to one.

Steelheaders have annexed most of the Atlantic salmon double-handed rod techniques and have also added a few new pleats to the steelheading quilt. With a two-handed rod you can effortlessly execute overhead casts, roll casts, switch casts, single Spey casts, double Spey casts—they all have their niche, especially when the steelheader is cramped for backcast space. (For clarity, Spey and single Spey casts refer to the same cast.)

Use a combination of push pull to help flex the two-hand rod. When the right side of the body pushes forward the left pushes back; when the left side pushes forward, the right pulls back.

The extra length of a double-handed rod acts like a giant conductor's baton, allowing the angler to "steer" the fly through steelhead holding slots that a nine-foot rod can't cover. Because the angler can hold more line off the water and make giant mends, a two-handed rod gives the angler more control over the fly line and the fly's drift. You effectively open up more water because you can control your fly at longer distances with a two-hand rod and because you can fish farther out when backcast room is limited.

For example, say you can only wade out 15 feet from shore. With a 16-foot two-hand rod, you are effectively covering water that a person fishing a rod 10 feet long would be if they could wade out six feet deeper. What that means is that you can not only cover more water on the same length cast, but you can control your fly at longer distances. Assuming that you start by covering the water close in, with succeeding casts you can effectively control your fly in an arced swath of river that exponentially jumps up in size: with a 10-foot rod a 40-foot cast covers an area of river that measures 1,964 square feet; with a 16-foot rod you can cover 2,463 square feet on the same 40-foot cast. For a 50-foot cast the difference is 2,827 square feet versus 3,421; at 60 feet the figures are 3,848 square feet versus 4,536, or 688 square feet more with a 16-foot rod as illustrated on the next page.

Line handling with a two-hand rod requires practice at first, but is easy to get used to. You keep the line pinched under the middle finger of the upper hand and hold extra line pinched in your lower hand. Photo by Barbara Meyer

The difference in amount of water covered is only part of the story, though, because with sufficient backcast room, the standard rod can cover the same amount of water with a longer cast. However, in most cases the shorter rod won't have the line control that the two-hand rod allows the angler. Sometimes that makes the difference between fishing water that holds steelhead and water that doesn't, and hooking steelhead by careful line control that the standard length rod can't accomplish because it's too short.

Even more crucially, if you can't backcast with a standard rod and are limited to a standard roll cast, you may not even get your fly to the holding water. With Spey casts the two-hand rod literally opens up miles of water that others can't cover.

LINES FOR TWO-HAND RODS

Because they "work" a long line when casting, two-hand rods require a double taper line. The front taper on normal weight forward lines is too short, causing the cast to collapse on the thin line behind the taper. A "long belly" weight forward taper works better because the front taper is extended to about 65 to 75 feet, depending on the manufacturer. But with an extended weight forward line you are limited to Spey casts within that range; however the thin running line is an advantage for overhead distance casting. A double taper line is the traditional setup for two-handed rods, and is the most comfortable to use when Spey casting.

Given the proper line setup, double-hand rods excel at distance casting with minimal effort. One approach is to retain the line-handling qualities of the double taper or long belly weight forward line, but modify it so the line is actually a long shooting head.

The first step is to determine how much line any given two-handed rod will comfortably pick up off the water. That is also the amount of line the rod will comfortably handle outside the guides for overhead, roll, switch, and Spey casts. Once that amount of line is out of the guides, the rest of the line can be considered shooting or running line because it is simply "shooting" through the guides and not contributing to line handling. In other words, once the line manipulations of the cast are over, once the overhead, roll, switch, or Spey cast is completed and the line is released, the "fatness" of the double taper line is a hindrance.

So some steelheaders have added monofilament running line to a shortened double taper. For instance, for a floating rig my 14-foot rod rated for a 9-weight is loaded with 45 feet of DT9 floating line, 150 feet of Cortland 25-pound Plion shooting line, and 100 yards of 30-pound backing. My 16-foot rod rated for a 10-weight is equipped with 50 feet of DT10 floating line, 150 feet of Cortland 30-pound Plion shooting line and 100 yards of backing. To get the ideal length of double taper line for these rods within my casting capabilities, I took the rods and reels loaded with full double taper lines and cast them until I determined the optimum length of line that each rod would pick up from the surface with one casting stroke of the rod, and the optimum length for executing roll, switch, and Spey casts. I added a bit of extra line so the shooting line knot would be inside the rod guides when casting. I then cut the double taper to that length and added shooting line and backing. (Because of the double taper configuration, you can make two floating heads from one line if the line is long enough.)

For different rods or for anglers with different casting abilities, the length of the working line might be longer or shorter. These particular rods were designed for distance work; although you can Spey cast with them, the rods are so stiff that the angler must put a lot of wrist into them so they bend while Spey casting. In fact, since rod tapers and rod design are changing so fast, you should consider this information as merely one approach to line setup. Another method is to go up a line weight or two, but with a shorter head. For instance, you might mate 35 feet of 10-weight or 11-weight line to a 9-weight rod, which would be roughly equivalent to a conventional 30-foot shooting head on a standard rod. That type of setup might work better on a rod designed primarily for overhead casting and distance work; most of the two-hand rods currently available are designed for overhead casting, but that is changing.

With a shooting head setup, casts of 100 feet are easy and not fatiguing over a day's fishing on broad rivers like the lower Deschutes, Clearwater, or many of the big rivers in British Columbia. It's debatable whether using a two-hand rod strictly for distance casting is any less fatiguing than using a standard rod, particularly when considering that the angler must hold the two-hand rod while the fly fishes out the presentation. But the two-hand rod does offer more line control at long distances. And with the longer floating head and a two-hand rod you can execute all the classic variations of the Spey cast when cramped for backcast room.

You can also modify standard fly lines to make sinktip lines or sinktip and full sinking shooting heads. These custom lines must balance the individual rod in both casting weight and length. There is no set formula because of variations in rod length and rod design, but with Scientific Anglers 30-foot long Deep Water Express in 550, 700, or 850 grains, we have a wide range of options, especially with the loop system described in the shooting head chapter.

With the added length of a two-handed rod, handling a custom floating or sinktip line is a dream, both in ease of casting and in mending and controlling the fly's drift.

Two-handed rods are not always the answer, but even on smaller rivers you can steer your fly into pockets and holding runs without spooking fish by wading too close.

CASTING TWO-HAND RODS

Two-handed rods are, in a sense, easier to cast than a one-handed rod. In contrast to the single-hand rod which uses primarily wrist and forearm, the two-handed rod uses the whole arm, the back, and side muscles. The two-hander still uses wrist and forearm muscles, but the stress of the casting stroke is spread over a larger area of the body. The stress on joints, tendons, and ligaments is also distributed over a larger area of the body.

Two-handed rods are also easy to cast from either side of the body, which lessens the pressure on one side. Very few fly fishermen can cast proficiently with either hand; because of the extended hours of casting necessary to catch steelhead, most of us fatigue one set of wrist, elbow, and shoulder muscles and joints.

Two-hand rods weigh more than a standard rod, which contributes to fatigue, but when casting a double-hand rod you push with one hand and pull with the other, so the extra weight is offset by extra casting leverage.

The only tricky part of using a two-hand rod is learning how to handle the loose line. With a standard rod you always have one hand free to handle the line; with a double-hand rod you control the extra line with the hand on the butt of the rod, or the "bottom" hand, no matter which side of the body you cast with. During the two-hand casting stroke you hold the line by pinching it to the rod with the middle finger of the

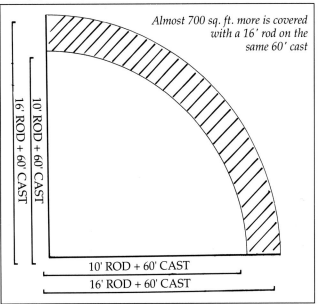

Almost 700 sq. ft. more is covered with a 16' rod on the same 60' cast

10' ROD + 60' CAST

16' ROD + 60' CAST

10' ROD + 60' CAST

16' ROD + 60' CAST

This diagram assumes that the river current is constant from 76 feet out from shore to the bank, which just doesn't happen on steelhead streams. However, the idea of comparing the differences in area effectively covered with 10-foot and 16-foot rods is valid, particularly with no backcast room.

"upper" hand, whether you are casting on the left or the right side of the body. When you first start casting a two-hand rod, use about 35 or 40 feet of line, which is plenty to learn the basic casting strokes.

Like most fly casting, to become proficient with a two-hand rod merely requires practice with well balanced gear. If you can't get to a river or lake, a good place to begin learning how to handle your double-hand rod is at a park or ball field because you can concentrate on casting without worrying about wading, river currents or other fishermen. Many parks or fields have trees or high fences where you can simulate casting with little backcast room, just as you often find when astream. Also, you can photocopy appropriate pages of this book and take them with you for handy reference. The only drawbacks are that fly lines handle differently on grass than they do on water, particularly for water-sliding casts such as the roll cast that depend on the friction of the water's surface, and casting on grass promotes fly line wear—be sure to clean your line after practice.

To joint up any multi-piece rod, always start with the tip section and work towards the butt. First, lightly press the sections together so the guides are about 90 degrees off center, then tightly press the sections together while lining the guides up. Be careful not to use the guides themselves for leverage—you might break the guide loose from the rod.

The only maintenance required on today's graphite rods is to rub paraffin on the male ferrules to keep the rod sections firmly seated together. Paraffin is used for sealing preservative jars, so it's available at the grocery store or wherever canning supplies are sold. Keeping the ferrules waxed is important with any graphite rod, but is particularly important with a two-hand rod because of the tremendous twisting-torque imparted to the rod and to the ferrules by change-of-direction casts. In the old days, fly fishermen used leather thongs wrapped around the metal ferrules on their two-hand bamboo rods to keep them tight. (Don't substitute bizarre concoctions for paraffin; beeswax is recommended for fiberglas rods, but I knew one fisherman who lubed his fiberglas ferrules with Vaseline. After the day's fishing he couldn't get the rod apart. In fact, the rod was so tightly jointed that he had to send it back to the factory, which was also unable to disjoint the rod. He had to replace it with a new one.)

Don't use a fly for casting practice unless you remove the rear of the hook; a good fly substitute is a piece of yarn knotted to the end of the leader or tippet. You need some type of fly simulator on the end of the tippet to keep it from fraying and to simulate the weight, bulk, and air resistance of the fly. If you neglect to put a leader on the line and cast just the fly line, you'll inflict severe damage to the line because of the tremendous speed of the kick-over on the backcast. And remember, the key is practice, and be sure to practice with both sides of the body because you will need to change sides when fishing.

After you've practiced enough to feel comfortable with your new rig you can proceed to steelhead country and begin pitching flies. River fishing is always different than casting on grass, but you will be more comfortable because you will have already learned the basics of two-hand fly casting. (Always wear eye protection when fishing—I know anglers who have been hooked in the eye—flying hooks are dangerous and it's terrifying to face the possibility of losing your sight.)

THE EXPERTS DISAGREE

Mike Maxwell, of British Columbia, has not only developed his own line of two-hand rods for Spey casting, but his own style of casting as well. He doesn't switch his upper and lower hands, but always keeps his right hand on the top grip, casting over his left shoulder when he needs to change sides. Both hands are positioned fairly close to the reel. He locks his left hand and the rod butt against his forearm. He stands with his right foot forward at all times when casting, and pushes the rod with his shoulder and body while rocking forward, then pushes the rod backward and rocks backward on the backcast, keeping the rod butt locked against his forearm.

The diagrams in Joan Wulff's book *Fly Casting Techniques* indicate that she puts her left foot forward when casting a two-hand rod with the right hand on top. English writers Falkus and Oglesby seem to be in agreement about putting your right foot forward when casting with the right hand on top, but all three advocate using wrists and forearms to make the rod bend, not using the whole body and rocking back and forth as Maxwell does. They make the rod flex by pushing with the top hand and pulling with the bottom on the forward stroke, then reversing it for the backcast, pulling with the top hand and pushing with the bottom. They also keep their hands wide apart on the grips of the rod.

Most double-hand casters find it easier and more efficient to switch hand positions when necessary. I, too, find it more comfortable and efficient to switch hands and less tiring over a day's fishing.

"Side of the river" always refers to the angler looking downstream. "Right handed" refers to the right hand on top. Here is the scenario:

Switch and single Spey casts: Left bank, cast right-handed; right bank, cast left-handed.

Double Spey cast: Left bank, cast left-handed; right bank, cast right-handed.

The switch and single Spey are change-of-direction casts executed without a backcast, when it's calm or when the wind is blowing upstream. The double Spey is necessary when the wind is blowing downstream because in that situation, when using a switch or single Spey, the wind might blow the fly into your rod or you.

Here are two tips that might ease your way into two-hand casting. First, you might consider trying switch and Spey casts with 20 or 25 feet of line with your standard rod, just to get the feel for the mechanics of the cast. That way you are concentrating on the casts instead of adapting to both the casts and the totally different "feel" of a two-hand rod.

Secondly, when you first attempt to transfer these directions and illustrations into actual casting, don't try it with line out, simply go through the casting motions with the rod. That gives you a road map of where the rod will travel during the cast. When you string the rod up you can then focus on working it because you will already know the path the rod should take.

After you've become comfortable with these casts and can handle 40 feet of line with your dominant hand on top, reverse it and place your dominant hand on the bottom. That way, no matter which side of the river you're fishing, you can perform switch and Spey casts.

OVERHEAD CAST

The overhead cast is fine when there is plenty of backcast room. The two-hand overhead cast is done much the same as an overhead cast with a single hand rod except the upper hand and wrists and the bottom hand and wrists push and pull against each other, forcing the rod to bend, using the spring of the rod to power the line through the air. As in a single-hand overhead cast, the rod should be stopped at about 2 o'clock on the backstroke and about 10 o'clock on the forward stroke.

ROLL CAST

The roll cast is done without a backcast, keeping your fly away from fly-snagging trees and hook-breaking rocks to your rear. The two-hand roll cast is similar to one done with a single-hand rod. The rod is brought back to just past vertical, behind the head, with the rod tip tilted out a little so the fly line won't hit the rod, and with some line hanging down just behind the angler. The rod is brought down, pulling and pushing with your hands and snapping your wrists, accelerating the line forward to form a rolling loop that deposits the fly on the water. While making the power snap forward, keep the line pinched under the middle finger of the upper hand. You can extend your roll cast by aiming higher above the water and releasing extra line (held by the bottom hand) when the power snap is completed.

the air back downstream, but in an arc that starts parallel to the shore and swings out over your head and continues across the stream, either straight across or slightly downstream.

To make that cross-stream arc on the forward cast, as the rod passes in front of you, the tip of the rod follows a small outward half circle, twirling the line out across or slightly downstream from the angler, all in one continuous movement.

The switch cast is ideal for two-hand rods because you can hold a lot of line in the air, and most importantly, you can keep the forward arcing cast high in the air, away from you or the rod tip. Although easily performed with a full double

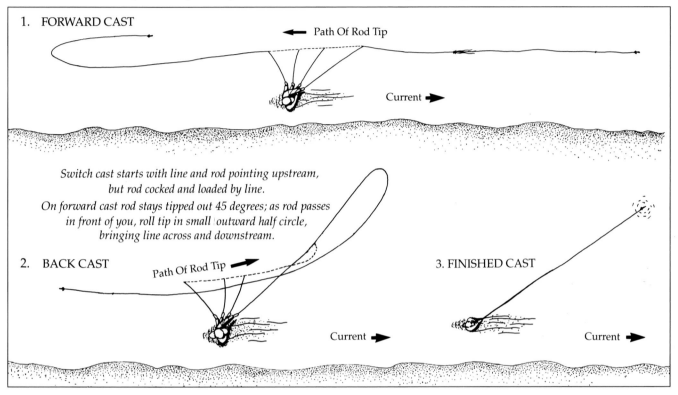

Switch cast: Once line and fly are picked up at start of backcast they don't touch down until forward cast is completed.
Facing downstream, right side of river, left hand on top, left foot slightly forward.

SWITCH CAST

The switch cast is a change of direction cast without a backcast and is made by bringing the fly from straight below you and delivering it straight across or slightly downstream, but without letting the fly snag the brush behind you. It is an aerial cast because once the fly is airborne at the beginning of the cast, it only touches down again at the point where it enters the water on the forward cast. It is an effective cast for shooting heads or full lines.

The switch cast starts when the line has finished its drift and is downstream from the angler (called the "dangle" by Englishmen). The rod is pointed at the fly, the line pinched by the middle finger, then the rod is brought upstream and around past the front of the angler, at about a 45 degree angle, in a brisk sweeping motion that stops when the rod is at the 2 o'clock position (with your right hand on top, 10 o'clock for left hand dominant). The line goes from straight downstream to straight upstream, but by tipping the rod out to a 45 degree angle, the fly and the line won't hit you.

Once the line is upstream and the rod cocked by stopping it at 10 o'clock, the idea is to make the line head through

taper line, the switch cast is excellent for shooting heads or weight forward lines because the line never touches down during the cast as in the Spey or double Spey casts.

SPEY OR SINGLE SPEY CAST

From straight downstream rod and line are brought back in front of the angler in what Joan Wulff calls a curving power snap, the line touches down briefly upstream from the angler as the rod drifts upward slightly, then the forward cast is made above the water, shooting line to a point directly across stream or slightly downstream, all in one continuous movement.

The "splash down" allows the line a pivot from which to change directions from upstream to across stream. Maxwell describes the splash down as an "anchor" that allows the rod to bend against it, which also allows you to change the direction of the cast. The Spey cast keeps the fly in front of the angler at all times and might be considered a type of aerial roll cast.

DOUBLE SPEY CAST

The double Spey is used when wind might drive the fly cast by a single Spey into the angler or the angler's rod. In the

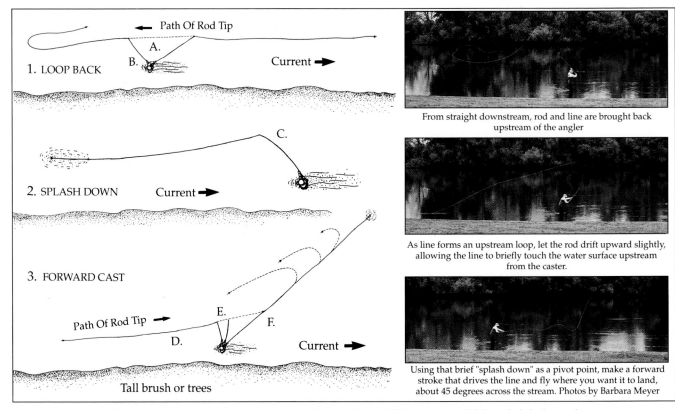

1. LOOP BACK — Path Of Rod Tip — A. — B. — Current →

From straight downstream, rod and line are brought back upstream of the angler

2. SPLASH DOWN — C. — Current →

As line forms an upstream loop, let the rod drift upward slightly, allowing the line to briefly touch the water surface upstream from the caster.

3. FORWARD CAST — Path Of Rod Tip → — E. — F. — D. — Current →

Tall brush or trees

Using that brief "splash down" as a pivot point, make a forward stroke that drives the line and fly where you want it to land, about 45 degrees across the stream. Photos by Barbara Meyer

Single Spey Cast: Facing downstream, right side of river, left hand on top, left foot slightly forward

double Spey the fly is always kept downstream from the angler so wind can't drive the fly into your personal danger zone.

Although actually one continuous movement, I think of the double Spey as having two parts: a backhand roll cast which positions the fly; and an aerial roll cast that delivers the fly across the stream.

As the first part of the double Spey, the backhand roll cast brings the fly upstream, placing it where you can make the forward cast: the rod is pointed at the fly, the line is tight to the dangle, then the rod and line are brought upstream by the rod sweeping upstream in front of the angler. The fly stays in the water downstream from the angler. Then the rod is brought forward in a roll cast with a soft power snap, while keeping the fly downstream from the angler. For the aerial roll cast that delivers the fly: swing the rod to the other side of your body, while raising it and pulling back so the reel is level with your face, then snap your wrists and power the line across the river, aiming slightly upwards.

Although different than the roll cast, switch and Spey casts can be considered modifications of the roll because in essence, switch and Spey casts are simply change-of-direction casts that never allow the fly to go behind the angler because none of these casts includes a backcast.

SHOPPING FOR A TWO-HAND ROD AND REEL

There are a variety of two-hand rod builders, rods and lengths to choose from. Even though many of these rods are labeled "Spey" rods, some of these rods are tapered for overhand casting and may or may not be good Spey casting rods, while some are designed specifically for Spey casting, while remaining efficient at overhand casting. Given the fact that there is an incredible variety of rod lengths, actions, and tapers

available from different manufacturers of standard rods, with each claiming that the rods they build are the best, why should there be any more agreement among "Spey" rod builders as to who is the best.

The rational approach is to cast a rod to see if it's comfortable for your fishing style and what you intend to do with the rod. Unless you are looking at a two-hand rod for distance casting only, beware of the trap that awaits rod buyers at most fly shops: the salesman, and often the customer, may try a few short casts, but within moments of stringing up the rod, the caster is firing out the longest casts he can make. With a two-hand rod used for Spey casting, distance is not the top priority; line handling is the crucial factor. That means choosing a rod with a more flexible mid-section and butt versus the relatively stiff butt and midsection of a distance-casting two-hand rod. (A rod designed for overhead distance-casting may Spey cast more efficiently if over-lined one line weight, which causes the mid-section and butt to flex more.) That is not to say that you can't distance cast with a more flexible rod, because you can, if you slow your stroke and let the more flexible Spey-tapered rod work through its tapers.

The dilemma facing us is that very few fly shops can afford to stock a selection of these two-hand rods, reels, and lines because of their cost, and many of us aren't located close to a shop that sells these rods, not to mention having them available for demonstration casting. Hopefully, as interest increases, more shops will carry two-hand outfits rigged for test-casting by potential customers. Otherwise, you are left with following the advice of the salesman—how can you be sure that what he wants to sell you is what you want to fish with, without trying it out first?

Another option is to build your own rod, which will require extra large corks of the finest quality for the extended fore and aft grips on a two-handed rod, an extra large reel seat, and larger-than-average guides. Because the fore and butt grip

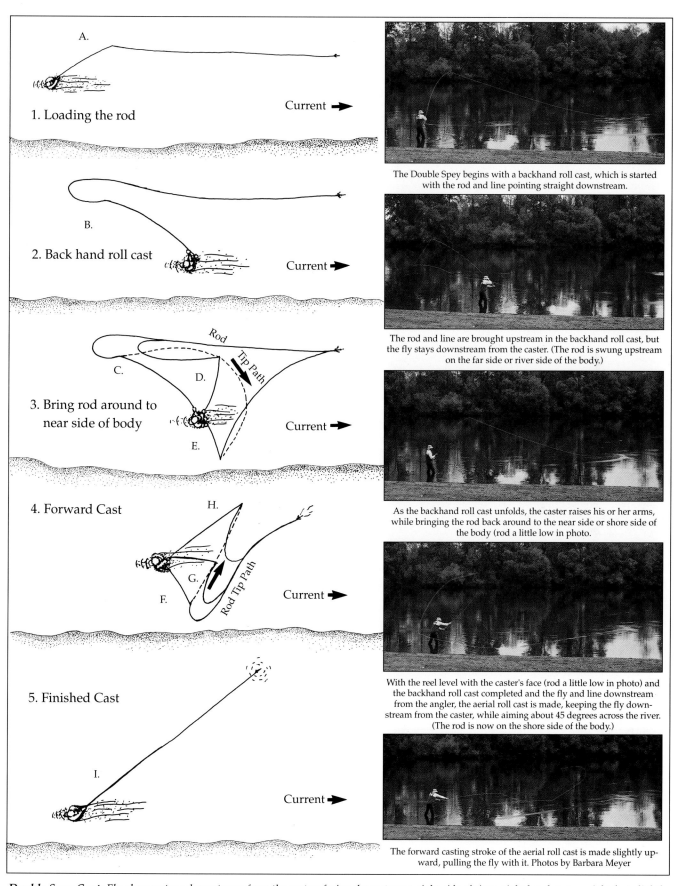

1. Loading the rod

A.

Current ➤

2. Back hand roll cast

B.

Current ➤

The Double Spey begins with a backhand roll cast, which is started with the rod and line pointing straight downstream.

3. Bring rod around to near side of body

Rod

Tip Path

C.

D.

E.

Current ➤

The rod and line are brought upstream in the backhand roll cast, but the fly stays downstream from the caster. (The rod is swung upstream on the far side or river side of the body.)

4. Forward Cast

H.

G.

F.

Rod Tip Path

Current ➤

As the backhand roll cast unfolds, the caster raises his or her arms, while bringing the rod back around to the near side or shore side of the body (rod a little low in photo.

5. Finished Cast

I.

Current ➤

With the reel level with the caster's face (rod a little low in photo) and the backhand roll cast completed and the fly and line downstream from the angler, the aerial roll cast is made, keeping the fly downstream from the caster, while aiming about 45 degrees across the river. (The rod is now on the shore side of the body.)

The forward casting stroke of the aerial roll cast is made slightly upward, pulling the fly with it. Photos by Barbara Meyer

Double Spey Cast: *Fly always stays downstream from the caster; facing downstream, right side of river, right hand on top, right foot slightly forward (opposite of Switch and Single Spey).*

configuration and guide spacing for any given rod is designed for that rod's tapers, I recommend closely following the factory's specifications for cork and guide spacings.

For most fly fishing, it's a good idea to balance today's lightweight graphite rods with an equally lightweight reel so the rod isn't overbalanced in the handle. The same theory of rod balance is even more critical when dealing with a 14 to 16-foot rod because the balance principle is more pronounced.

Instead of a light reel, though, these extra long rods need a heavy reel to offset the leverage of casting a long heavy line, and to balance the rod after you complete the cast, when you are holding it while fishing. The length and weight of a two-handed rod, the casting, and the fishing of a double-handed rod puts a lot of leverage on the handle end of the rod. So to that extent, a comparably heavy reel is an advantage.

Another factor in matching a reel to a double-hand rod is the bulk of double taper 9, 10, and 11-weight lines, plus the 100 to 150 yards of 30-pound test backing. You're looking at reels that measure at least four inches in spool diameter.

Prices range from inexpensive line holders to exotic big game reels that cost more than the rod. As you pay more, you get better metal, workmanship, and smoother, more efficient drag systems. The better reels are machined from solid bar stock instead of die cast, and offer a high degree of workmanship and precision engineering. There are many big game reels to pick from; many models are state of the art creations from small shops that offer a specialized product for a demanding group of salt water fly fishermen. The larger salt water reels work well on two-hand rods because they have the line capacity needed and they have finely tuned drag systems.

There is an ongoing discussion in fly fishing about which is the correct way to reel—with your right hand or left hand. If you are right-handed like me and fishing a standard rod, the argument goes something like this: you are casting with your right hand, so why switch over and reel with your right when you hook a fish; why not reel with your left instead of changing hands in the middle of the battle?

One argument for switching back and forth is that it is more crucial determining when to reel and when not to reel than operating the rod during the fight, particularly when the steelhead makes a sudden lunge.

I agree with the theory that reeling is more crucial than rod work when fighting fish. Another telling factor is one that appears after you've landed a steelhead-sized fish and becomes even more evident if you catch more than one steelhead. If you don't switch over, you reel left-handed and fight the fish with your right hand, so that your right side endures the fatigue of battle. When you try to cast again, and with steelhead you are often casting heavy lines and long distances, you are casting with the fatigued side. If you switch hands, fighting the fish with your left side, the right side is still fresh, ready to resume casting.

For a double-hand rod, which side you reel on is not as important because you will be casting with both hands and from both sides of your body. However, even though you can easily exchange lower and upper hand positions on the rod when the fish is running against the reel's drag, I still prefer to reel right-handed because, for me that hand is more sensitive to the crucial give-and-take of line, which I believe is the most critical aspect of landing steelhead.

LEVERAGE AND WHY FISH FEEL BIGGER ON A TWO-HAND ROD

With a double-hand rod you have the added casting leverage of an extra long rod, but the fish also have more leverage on you. Which means that the fish seem bigger and more powerful, just the opposite of what you might expect when you first heft a two-hand rod. (Which seems like a graphite telephone pole after handling standard steelhead rods.)

I discovered that leverage principle when I hooked my first two-hand rod fish, a Deschutes summer run steelhead. The rod kept bending deeper and deeper, putting more and more pressure on my arms and back—it felt as if the fish weighed 18 pounds instead of 8.

Although a double-hand rod weighs more than a single-hand rod, the fish feel bigger because they have more leverage on the angler than with a standard rod. Through a series of graphs and ratios, Gary Hewitt explained it to me this way: to compare a nine-foot rod to a sixteen-foot rod, both must exhibit the same amount of stiffness. If the angler fights the fish by bending either rod at a 45 degree angle from a straight pull, the fish feels heavier with the two-hand rod because the fish exerts twice as much leverage on the angler than with a standard rod.

You can decrease the steelhead's leverage by gripping the rod above the handle on a standard rod, but you run the risk of overstressing and breaking it because you are putting the maximum pressure on the midsection or tip of the rod instead of the butt, which is where the strength lies. By increasing the bend in the rod from 45 degrees to 90 degrees from a straight line of pull, the fish's leverage advantage drops by 50 percent because you have essentially shortened the leverage-length of the rod. However, you are also in danger of breaking the rod by making it bend in a tight hoop, overstressing the midsection and tip.

At the other extreme, if you point your rod straight at the fish, the fish's leverage advantage is zero, but the shock-absorbing capacity of the springy fly rod is nil and the stretchy monofilament tippet is all that keeps you tethered to your steelhead—if the fish pulls the tippet more than it can stretch, it breaks.

FIGHTING STEELHEAD ON A FLY ROD

When fighting a steelhead with either a standard or two-hand rod, the idea is to pump the fish towards shore without overtaxing your rod. Either you should be gaining line or the fish should be gaining line—don't let the fish sulk. To pressure your steelhead, reel down, keeping a tight line until your rod is pointed towards the fish, but about 10 degrees above the fish so that if it bolts away the spring of the rod will allow you a split second to release the reel handle. Then pull back on the rod until the butt of the rod reaches a 45 degree angle to the fish. While you keep the line tight, reel down while lowering the rod to once again point at a 10 degree angle above the fish, then pull back to the 45 degree angle. If the fish starts to run, let it power away; by fine tuning the reel drag or palming the spool you'll force the fish to expend energy by swimming away against the drag, but without breaking the tippet.

You can pull the rod straight up, but it's more effective to pull it towards shore. If you pull straight up, you merely force the fish up in the water column, which causes the fish to expend little energy because it is still upright and using its body weight and the river current to defeat you. By pulling towards the shore you force the fish off balance and press it to swim against the pull of the rod. By never going over a 45 degree angle from a straight pull to the fish, you won't overstress your rod, and by forcing the fish to either take line or surrender to the rod, you force the fight to its conclusion in the minimum amount of time, which is particularly important if you intend to release your fish.

The graphite fibers that run the length of the rod give it casting strength and line speed. By wrapping graphite around the rod, perpendicular to the shaft, manufacturers build hoop strength into the rod. Hoop strength keeps those lineal fibers in place; hoop strength keeps the rod from breaking. George Cook draws an explicit analogy when he compares the hoop strength of a rod to a straw.

He says, "Take a straw and bend it. It starts out round, then it forms an oval, and then it cracks and breaks. That's exactly how a rod acts. When bent, the upper side of the rod is elongating while the bottom side is compressing. The idea is to build sufficient hoop strength to keep that resistance from being overbearing, causing a total system breakdown. I think the designs today—Sage, Loomis, Orvis, everybody else—have gotten to the point where technology with hoop strength has become of key importance throughout the rod because that's what got the early graphites in trouble. The hoop strength just wasn't there."

LANDING TWO-HAND ROD STEELHEAD

With two-hand rods the challenge is to find a decent place to beach the fish because you can't land it easily any other way. Lead the fish into shore with the rod, then set it down and hold the fish. That's fine if you are standing on an uncluttered beach, but in many Spey casting situations you are backed up against some brush, a line of trees, or a cliff. You may be forced to employ more radical tactics.

After the fish is tired and in the shallows and I'm "up against it," one approach I've tried with some success is to clamp down on the line with the upper hand, hold the rod parallel to shore, strip off about 20 feet of line with the bottom hand, then quickly point the rod straight up while releasing the extra line. The line outside the rod tip should droop enough for you to reach it. Lay the rod down, then land the fish via the line in your hands.

There are obvious pitfalls—if you don't get enough slack out, you can't reach the line and the fish glides out into the current, or the fish isn't tired and bolts back out into the river, taking all the slack line. That isn't so bad if you still have the rod in your hands; if not, you must quickly decide whether to fight the fish with your hands or pick up your rod and work the fish back into the shallows. I dislike laying a rod down because in the excitement of landing a steelhead it's just too easy for me or fellow anglers to step on it or the reel or both, but sometimes it's the only alternative.

THE FUTURE OF TWO-HAND STEELHEAD RODS

I predict that there will be a minor revolution within the next few years in the types of two-hand rods offered specifically for steelheaders; and these rods will excel at Spey casting as well as overhead casting. In conjunction with that trend, Cortland and Scientific Anglers will market fly lines tailored for steelhead Spey fishing. In addition, an increasing number of fly shops will not only display rigged-up two-hand rods, but offer instruction on Spey casting.

Two handed rods are not new to fly fishing, nor or they new to fly fishing for steelhead. And they are certainly not going to replace the more common 9, 9 1/2-foot and 10-foot rods. But they do have a place in steelheading, and it's a niche that many steelheaders will enjoy exploring, particularly when the fisherman wants to probe waters that others overlook because of limited backcast room. Not only do two-hand rods open up more water, they offer a high degree of line con-

trol. They have a totally different "feel" to them, but are pleasant fishing tools when well matched to the angler, the river, and the techniques needed to comfortably steer a fly in front of the steelhead.

FOR MORE INFORMATION ON CASTING TWO–HAND RODS:

BOOKS

Fly Casting Techniques, Joan Wulff, Nick Lyons Books, 1987.
Salmon Fishing, Hugh Falkus, Greycliff Publishing, 1984, 1985.
Fly Fishing for Salmon and Sea Trout, Arthur Oglesby, The Crowood Press, 1986, 1987.
The Salmon Fly, George Kelson, The Anglers and Shooters Press, (1895) 1979.
Salmon Fishing, Eric Taverner, 1931

A NOTE ON SPEY CASTING BOOKS:

Joan Wulff's book is highly recommended for two reasons: first, it does a fine job of describing casting with a two-hand rod; and second, it's readily available in the United States. For an autographed copy, contact Royal Wulff Products, HCR #1, Box 70, Lew Beach, NY 12758, phone (914) 439-4060.

Books printed in England are almost impossible to obtain in the US, but it's possible to get them from England. The most useful is *Salmon Fishing*, by Hugh Falkus. Surface mail can take two months or longer; airmail is usually less than two weeks. The fastest way to get service is to FAX an order with your credit card number. I haven't ordered from this company, but they did write and say they would be happy to deal with American fly fishermen:

McHardys of Carlisle
South Henry Street
Carlisle
Cumbria, England
phone (0228-23988) FAX NUMBER—011-44-0228-514711

VIDEO

Fly Fishing: The English Way, 3M/Scientific Anglers Has a very short section on Spey casting, demonstrated with a single hand rod.

There are English videos available on Spey casting, but they are formatted on a different system; It cost $150.00 in 1990 to have an English video reformatted for American VHS.

Mike and Denise Maxwell offer a "homestudy course", an unpolished video they made showing the advantages of Spey casting, and a manual on Mike's method of Spey casting.

Mike and Denise Maxwell
Gold-N-West Flyfishers
5169 Joyce Street
Vancouver, B.C. CANADA V5R 4H1
(604) 435-7173

SCHOOLS

The Maxwells teach Spey casting at their fly shop in Vancouver, B.C. and during September and October on the Bulkley River in British Columbia, where they fish dry flies for steelhead.

Sage offers half-day and full-day casting clinics across the country, which include two-hand rod casting. Anglers wishing two-hand rod instruction may bring their own rod to the class or Sage will supply one. In either case, please contact Sage in advance.

Sage
8500 NE Day Road
Bainbridge Island, WA 98110
phone (206) 842-6608

Nymphing System For Steelhead

X

One of the most effective methods for catching summer or winter steelhead is presenting the dead-drifted fly close to the bottom of the river or at the fish's holding depth via a floating line and long leader. It's a simple method requiring a minimum of gear and accomplished with straightforward tactics. The steelhead nymphing tactic is particularly deadly on steelhead that you've spotted, that aren't spooked, and that you can approach to within 25 to 35 feet without scaring the fish.

It's also a deadly tactic for bottom-hugging fish in deeper slots that don't lend themselves to a wet fly or skated fly presentation, providing that your leader can reach close to the bottom and that you can still effectively handle the long leader with your rod.

Rod length is a variable with the nymphing tactic because the length of the rod determines how much line you can flip-cast, roll cast or mend properly, and rod length also determines how long a leader you can comfortably cast with a large fly, weighted fly or with weight added to the leader or tippet.

For example, standard steelhead rods of 9 to 10 feet will handle leaders up to about 15 feet with a weighted fly. Two-handed rods of 14 to 16 feet will handle leaders up to 20 feet or more, but can be tiring to fish when you hold them in a 45 degree angle to the stream, following the fly downstream, then mending, roll casting, etc. The shorter two-handed rods of 12 1/2 to 13 1/2 feet are another option, giving the angler the advantages of extended line and leader control while weighing less than the longer two-handed rods. In many instances, either the stream will be small enough to be compatible with nymphing tactics with a 9 to 10-foot rod or the angler can search out slots in larger rivers that are close enough to cover properly.

Another variable in the nymphing tactic is fly line weight. For instance, a 9-weight rod and line will handle a much heavier fly or added lead than a 7-weight outfit, but the 9-weight will tire you out more quickly.

So for example, when winter steelhead nymphing with a size 2 or 4 weighted fly on a 10 to 15-foot leader, a 9-weight is appropriate; for summer nymphing with a size 6 or 8 fly, a 7 or 8-weight system will work. These are only generalities, though, because to an extent you can modify your casting stroke to compensate for variables such as weight of the fly, lead added to the leader, or stiffness of the rod. A softer rod is better for mending but a stiffer rod is better for sinking the hook into the fish's mouth. The best graphite rods can do both.

The most common mistake made when nymphing is to over-reach your "line control length" by casting and fishing too far out. You can only properly control the fly's dead-drift and see the line react to the steelhead's strike in the 25 to 35-foot range, 40-foot maximum. Sure, you can fish farther out, but your chances of making a proper presentation and then detecting the strike to your dead-drifting fly drop dramatically. In most long-line situations, you are better off trying to get a little closer to the fish or going with another tactic, such as the wet fly swing.

THE TRADITIONAL NYMPH LEADER

The most common approach to the nymph leader is to use the same setup as you would with a floating line presentation, usually based on the formula of 60% butt section, 20% mid-section to step down to the tippet, and 20% for the tippet. That system works, and it's most commonly used because you simply add a strike indicator and lead to the leader, if necessary. In many cases, the fly may be very similar to one used with a floating line tactic such as the wet fly swing.

The biggest disadvantage to the traditional nymphing leader is that it "bends" downstream in the current, particularly in the heavy butt and midsection of the leader. Given equal force by the current on the whole leader, the tippet and fly drift downstream at a slower rate than the heavier part of the leader. Because there is more surface area to press against,

---

Nymphing for steelhead is particularly effective when fishing smaller streams. Photo by Scott Ripley.
Facing page: *One of the deadliest methods for catching steelhead is presenting the dead–drifted fly close to the bottom of the river or at the fish's holding depth via a floating line and a long leader.*

the force of the current pushes harder against the bulkier part of the leader, causing it to "bulge" downstream ahead of the fly. So in spite of mending the line and leader to keep the strike indicator dead-drifting, the indicator may or may not be lined up properly so that the fish taking the fly will move the indicator far enough to signal a strike.

The ideal nymphing tactic presents a fly that is dead-drifting at the speed of the current or a little slower, with the strike indicator in a straight line to the fly so that the instant a fish stops it, the indicator dips under the surface, signalling the take. But because of variances in water velocities of the fly and the leader, the traditional setup loses that "straight line" approach.

RIGHT ANGLE NYMPHING SYSTEM

The "right angle" nymphing system still uses a butt section, a mid-section, and a tippet, but instead of a gradually tapering leader in a linear configuration, this nymph leader forms an abrupt right angle. The advantage is that the strike indicator is directly above the fly without the "bulging" effect of the traditional leader.

Also, this leader formula incorporates a loop to loop system for interconnecting the different sections of monofilament. The greatest advantage is that you can quickly add or subtract looped sections of monofilament to change the length of the leader. Besides which, you can quickly exchange worn monofilament for new material and you don't eat up your flat butt or mid-section by using three or four inches of monofilament every time you tie a blood knot. In addition, you can mate monofilament of greatly varying diameters, such as 20-

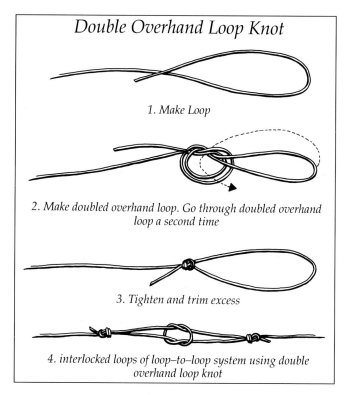

Double Overhand Loop Knot

1. Make Loop

2. Make doubled overhand loop. Go through doubled overhand loop a second time

3. Tighten and trim excess

4. interlocked loops of loop–to–loop system using double overhand loop knot

pound test to 10-pound test, which you can't do with a blood knot. You can also mate different brands of monofilament, such as a stiff midsection looped to a limper tippet.

At the end of the floating fly line you nail knot a 12-inch butt section with a loop on the end of the monofilament. The loop allows you to quickly change from the traditional leader for a standard wet fly or a skated dry fly tactic to the right angle nymph leader. Flat monofilament is best for leader butt material because it holds no line memory, stretching out straight and staying limp even on the coldest of fishing days. It holds knots well, and makes a nice flat nail knot on the fly line.

I first started using flat butt material in 1975 after reading Swisher and Richards book, *Fly Fishing Strategy*. Their original leader formulas revolved around Berkley flat butt trout leaders. I modified their formula to accommodate bulkier fly lines and for the flat butt to mate with Maxima, a stiff monofilament. I prefer Maxima because it is abrasion resistant. There are many types of leader and tippet materials to choose from, so I offer this guideline: every brand of extruded nylon has its advantages and disadvantages; decide what is the most important quality you desire in the material you use and get to know the strengths and weaknesses of that particular brand. The tradeoff with Maxima's toughness is that it is stiff. Many of the newer monofilaments flow better in

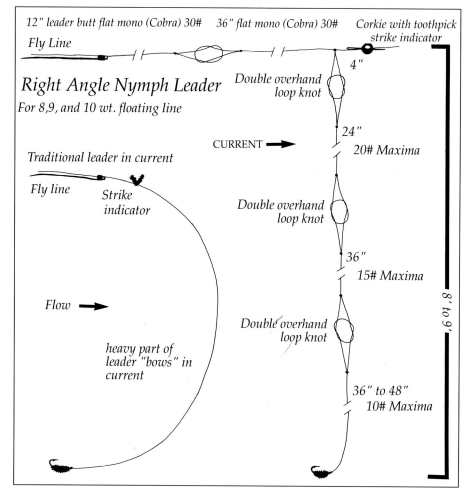

12" leader butt flat mono (Cobra) 30#   36" flat mono (Cobra) 30#   Corkie with toothpick strike indicator

Fly Line

Right Angle Nymph Leader
For 8,9, and 10 wt. floating line

Double overhand loop knot

4"

CURRENT ➡

24"
20# Maxima

Traditional leader in current

Fly line   Strike indicator

Double overhand loop knot

36"
15# Maxima

Flow ➡

Double overhand loop knot

heavy part of leader "bows" in current

36" to 48"
10# Maxima

6', 8, to 9'

the current, but are weak when nicked, scraped, or have wind knots, and some tend to curl badly. None are perfect.

Cortland's Cobra flat monofilament is available in 20- or 30-pound test in either mist blue or red. Red Cobra offers greater visibility and is an advantage for those not wishing to use a strike indicator. Another option is Cortland's Plion running line for shooting heads, a limp fluorescent green monofilament available in 20-, 25-, or 30-pound test. Plion running line and Cobra come in 150-foot spools for use as shooting head running line or leader material. Fly lines of 8, 9, or 10-weight are better matched with 30-pound material; 25-pound Plion (or 20-pound mist blue Cobra for a less conspicuous leader butt) works well for a 7-weight line; and the 20-pound matches with 6-weight lines.

The setup I'm describing as an example works well with an 8-, 9-, or 10-weight rod between 9 and 10 feet long. Because this system uses interlocking loops, you can adjust the dimensions according to any specific rod length or line weight, and to accommodate varying water depths, current, and type and weight of fly.

The right angle nymph leader has an additional flat monofilament butt section of 36 inches looped onto the original 12-inch section that is nail knotted to the fly line, making a total butt of 48 inches of 30-pound Cobra. (Because I use a Corkie and a toothpick as a strike indicator, I use blue mist Cobra.) A dropper loop is installed 6 inches from the end of the flat butt section of leader, leaving a tag end of about 4 inches to attach the strike indicator.

A 24-inch mid-section of regular monofilament with loops on both ends is added onto the dropper loop: one loop interlocks with the dropper loop in the Cobra; the other loop interlocks with either another mid-section of monofilament or with the tippet.

Even though the Cobra is 30-pound test, there may be an abrupt step-down difference in the line-stress-rating of the mid-section of monofilament, depending on the stiffness and diameter of the monofilament that you use. Cobra is not only flat and limp, but it's also much softer than many monofilaments. Typically, I have 24 inches of 20-pound test Maxima looped onto the Cobra, then another mid-section of 36 inches of 15-pound Maxima looped onto the heavier mid-section.

The length of the tippet will vary according to the depth of the steelhead holding water and to some degree, the speed of the current. For example, even though you might add lead to compensate for current speed, you might also use just a little bit less lead and lengthen the tippet a foot or so, which allows the fly more movement in the water and may lessen the number of snags.

I prefer to loop on at least a 36-inch tippet of 10- or 12-pound test Maxima to allow some stretchiness in the monofilament when fighting a fish and to allow for a fly change or two before replacing it. In this example the overall result is a 4-foot butt section, then a 5-foot mid-section, and a 3-foot tippet, for a total leader length of 12 feet.

Actually, there are two distinct parts to the right angle nymph leader. The butt section allows for passing the energy of the cast from the fly line to the leader, and because it's 4 feet from the fly line tip to the strike indicator, you can mend and keep the indicator drifting drag-free. However, the part of the leader that determines where the fly actually drifts is the "right angle" portion of the leader. The "fishing" part of the leader is the length that drops straight down at a right angle from the flat butt section. The 4-foot butt section is a constant; when fishing, you zero in on the water depth and velocity and adjust the length of the "right angle" to compensate. If the mid-section is 5 feet long and the tippet is 3 feet long, the resulting right angle length is 8 feet of actual fly-drifting depth.

One of the skills basic to the steelhead nymphing tactic is adjusting the length of the leader and the weight of the fly or lead to get the desired drift of the fly.

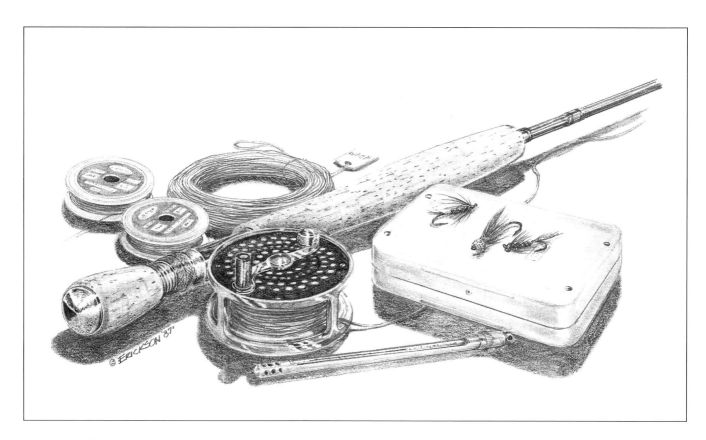

For a 7-weight system, I drop down from the Cobra with a 15-pound Maxima mid-section and an 8 or 10-pound tippet. I drop to a 6-pound tippet if I change to a size 8 or 10 fly for fish holding in clear water. These are variables you can adjust given different water conditions or fish holding stations. The main point is to use a flat monofilament butt with a dropper loop and looped mid-section and tippet to get a right angle nymph presentation, using the quick-change loop system for adjusting the leader length according to fishing conditions.

STRIKE INDICATORS

With a fluorescent leader butt, a strike indicator is not mandatory, but it can sure help you detect strikes. Some of the most effective indicators include adhesive backed foam pads dyed fluorescent red, orange, yellow, or green; a drift fishing Corkie bobber with a toothpick inserted; or a tuft of bright fluorescent yarn tied onto the leader butt.

THE SUNKEN FLY;
LEAD OR UNLEADED

There are three ways to get your fly down when using the dead-drift nymphing technique: 1) use a large hook; 2) weight the fly with a lead wire underbody or with lead eyes; 3) add lead to the leader or tippet. All three methods have advantages and disadvantages and it seems that each of the three have a following of hard core steelheaders that are proponents for each method. There is no "right" or "wrong" system, just differences of opinion.

Using a large hook to get down to the fish is probably the oldest method and carries with it a sense of steelheading history. It can be very gratifying to fish in a traditional manner because it not only dusts the angler with a mood of tradition and history, but imparts a feeling of continuity in time and ritual that was laid down by fly fishermen who have gone

before us. That can be a rare delicacy in our age of plastic haste.

One disadvantage to using a large hook is that often steelhead will refuse a bulky fly because of its size. Fish that are put off by a jumbo fly will often nail a fly that is smaller. Another disadvantage is that a large hook makes an ideal anchor, making it very snag-prone.

The advantage of adding lead wire to the underbody of the fly is that it sinks quickly and stays down in severe current. One disadvantage is that when fishing you are often not completely certain how much lead you have added to the fly. Also, a heavily leaded fly retards the fly's reactions to the current, suppressing its life-like twisting and turning in the river. Another option is to add lead eyes, such as in Black's Buster Leech, the Steelhead Woolly Bugger, or the Comet series.

Adding lead to the leader is an advantage because you not only get the maximum movement from the fly while it drifts downstream, but you can adjust the amount of lead needed for each steelhead holding slot.

Some anglers feel so strongly against adding lead to the leader or tippet that they refuse to do it, saying it's not really fly fishing. Regulations for Oregon read:

Fly Angling: Angling with a fly rod, fly reel, (no spinning or fixed spool reels) floating or sinking fly line, and an artificial fly. In waters restricted to 'fly angling only' no additional weights or attractors shall be attached to the hook, leader, or line, and no metal core lines may be used."

Washington regulations are very similar: "In waters designated as 'Fly Fishing Only' an angler may use: a dry fly, bucktail fly, wet fly, nymph or streamer with a single hook; a conventional fly line at least 25 feet in length, with a back-up line of any kind behind the fly line. In waters designated as 'Fly Fishing Only' an angler may not: use a fixed-spool reel; use weight attached to the leader or line; use bait; use any other than the artificial flies described above; fish with any floating device equipped with a motor, except where specifically allowed under special regulations for individual waters."

For general angling Oregon regulations further state: "When angling for salmon or steelhead the following regulations apply: a) Single-point hooks larger than 1-inch and multiple-point hooks larger than 9/16-inch are prohibited. b) All weight, if not part of a conventional lure, must be attached above the hooks. When using single-point hooks larger than 5/8-inch or multiple-point hooks, the attachment of the weight must be 18 inches or more above uppermost hook."

Oregon regulations list further restrictions on hook sizes for specific waters. Washington regulations list no restrictions on hook sizes or weight attachments, but have "Selective fishery regulations" that specify: "Only artificial flies or lures with a barbless single-point hook are allowed." (At the gape, the Tiemco 7999 size 2/0 hook measures 1/2 inch; the Partridge Low Water 3/0 hook measures 9/16 inch; the Mustad 36890 size 6/0 measures 5/8 inch.)

If the logic is to prevent snagging, and particularly in fly-fishing-only areas, then it makes no sense to ban adding lead to the leader—if snagging was the object of the game, a heavily weighted fly would work far better for snagging than adding lead to the leader. If the logic says that fishing with lead on the leader isn't fly fishing, then it makes little sense to draw an arbitrary difference between lead in the fly versus lead on the leader.

In Washington, you can't fish a fly-angling-only river such as the North Fork of the Stillaguamish from mid-April to the end of November with any size double salmon hook. In Oregon the rules for the Deschutes allow for barbless flies and lures (so you can add lead to the leader); the North Umpqua rules allow for artificial flies only, any type of rod or reel permitted but with no metal core lines and no added weights or attachments, except a bubble or similar floating device.

My conclusion is that there is no widely accepted vision of what "true" fly fishing entails, so each angler must find the soul of the sport on their own.

The Metolius River in central Oregon is a fly-fishing-only trout river so it has a ban against lead added to the leader. Nymph fishermen work around the spirit of the regulation by using heavily weighted stonefly nymphs to get their lighter nymphs down to the proper fishing depth. Sometimes they catch trout on the stonefly nymph, but they commonly refer to that heavily weighted fly as the "anchor."

A universally adopted rule that would require that lead must be attached at least 12 inches from the fly seems more logical and more accurately addresses the question of snagging.

Unless restricted by specific regulations, I often combine methods for sinking the fly in a nymphing presentation for steelhead. In other words, I feel free to use a large fly, a weighted fly, add lead to the leader, or fish a weighted fly and add lead to the leader. I believe these are merely some of the components of fly fishing and that their use doesn't violate the joy of fly fishing or infringe on other's enjoyment of the sport or take undo advantage of the fish. Nymphing for steelhead requires a measure of skill and patience, not unlike any other steelheading strategy.

FLY TYPES FOR STEELHEAD NYMPHING

Steelhead flies have a fascination all their own, partly because they are inherently beautiful, and partly because the fly is our direct link to the fish. Even if a steelhead doesn't take the first fly we offer, we always believe that a change in flies might change our luck. I delve into the subject of steelhead flies and fly design in another chapter, and particularly how to design flies that are less snag-prone than standard flies. I also cover how the size of the fly and its brightness affects how steelhead see it, which in turn determines which pattern the angler should choose. The winter steelheading chapter also covers specific fly types that work well with the nymphing technique. Both chapters address the most bothersome problem when nymphing—fishing close to the bottom and hooking more snags than fish.

Using this technique you can catch steelhead with a tremendous diversity of flies, including the traditional steelhead hairwing streamer; patterns that resemble aquatic nymphs such as the Black Stonefly tied on the Tiemco 207BL English Bait Hook; shrimp patterns tied on the same hook, soft hackles tied with marabou, grouse, pheasant rump, or duck flank feathers; egg flies tied with a tuft of fluorescent yarn; or even Spey flies. As I have emphasized throughout this book, pattern is secondary to presentation.

NYMPHING TACTICS

As I mentioned earlier, because line control and control of the progress of the dead-drifting nymph is the key to the nymphing technique, you should concentrate your efforts in steelhead slots that are less than 40 feet away. Because we often spend hours trying to hook steelhead, it makes sense to be close enough to instantaneously detect the strike. Strike detection is particularly crucial since the take is often very subtle because steelhead frequently just stop the fly by biting it, while never leaving their holding station.

You can nymph just fine with a straight-line cast, either upstream or across, but it's often an advantage to put slack in the line and leader close to the entry point of the fly into the water. That allows the fly time to sink to the fish's level, which will vary from slot to slot.

Whether you use a tuck cast, a parachute cast, a check cast, or throw a mend in the line while the forward cast is in the air, these tactics all allow slack line to allow the fly to sink. There is no "right" way to do it, particularly considering the variables of rod length, line weight, weight of the fly or additional lead, the distance cast, and the vectors of converging current lanes. Just do what is comfortable for you, especially since river conditions vary widely among different streams and each will hold diverse steelhead resting areas. As you guide the dead-drifting nymph on a series of casts through water of varying current speed and depth, you may alter your cast, length of leader, or type, size, and weight of the fly, or you may add or subtract lead on the leader.

Another variable that affects your cast is your approach to the holding lie, whether it's from an upstream or downstream angle, or whether you have any back cast room. The nymphing technique is one of the most effective strategies for fishing small streams for steelhead, where you'll find yourself using the roll cast much of the time.

You may also find yourself combining tactics: throwing a slack-line cast, mending first upstream, then downstream as currents of different speeds intersect the drifting fly line. The intent is to keep the fly and strike indicator dead-drifting, all the while steering the fly through the steelhead's lair. It sounds deceptively simple and easy, and is in many situations. Best of all, the steelhead nymphing tactic catches fish.

Jim Teeny—Breaking Tradition

XI

With his specialized non-traditional fly fishing techniques, Jim Teeny has stirred up more controversy among fly rod steelheaders than any other fisherman I know. Partly it stems from Teeny's attitude about fishing. He says, "My goal when I go out fishing is to hook as many fish as possible with whatever legal method it's going to take, and I'm happy to do it—I'll adjust. I've taken steelhead greased lining and I've taken them with split shot and there's a heck of a difference between the two. If I see fish down there and I just can't get to them, and they're down there in a deep slot and I have to put split shot on, I'll do it.

"One thing you have to remember is that you can't put split shot on your leader if you're in a fly-fishing-only section. So you have to be careful and watch your regulations. On all general fishing waters that are open to all methods, you can fish any style you want, but you have to have the lead at least 18 inches from the fly and I always have my lead from 24 to 30 inches from the fly.

"The way to become a consistent fisherman is to be able to adapt to a changing situation. The quicker you can look a situation over and say 'I don't have the right line on, I'm not fishing right, I've got to go to a longer leader or a shorter leader or I better add split shot or this heavy line isn't working I better get to the top,' the better off you are. The sooner you're able to realize that you're not fishing right and change, and start hooking fish, the better the fisherman you're going to be and the more fish you're going to end up hooking."

THE TEENY CONTROVERSY

The title of Jim Teeny's Scientific Anglers steelheading video states it up front, "Catching More Steelhead: Breaking

Tradition With Jim Teeny." Right from the start you know you're in for something different: he's throwing rocks into the river, moving steelhead into more favorable holding lies for fly fishing.

That illustrates why Teeny upsets people—he is less concerned with aesthetics and tradition than catching fish. Personally, I wouldn't throw rocks in any river because it goes against the grain of what might be called my "fly fishing ethics" or what I think is proper river conduct. However, whether I do it or not doesn't answer the question of whether you or Jim Teeny or anyone else should do it—I believe that is a question for each angler to answer in their own heart. The fish aren't being physically harmed—are they being any more harassed than by the endless cascade of flies and flashing lures and deadly baits that bombard most steelhead rivers?

Because I myself wouldn't feel comfortable stoning a pool, does that make it "wrong" for Teeny or his followers to do it? When do you cross the arbitrary dividing line between being an ardent angler and become one who interferes with game fish? Isn't one definition of angling the act of harassing game fish?

In the nymph chapter I discuss the use of lead on the leader and the "soul" of fly fishing; much of the Teeny controversy can be laid to philosophical differences between what fly fishermen construe as the true meaning of fly fishing, and consequently, proper conduct on the river. The vision of hordes of fishermen pelting rocks to move steelhead is obviously upsetting, but as I state in the conservation chapter, our steelhead are in far more danger from human offshore predation and our own increased population that in turn will cause

---

Jim Teeny has spent over 15 years perfecting his specialized techniques that are particularly effective when other steelhead methods don't work. He says, "I would rather work all day over steelhead I can see than to fish the water blind. This gives me the confidence of knowing that the fish are really there. Instead of guessing where they are, I know for sure. When I can see that fish, I make better presentations, I can watch how the fish behaves and follow him if he moves."
Facing page: *Jim Teeny stalks a steelhead in the Scientific Anglers video,* Catching More Steelhead—Breaking Tradition with JimTeeny.

excessive angling pressure and other ecological inroads on our steelhead streams, than from Jim Teeny's unorthodox angling methods. Be that as it may, there is historical precedent for stoning pools for Atlantic salmon in the British Isles and Canada because ghillies used to do it to stir up dour salmon, but as I understand it, stoning pools is now illegal in Atlantic salmon waters.

In 1939 in his book *The Floating Line For Salmon And Sea-Trout*, Anthony Crossley quotes from letters of A.H. Wood:

"I do not think for a moment from my experience in shallow water among fish that a noise or vibration disturbs the fish. All it does is to distract the fish's attention from the fly and I have never seen the fish quit their lair from noise or vibration. To go to extremes, we had two years of waterwork blasting on the top of my water and it was funny but we thought it would spoil those pools, instead of that we all found that the salmon took well after a big blast. The actual blasting taking place in a deep channel cut within four or five yards of the bank of the river and the stones blasted fell like a broken shell into the pool. Each time we were warned they were going to blast and we had to clear out to safety, but on coming back and starting to fish again we invariably got fish. They are funny devils."

With his specialized non–traditional fly fishing techniques, Jim Teeny has stirred up more controversy among fly rod steelheaders than any other fisherman the author knows. Partly it stems from Teeny's attitude about fishing. He says, "My goal when I go out fishing is to hook as many fish as possible with whatever legal method it's going to take, and I'm happy to do it—I'll adjust. I've taken them greased lining and I've taken them using split shot and there's a heck of a difference between the two."

"An iron shod wading staff makes continuous noise, distracts the fish but does not frighten him. Nothing does.

"Try stoning a fish that you can see, when you have succeeded to move him which does take some time unless you hit him with a stone, sit down and watch him return, then try for him with the fly. I think you will find that he has got over his fright very quickly."

Teeny says he never throws rocks directly at fish and he always asks permission of other anglers before he rocks any fish. He says, "There are two things to remember about rocking steelhead. First, it is easier to move the fish from shallow water into deeper water. Second, if there are other fishermen fishing nearby, it would be wise to ask if it's ok to throw a couple of rocks to move the fish. They will think you're crazy, but if you move a steelhead, and then catch him, they will be amazed."

I predict that even though the method stirs up steelhead and makes them aggressive to the fly, if very many fishermen start doing it, regulations will be enacted to prohibit rocking rivers, based on the ethical and philosophical opinion that such action unduly harasses steelhead. Until the regulations change, though, "stoning the pool" is legal.

If we do enact a prohibition against rocking the river, however, you can imagine the quandary that would ensnare a game warden. Suppose a kid started skipping rocks across the river—he would be breaking the law. How can a warden or a judge determine whether the law has been broken with an arbitrary situation like rocking a pool?

To take this philosophical discussion one step further, it boils down to a question of degree: can we morally sit in judgement when we fashion pieces of steel to stick into a steelhead's mouth so that the fish will jump and run, burning up valuable energy best left for spawning, especially since 99% of steelhead don't refuel by feeding in fresh water? Hooking and playing a steelhead certainly doesn't increase the steelhead's chances at successful spawning.

Perhaps Jacques Cousteau is right when he says that anyone who fishes for fish for mere sport instead of for food is perverted. We fly fishermen place artificial and arbitrary rules on our sport and its accepted conduct, whether it's the rule that allows only casting a dry fly and only to rising trout on the English chalkstreams of the early 1900's or the definition of fly fishing for steelhead.

There are some who ethically disagree with continually casting to a fish or using split shot to run your fly right into the fish's holding lane. In fact, Teeny's critics accuse him of snagging fish. When you get into a real intense nymphing presentation, repeatedly drifting steelhead-sized flies to fish that weigh from six to sixteen pounds, you can't always determine the exact location of your fly. When your fly is close to the steelhead and the fish opens its mouth or the steelhead moves towards the fly, your natural reaction is to set the hook—sometimes the steelhead isn't taking your fly and you will accidentally snag the fish. I've watched Teeny—he's good at what he does and he doesn't intentionally snag fish—he's simply very intent on hooking his quarry, which often means drifting his Teeny Nymph or Teeny Leech right into the fish's mouth.

Teeny has spent over 15 years perfecting his specialized techniques that are particularly effective when other steelhead methods don't work. Teeny's strategies take advantage of angling opportunities often missed by the traditional steelheader; for example, Teeny fishes the "bright water" hours of mid-day, and he catches fish in waters pummeled by intense angling pressure.

THE TEENY KEYS
TO SUCCESSFUL STEELHEADING

Teeny is successful primarily because of two main ingredients: he spots his fish before he casts his fly; and he has a hefty dose of confidence. He says, "Confidence is one of the most important elements of successful steelheading.

"I would rather work all day over steelhead I can see than to fish the water blind. This gives me the confidence of knowing that the fish are really there. Instead of guessing where they are, I know for sure. When I can see that fish, I make better presentations, I can watch how the fish behaves and follow him if he moves."

Teeny prefers spotting fish in a smaller river because it's easier to "read" the water. A smaller river is also easier to wade and will generally clear more quickly after a hard rain.

He says, " The ability to see fish is the single most important aspect of my method of steelhead fishing. Sight fishing gives you confidence. You know you're casting to fish instead of guessing where they are and maybe wasting your time on empty water. It's the most challenging fishing I know.

"Traditionally, anglers have said, 'If you can see that fish, it can see you,' but I say, if I spot 'em, I got 'em. If I spot a steelhead and can cast to him without him spooking away, I've got about a 75 to 80% chance of hooking that fish."

TIPS FOR SPOTTING STEELHEAD

Teeny prefers clear rivers and bright sunshine to spot steelhead, especially in mid-day when the sun shines directly down on the river, illuminating as much of the holding areas as possible. As an added bonus, that's when many fishermen have given up on the fishing because of the traditional belief that the fishing is not good in the middle of the day.

Teeny recommends wearing polarized glasses for spotting fish, and wearing clothes that blend into the streamside foliage, avoiding brilliant colors like white and yellow that might startle holding steelhead. Using a high vantage point like a bridge, large rock, or even a tree can be a considerable help in spotting fish. Binoculars are helpful for viewing fish from a distance, such as in the canyons of rivers like the North Umpqua.

One spring I watched Teeny show an angler how to use his methods on the Sandy River in Oregon for wild winter run steelhead. Teeny climbed a tree near the tailout of a run to spot

Teeny prefers to fish for steelhead that he's spotted so that he can present his nymph to a known holding lie. He uses polarized glasses and whenever possible, a viewing station that is elevated above the river because he is better able to spot fish from above.

some fish. Then Teeny directed the angler's casts to cover the fish.

The steelhead turned, moved crosscurrent several feet and inhaled the fisherman's size 4 black Teeny Nymph. After the hookup the steelhead cleared the water in a four foot leap; the angler got too excited and broke the fish off. Using Teeny's

John Fabion, director and producer of Scientific Anglers videos, films Jim Teeny.

specialized fly lines and techniques, by day's end the fisherman landed steelhead of 10 and 12 pounds.

Teeny concentrates on watching the "window" in the current. The boils and conflicting currents in the surface of the stream will often clear momentarily, leaving a flat spot in the surface that allows you to see the bottom of the stream.

On that same spring trip, Teeny's friend Don Anderson had spotted a dark shape in the current that suggested fish.

"You really ought to try that one, Jim," Anderson said.

"Are you sure you don't want to go for him?" Teeny answered.

"No, you go ahead and get him," Anderson said.

Teeny cast several times, then moved in closer to his target. By then he was only 10 feet away from it.

At that point, knowing that it was a rock, Anderson burst out laughing, "What's the matter, Jimmy, won't it bite for you?"

It takes practice and patience to spot fish. And sometimes even experts like Teeny can be fooled.

Teeny recommends moving in closer if you are in doubt about a rock versus a fish. And he says that once you've spotted a fish, keep your eye on it, even when you are rigging up

the Lani Waller series of traditional steelheading films. The Teeny video is a valuable tool for those wishing to explore new methods for taking steelhead, and particularly in waters that receive severe fishing pressure. The video was not filmed on a pristine wilderness river, but on seven heavily fished rivers within an hour's drive of Portland, Oregon. The day the pocket water sequence was filmed I watched Teeny hook 15 steelhead. On the tape Teeny lays his strategy out in these 10 steps:

One: Locate a steelhead without spooking it. Be sure to keep watching the fish as you move into position, so that if the fish moves, you can track it to its new holding spot.

Two: Position yourself as close to the steelhead as possible without spooking it and slightly downstream from the fish.

Three: Estimate how far upstream you must cast to allow the fly to sink to the fish's depth. Zero in on a target zone for your first cast, mentally noting any nearby landmarks like a rock or bush so you know where your first cast landed. That way you can adjust your next casts as needed.

Four: Let the fly sink before you start the retrieve. Try to match the depth of your fly with the depth of the fish.

your rod or changing flies. That way, although the fish might change its holding station, you still have eye contact with that fish.

10 STEPS FOR CATCHING STEELHEAD
THE TEENY WAY

The Scientific Anglers video "Catching More Steelhead: Breaking Tradition with Jim Teeny" is a companion piece to

Five: Work to get a dead-drift with the fly, allowing it to drift naturally in the current. Keep slack out of your line to detect the strike. Keep the rod tip low for maximum sensitivity to the strike and for a quick hook up.

Six: Concentrate. Watch your cast, the fly, and the fish. You may see the take before you feel it. Be ready for the slightest hesitation of the line or the least movement of the fish; steelhead takes can be very gentle.

Seven: Set the hook on the slightest pull on the line. It may only be the bottom but it may be a steelhead.

Eight: After covering the fish well, experiment by changing the color or the size of the fly.

Nine: Try changing position up or downstream to change the angle of presentation.

Ten: Never give up on a steelhead. The Jim Teeny motto: "If I see 'em, I got 'em."

SPECIALIZED TACTICS FOR SPECIAL WATERS: DEEP POOLS AND POCKET WATER

For deep pool fishing, Teeny uses his Mini-Tip fly line and a 10-foot leader, although he will lengthen his leader if conditions warrant it. About 80% of the time Teeny uses a roll cast to cover the fish. The roll cast keeps his fly out of the streamside brush. Also, it takes less time to make a roll cast than an overhead cast, which means his fly is in the water more of the time, resulting in more hookups. And by using a gentle retrieve, Teeny will often give his fly some action when it swings in front of a steelhead.

One of the biggest challenges to pool fishing is the soft take of the fish.

Teeny says, "In these situations the take is incredibly soft—it's like a little leaf, a little tick on the end of your fly line. Something that you think isn't a fish could be a big steelhead just lightly picking up your fly. It's incredible that fish so big can be so gentle."

For pocket water Teeny says, "I've found that steelhead bite very well in faster water because they feel safe beneath the turbulent surface. And, in the faster current, they have so little time to study your fly, it's easier for the fish to make a mistake and that's when you got 'em."

He says, "When looking for fish in pocket water, look in the slots or depressions or around the rocks or boulders where the fish will be holding out of the heavy current."

For pocket water Teeny uses a floating line, a 7-foot leader, and split shot to get his fly down to the fish. (Split shot may not be legal in some fly-fishing-only areas.) As illustrated in the video, he uses a lob cast and guides his fly through the holding slot in the pocket water.

Teeny says, "Pocket water fishing is the single most productive way to catch steelhead when they are under pressure from other anglers."

THE TEENY TECHNIQUE—A UNIFIED NYMPH SYSTEM

Teeny first became known for his Teeny Nymph, with it's body and beard hackle composed of Chinese ringneck pheasant tail feather fibers. Teeny invented his fly in 1962, calling it "Abduli". He went public with it when he formed the Teeny Nymph Company in 1971. Besides the natural color, he has since added black, insect green, antique gold, flame orange, hot pink, hot green, ginger, and purple. Some Teeny Nymphs include an optional wing of ringneck fibers. With a ringneck fiber tail, the Teeny Leech is very similar and is tied in the same colors as the original nymph. The Teeny Flash Flies add Crystal Flash to the wing on the nymph.

He has developed a series of specialized fly lines for probing steelhead water, including the Teeny Nymphlines from 130 to 500 grains, and Mini-Tips and floating lines in 5 to 9-weights.

Perhaps Teeny's greatest contribution is to reexamine traditional steelheading techniques, showing us new methods that catch steelhead.

Larry Dahlberg says, "If there's ever been an ultimate philosophy, with the purest form of direct effect to catch steelhead, I truly believe the Teeny system is the closest to being a unified whole theory.

"The system I'm talking about is the idea of having from large to small, from dark to light, in a specified universal pattern that doesn't change from size to size or from color to color. Then you have a semblance of control in the size and the color and you've got a predictable drift rate. You know the way the fly's going to work and how fast it's going to sink as you're running through the spectrum. It's a pretty fast way to get to where you need to be. That system could easily be applied and is already, without needing to be said, to dry fly fishing or to flies right in the surface film. We're talking about size and color.

"It's a search method and that's what you do with every type of fishing that you do whether it's fly fishing or spoon plugging. That is how a fisherman looks at fishing if he's going to be successful and not superstitious."

Several years ago Teeny and John Dusa spent the last two weeks of October on the Skeena system in British Columbia fishing for steelhead. Using Teeny's specialized strategies, he and Dusa landed steelhead up to 24 pounds, including one memorable day when they hooked 21 steelhead on the Kispiox. Although Teeny didn't set the new world's record that he was seeking, he hooked a behemoth steelhead estimated between 27 and 30 pounds, but he lost it. The Teeny methods do work.

Steelheading Survival Kit

XII

Fly fishermen are an optimistic lot. We seem to have no qualms about wading deep, wading far, and wading along ledges, above rapids, and in short, always being near a good dunking.

Modern neoprenes and wading boots allow us to wade deeper and farther because neoprenes fit better than baggy chest waders and the boots offer better support and traction in the stream. But in many cases these advantages also impart a false sense of security for anglers, causing them to overreach themselves.

Every year fishermen drown; in almost all cases the death could have been prevented. It is my fervent hope that someone reading this, and possibly you, dear reader, will be saved by using the gear available to us.

Patrick McHugh of MPI, makers of the Space Blanket, says, "For some reason, hunters and campers seem much more safety conscious than most fishermen. Everybody thinks that an accident will never happen to them—it always happens to the other guy."

For Scott Swanby it did happen to the other guy. On Thanksgiving day, 1985, Swanby's best friend died in a boating accident—the life jackets were tied up in the front of the boat. Inspired by that shock, Swanby started Sporting Lives, the company that makes SOSpenders.

But the stories of "the other guy" continue. Swanby tells of a man who was steelheading in the fall of 1988 on the Snake River, fell, filled his waders, and drowned in front of his wife and five kids.

Swanby says, "You can bet they would have paid anything to save their dad's life."

The prototype SOSpenders was originally invented by Merrill Salleen, who saw a fly fishing friend slip and drown in the Middle Fork of the Salmon River. Salleen spent five days with his friend's wife and children looking for the body.

At that time Salleen vowed to invent a life preserver that a person could wear and fish in comfortably. In 1970 Salleen developed his first prototype, which consisted of two plastic baggies and some straps. After many hours and numerous product upgrades, Sporting Lives, Inc. perfected SOSpenders.

Swanby says, "We wanted to make a life preserver that active sportsmen would be willing to wear because it's lightweight and comfortable."

SOSpenders address the main reason fishermen don't wear life preservers: anglers think most preservers are too cumbersome or uncomfortable to fish in. And that is probably the main reason why fishermen will continue to drown.

INFLATABLE LIFE VEST AS FLY FISHING VEST

Inflatable fly fishing vests aren't approved by the Coast Guard because there is the possibility that the vest may not work. When the cord is pulled there is a slight chance that the CO_2 cartridge won't expand the air chamber. Statistically that possibility is very remote, but it's there and in an emergency you really don't have the time or presence of mind to orally inflate the air chamber.

Besides SOSpenders, I regularly use the Shorty Inflatable Fishing Vest by Sporting Lives, the Mustang MIV-120 Inflatable Vest and the Stearns AV-4442 Inflatable Anglers Vest. SOSpenders Shorty vest is handy for deep wading steelheaders that dislike a regular length vest. These inflatables are manufactured in the United States, are well made, and have most of the features of better fly fishing vests. All use a 16 gram CO_2 cartridge and the same Roberts valve that has been proven to be utterly reliable over the years.

Will he slip or will he make it? The main reason fishermen don't wear life preservers: they are too cumbersome or uncomfortable. And that is probably the main reason why fishermen will continue to drown. The author offers several options that may save your life, including inflatable fly vests which are quite comfortable.
Facing page: *The main danger to steelheaders is drowning, but an associated danger, and particularly to boaters, is hypothermia resulting from a dunking in cold water.*

Inflatable vests require minimal maintenance. Before a fishing trip take a moment to check the inflation chamber. Via the oral inflation valve, blow up the vest with the few puffs of air that it takes, leaving it expanded while you organize your gear. When everything is ready, listen closely for any escaping air from the vest, and check to see if the air chamber has lost any volume. Deflate the chamber by pressing in on the top of the oral inflation valve while compressing the air chamber.

You should periodically check the lanyard assembly to make sure that when the cord is pulled, the piercing pin protrudes upwards to enter the CO_2 cartridge. Before pulling the cord, unscrew the CO_2 cartridge and remove the red plastic keeper on the valve assembly. The plastic keeper is in place so that you must yank the cord to pierce the CO_2 cartridge, thus eliminating accidental inflation of your vest.

The greatest advantage of the inflatable fly fishing vest is that an angler is much more likely to wear one because they are not as bulky as a regular life vest. If you wear one when wading tricky water, the odds are excellent that it will be there when you desperately need it. If your only excuse is, "I don't wear one because it's too bulky," then the inflatables deflate that argument. One advantage with an inflatable is that you can orally inflate your vest before you wade through tricky water, before you cross the river through deep water, when you fish along a slippery underwater ledge, or if you are fishing upstream from deep, heavy currents. When finished, you can easily deflate the vest.

Even if you don't inflate your vest, wearing a PFD will give you more confidence while wading deep water, allowing you to more fully concentrate on fishing. If the only reason you don't wear one is because the vest might not inflate, then you should wear a life vest that is modified as a fly fishing vest.

LIFE VEST AS FLY FISHING VEST

Various companies offer life vests that double as fishing vests, with extra pockets, fly patches, and specialized attachments. The biggest advantage of these life vests is that there is no danger that the CO_2 cartridge won't work because the vest already has built-in floatation. The only disadvantage is that life jackets are bulky to fish in.

These vests are Type III PFD (Personal Flotation Device), designed to float the wearer in a vertical and slightly backward position. A Type III PFD will not turn an unconscious person over and into the upright position. Fishermen use Type III vests because they are more comfortable and less bulky than the Type I or Type II, which will turn the wearer upright. If you are only wearing a PFD when in a boat, a Type I or Type II is a better life jacket than a Type III because of the extra flotation, and if the boat overturns or you are thrown out and hit your head, a Type I or Type II will keep your unconscious self upright.

My most exciting Type III adventure occurred when floating the Deschutes River with Forrest Maxwell of Salem, Oregon. He was rowing and advised me to jump over and fish some particularly succulent-looking trout water. I hesitated because the distance to the bottom of the river looked like it might exceed the length of my waders.

"You can do it, just jump in and start fishing," Maxwell said, "I'll row ashore farther downstream and you can join me after you catch some of those big rainbows."

I succumbed to temptation; I checked to be sure my Type III PFD was zipped up, then lowered myself over the side of the drifting drift boat. While dangling off the side of the boat I quickly discovered that the bottom of the river had disappeared. What's worse, the river current pinned me to

Anglers think most preservers too cumbersome or uncomfortable to fish in. That is probably the main reason why fishermen will continue to drown. Inflatables are lightweight, inconspicuous life preservers that don't hinder your fishing pleasure.

the sloping side of the boat so I couldn't get enough leverage to climb back in. By now we were approaching a set of rapids.

"You have to either get in the boat or let go because I can't row through these rapids with you hanging on the boat," Maxwell said.

While visualizing a ride through the rapids in my life jacket I noticed we were fast approaching an underwater gravel shoal that looked to be a little higher than the rest of the river bottom.

When we got over the shoal I dipped down into the river, briefly touched bottom, then shot up into the boat.

The thought of running the rapids in my PFD was scary, but the option of running the rapids without a life jacket is terrifying.

WADING BELTS, WADING STAFFS AND STUDDED FELTS

The main advantage to a wading belt is that if you fall in, the belt will help to keep your lower extremities dry. If you fall in wearing neoprenes, they tend to collapse around your body and don't balloon out and fill with water as rubber chest waders are prone to do. The new stretch nylon wading belts with Fastex Quick Release buckles are comfortable to wear, easy to put on and off, are inexpensive, and are dandy for attaching a Folstaf.

I've used the Folstaf wading staff for years and highly recommend it. The only maintenance required is to occasionally rub paraffin or candle wax on the male ferrules of the staff, just as you would on a graphite rod. The wax lubrication aids in unjointing the staff.

When I first started steelheading, I would find a tree branch and use it as a staff. But a branch can be difficult to come by when on a desert river like the Deschutes or when you are already out in the river without a branch and suddenly find yourself in desperate need of a helping staff. Becoming upwardly mobile, I invested $3.00 in a ski pole and found out two things: it worked as a wading staff but it was a total pain in the rear. It clanked and banged around when I wasn't using it and always managed to either wrap itself around my legs or tangle in the fly line. I still see fishermen clanking around on steelhead streams with ski poles—I often wonder how the steelhead react to all that underwater noise—I suspect by fleeing from the site of the disturbance.

The advantage of the Folstaf is that it's there when you need it and out of the way when you don't because it folds into short sections, carried in a belt holster. My Folstaf has more than paid for itself over the years, preventing a dunking a number of times. On several occasions when I slipped I came down hard on the staff, not on an expensive fly rod or on non-expendable body parts. Other times I've slipped and bruised myself when I wasn't using the staff. We optimistic fly fishermen always try to go as light as possible, gazing into our crystal ball to determine what will happen next on any given river. If we can be so accurate in our predictions of upcoming hazards, why can't we predict the fishing as well?

Besides felt soles we often need more traction for slick-bottomed rivers. Options include Bailey Stream Cleats rubber galoshes that go over wading shoes, Korkers wading sandals or Weinbrenner wading shoes equipped with Korkers carbide studs.

The tradeoff with Stream Cleats or Korkers studs is underwater noise caused by studs grating over rocks. Of course, the noise is less than the splashing and yelling of a fisherman dumped into the river. On many streams the additional traction offered by these studding systems eliminates the need for a wading staff.

There are numerous fly fishing areas where the angler doesn't need a wading staff or life preserver. However, most steelheading demands wading precautions; many of us are simply playing the odds that we won't need a flotation device or a wading staff. But I sincerely hope that when the time comes, you will be one of the smart ones wearing your life preserver.

HYPOTHERMIA

The main danger to steelheaders is drowning, but an associated danger, particularly to boaters, is hypothermia resulting from a dunking in cold water. Even after gaining dry ground, hypothermia is a danger.

Hypothermia is lowered deep-body temperature. In a life-threatening cold water immersion, skin and external body tissues cool very rapidly, but it takes 10 to 15 minutes before the heart and brain begin to cool. By intense shivering, the body attempts to increase heat production and counteract the extensive heat loss. Unconsciousness occurs when the body's core temperature drops from the normal 99 degrees to 90 degrees. Heart failure is the usual cause of death when the deep-body temperature cools below 86 degrees.

Another factor to consider is wind chill. For instance, even though the air temperature might be 40 degrees, a 15 mph breeze can drop the chill factor to 25 degrees, causing you to cool more quickly.

Steelheaders often get cold and sometimes cold enough to shiver. Shivering is a warning sign: get out of the water and warm up before you fall in. Although I'm sure that many dunkings in cold water ensue from slipping, I suspect that in cold weather or cold water conditions most of those dunkings are a result of the angler being overly chilled, which causes the feet to become slightly numb, joints, fingers, and leg and arm muscles to get stiff, and judgement to get fuzzy. With stiff legs, arms, and back muscles, it's quite easy to misjudge a step, trip, and fall in the river.

If you start shivering, feel chilled to the bone, or your fingers are so numb you can't feel the fly line in your hand, get out of the water and warm up. When you take a step and your feet are so numb you can't tell what type of terrain you're on—whether it's rocky or a gravel bottom—your body is flagging you to warm up. At that point, you're a dunking just waiting to happen.

If you're steelheading on foot and fall in, you can regroup at the car with dry clothes and comfort of the car heater. But if you're boating or a goodly ways from the car, camp or lodge, you need to take some preparedness precautions.

COLD WATER SURVIVAL

Fishermen fueled by big-fish-fever consistently ignore the two most dangerous hazards to anglers, primarily due to a lack of forethought. The greatest danger is from drowning because we don't wear a PFD while wading or boating. Invariably, the life jackets are stowed instead of worn. And because we are all secretly convinced that accidents always happen to the other guy, we don't worry about hypothermia or simple survival strategies.

I vividly remember being lucky one time in Alaska. The guide operating the 16-foot jet sled on a large river with myself and two clients decided that he wanted to fish, too. So we began drifting downstream with the engine off. The sled eased close to shore, bumping against the brush. That wasn't too precarious because the current was slow and the brush wasn't entangling the boat enough to tip us over.

As we drifted back out into the center of the river we picked up speed in the faster current. The others didn't seem to mind that their guide was fishing instead of tending to business. We eventually came to a parting of the river where an island of fully grown, flooded trees bisected the current.

"Don't you think we had better start the motor now," I suggested nervously.

"Naw, there's plenty of time, and besides, you never know when you might catch a big fish," he remarked with off-hand bravado as we gathered more speed in the current.

Now we were being swept into one of the river channels, heading directly for a line of trees. I became acutely aware that the life jackets were stowed in the bow under a pile of equipment and that the bag sitting at my feet contained over a thousand dollars worth of camera gear. If we dumped the boat the current-swept trees would offer some sort of refuge, but the trees were separated from either bank of the river by deep, swift water, and we were miles from camp.

By now we were so close to the trees that I could see where with icy fingers, Alaskan winds had etched deep patterns in the bark.

The guide was stroking on the pull cord of the outboard like a crazed idiot; when we were 12 inches from the trees the motor stuttered to life. We banged into the trees, tipping the sled, but only shipped a little water and roared off down the river.

The thought of being chucked into the river without a life jacket and losing all my camera gear and expensive rods and reels is still frightening. I wonder what would have happened had we survived the boat dumping, particularly since one of the clients was in his 70's. We would have been soaking wet, miles from camp, with fading light and dropping air temperatures.

Given the grace of afterthought, I have developed a fishing vest survival kit along these guidelines: the items must be functional, not bulky, and not heavy—if not, fishermen won't carry them.

FISHING VEST SURVIVAL KIT

The most important item for your survival is an inflatable angling vest. Other items include a pair of neoprenes and studded wading boots. Sunglasses, raincoat and warm clothes are essential, but aren't considered part of the vest survival kit.

This survival kit can be carried in a daypack, but just as most anglers stow their life jackets, the daypack will also be packed away. The best place for this kit is in your vest.

MPI Products Space Blankets are highly recommended: the Space Emergency Blanket at two ounces, folds to 4x2x2 inches, measures 56 x 84 inches when laid out and retains 80 percent of radiated body heat; or the Space Emergency Bag (which you can crawl into) weighs three ounces, unfolds to 36 x 84 inches, and retains 90 percent of radiated body heat. Either will make a tremendous difference when you get wet, particularly if there is a wind chill factor. Space Blankets don't absorb water, so even if you and your gear get soaking wet, the Space Blanket will still reflect heat at optimum efficiency.

To keep your body's heat pump primed eat the candy bars, hard candy, snack bars, or beef jerky that you have stashed in your vest.

I know of one steelhead outfitter on the Rogue River who suggests carrying several skyrocket flares in your vest to signal for help, but I recommend MPI's Emergency Strobe. On one "D" cell battery the Emergency Strobe flashes its Xenon personal strobe light between 50 and 70 times per minute, visible up to three miles. It's hand-sized, waterproof, weighs eight ounces with battery, will flash up to three days on an alkaline battery, and is made of tough plastic that won't rust or rot. It has a sealed on/off switch and a stainless steel locking pin for attachment to a vest, life jacket, belt, or pack.

There are disadvantages to flares: you never know if they will work—you can always check a battery powered device without expending it; you might injure yourself when you set off a flare, particularly if you're not functioning well because you're injured or shaken; and flares are bulky. The worst drawback to a flare is that it only works once—if you carry three flares, then you only have three chances to signal for help. What if you need four?

Another recommended signalling device is one of the pocket-size waterproof signal horns manufactured by Falcon Safety Products for small boats. They weigh four ounces and power 100 two-second blasts heard up to a mile away. (Refill cartridges weigh 2 ounces.)

Signal horns are invaluable if you are hurt or stranded in dense fog, in a winding canyon where straight line visibility is poor, or for other types of signalling: two blasts—bear alert; three blasts—bring the boat; four blasts—emergency, come quick. A signal horn is a mandatory fishing vest item for someone with a medical problem that might need immediate attention. When the guide is tending to several widely spread out clients, sometimes yelling and jumping up and down while waving your arms just isn't enough.

One morning at a lodge in Alaska we bid good luck to four anglers flying out to a distant river to retrieve mouse patterns in front of steelhead-sized rainbow.

That evening we were told, "Go light on the food, we need to save some for those guys that flew out today and their pilot. They should be coming back any moment, now."

At twilight the plane still hadn't returned. The lodge owner and friends of the anglers were getting nervous. The river they were fishing was known to have a lot of bears fishing for spawning salmon.

Finally, just as it was getting difficult to see, the float plane roared in over the river, dropped onto the water and then taxied up by the lodge.

The pilot was angry and defensive; the anglers were hungry, tired, cold, and angry. Both parties claimed the other had screwed up.

The pilot had been flying Alaskan skies for over 30 years—when he flew over a specific spot on the river and told the fishermen that he would pick them up "right there, by that island," it was perfectly clear to him.

The anglers quickly agreed, minds filled with scenes of 12-pound rainbow slashing into their mouse flies, bent rods

and screaming reels. That was why they had come all the way to Alaska.

The dilemma became apparent when the anglers thought they were waiting on the right island for the pick up. When the plane flew over them, they had no way to signal the pilot.

As light faded and the pilot made pass after pass over the "right" island, he couldn't figure out where the anglers were—he was making his last pass over the river "before leaving them there until morning" when he finally saw his passengers.

The fishermen wore neoprene waders, which could be considered a limited survival suit, but they still came close to spending a long, cold night with a lot of roaming bears and no food.

The beauty of this survival kit is that you would have been prepared with snack food, Space Blanket, matches or

The author's survival kit fits in the back pouch of an inflatable fly fishing vest. Some of the kit is pictured: Space Emergency Blanket, snack bars, toilet paper, knife, bandages, MPI Emergency Strobe, Falcon signal horn, cigarette lighter, and flashlight.

cigarette lighter for starting a fire, flashlight and a signal horn for scaring off bears. With an Emergency Strobe you would have avoided it altogether.

I've heard other stories: excited about leaving at dawn for a day of fishing, an angler fell off an icy dock into a cold Alaskan river and was swept downstream; a bush plane filled with gear couldn't get off the water on takeoff—while taxiing back to the dock, the plane began to sink because of an undetected leak in the pontoons.

Whether you're in a bush plane swooping down on a steelhead stream in Alaska or helicoptering into a river valley in British Columbia, fly with your inflatable vest on, with your survival kit in the vest. If the craft crashes in water and you get out, even if you are a good swimmer, you may be injured and not able to swim. With your inflatable, you merely yank the lanyard.

The kit also includes toilet paper, Band-Aids, insect repellent, sunburn protection (some have moisturizing ingredients which salve windburn), headache or pain reliever tablets, tablets for a cold, antihistamine tablets for allergies, upset stomach tablets, lip balm like Chapstick and chewing gum to plug a missing tooth filling.

I carry 100% DEET to combat heavy infestations of mosquitoes, black flies, or no-see-ums. However, DEET is toxic, can ruin the finish on your fly line, take off paint (such as the f-stop number on one of my camera lenses), and has a noxious smell. In many instances you can repel insects with Green Ban, an organic citronella repellent from Australia; or Natrapel, a citronella repellent, with aloe vera for moisturizing the skin. These citrus scent repellents rub off easily and must be applied more often than DEET.

Based on an old remedy of ammonia hydroxide and mink oil, After Bite takes the sting and itch out of insect bites and comes in a handy pen-like cartridge.

Other needed items include a Flexlight or miniature waterproof flashlight and small folding pocket knife. The final must-have item is matches or a cigarette lighter.

Organizing your survival kit centers around one of the finest achievements of modern man, the Ziploc bag. Waterproof items such as the Emergency Strobe, Space Blanket, flashlight, knife, and signal horn don't need a Ziploc bag, but having the whole kit in a large Ziploc bag keeps everything compact and prevents loss. Matches, cigarette lighter, medicinal items and snacks fare better when dunked underwater if protected in a Ziploc bag.

Plastic 35mm film canisters are ideal for storing matches (include the rough striking edge for lighting), pain reliever, cold, antihistamine, and upset stomach tablets. You only need a few tablets of each type for the survival kit, but be sure to label them.

If you're separated from your main gear bag, take a dunking from an overturned boat, or are somehow stranded while fishing, with this survival kit in waterproof containers in the back pocket of your vest, you'll have what you need to make it back to civilization safely. And because you're wearing an inflatable vest you can wade as far and as deep as you wish without the fear of drowning.

FIRST AID ITEMS FOR THE TACKLE BAG

You can buy scaled down versions of many health products in "travel sizes" for your tackle kit. Or you can put limited quantities in 35mm film canisters labeled with masking tape or in labeled Ziploc bags.

Items for your gear bag include a wound protectant like First Aid Creme or Neosporin, tweezers for extracting ticks or splinters, aloe vera gel or After Burn for windburn or sunburn, and medication for poison oak.

Clean water is critical for comfort and survival; the First Need Purifier has performed well for me. It filters out Giardia and other nasties down to .4 microns and has a replaceable filter canister. I recommend the optional Prefilter to screen coarse debris before it enters the purifier. (Water purification tablets make water stink but are suitable as backup.) Include a small canteen or collapsible cup.

Use barbless hooks; otherwise, you need this item: the two-ounce Emergency Hook Remover and First Aid Kit, a plastic pouch containing hook remover, first aid items and instructions for removing an embedded hook from the human anatomy.

TACKLE FIRST AID KIT

On the first day of my first trip to Alaska, the tip guide on my 9-foot, 8-weight rod fell off and was lost. Because I didn't have a spare guide, that rod was worthless the remainder of the trip. Fortunately, I was able to borrow a rod.

A tackle first aid kit includes: rod tip and snake guides, ferrule cement, Superglue, Aquaseal or Sportsman's Goop or Shoe Goo for wader repair (Aquaseal dries overnight; Goop or Shoe Goo dry within minutes), a 24-inch piece of filament tape or duct tape, (wrap around film canister containing guides and ferrule cement), and two-ounce can of WD-40. You can take a midget screwdriver set with various bits, needlenose/sidecutter pliers (among other things, for removing hooks if you don't have your Emergency Hook Removal

Kit) and a Swiss Army knife. Or you can take my favorite, the Leatherman Pocket Survival Tool which incorporates 12 tools within its five compact ounces. I would also add a pair of small folding scissors, spare batteries, spare CO2 cartridges for the inflatable vest, a two-ounce refill signal horn cartridge, and a Space Blanket for a companion not smart enough to bring his own.

Marty Sherman, editor of *Flyfishing* magazine, once told me that whenever he gets into one of those little bush planes, he says to himself, "Well, today looks like a good day to die."

Undeniably, we all have our day coming, and a person could do a lot worse than to check out while fishing, but I would hate to die because of my own stupidity or lack of forethought. And even if you aren't in a life-threatening situation, your vest survival kit could make the hours after a dunking or while waiting for help a lot more pleasant.

Emergency Hook Remover And First Aid Kit available from: Sports Aid, Inc. 7110 East 13th Street Indianapolis, IN 46219 (317) 356-3137 (John H. Leane)

ITEMS FOR THE SURVIVAL KIT

1) Inflatable vest
2) Space blanket (Space Emergency Blanket, Space Emergency Bag)
3) Snack bars
4) Emergency Strobe, MPI Products
5) Boat horn (Falcon Sound 911, Supersound, Sound Off, Mini Sonic Safety Horn)
6) Matches or cigarette lighter
7) Toilet paper
8) Band-Aids
9) Insect repellent (100% DEET; Green Ban or Natrapel)
10) Sunburn protection (without PABA)
11) Pain reliever tablets (Exedrin)
12) Antihistamine tablets if allergic to pollen or insect stings
13) Upset stomach tablets (Rolaids)
14) Chapstick
15) Flexlight or small flashlight (Mini-Maglite)
16) Pocket knife (Gerber LST or Ultralight)

ITEMS FOR THE TACKLE KIT

1) Wound protectant (Neosporin, First Aid Creme)
2) Tweezers (Tick Kit or The Tick Solution)
3) Cold medicine (Comtrex tablets)
4) Poison oak medication (Jake's Poison Oak Remedy or Oak-n-Ivy Cleanser)
5) Emergency Hook Remover and First Aid Kit
6) First Need Purifier and Prefilter (or Giardia-proof water purification tablets)
7) Guides, tip and snake
8) Ferrule cement
9) Superglue
10) Aquaseal or Shoe Goo or Sportsman's Goop
11) 24 inches of filament or duct tape
12) WD-40, two ounce can
13) Midget screwdriver kit with various bits
14) Combination needlenose and sidecutter pliers
15) Swiss Army Knife
16) Substitute Leatherman Pocket Survival Tool for #13, 14, and 15
17) Small folding scissors
18) Spare batteries for Emergency Strobe
19) Spare CO2 cartridges for Inflatable Vest
20) Refill cartridges for Falcon signal horn
21) Spare Space blanket
22) Small canteen or collapsible cup

Conservation & Steelheading in the Twenty–First Century

XIII

You and I are at once the biggest threat to steelhead and their greatest chance for their survival. We slice into schools of steelhead on the high seas, trapping their gills in mesh, strangling them; we build more dams; log more timber; and run more highways along steelhead streams and rivers. But possibly worst of all, we continue to expand our population, a population that constantly sucks on a limited pool of running water, while swelling the ranks of fishermen tossing hooks at steelhead.

But we also band together to fight high seas steelhead and salmon piracy, contest dam building in court, and watchdog logging and road building and stream flows. We unite with like minded fishermen to form a social consciousness that wields a mightier political sword than the outcry of an isolated voice. We do it for ourselves because of our intimate affection and compassion for the fish we treasure.

We fly fisher persons are a strange lot: we plead catch-and-release for wild fish while angling with flies tied from the fur and feathers of wild animals, some of whom we have pushed to the brink of extinction. I'm not burning my stash of seal fur and polar bear hair in a funeral pyre of contrition but I am saying that we shouldn't automatically feel superior to our fellows because we fly fish for steelhead, prefer to catch wild fish, and finally, grandly turn them loose. Being of the set of mind to enjoy fly fishing for steelhead, preferably over wild fish on an equally wild river, you and I should enjoy the fly tying arts and aesthetics of our fish-quest and all its assorted gear, but with one foot rooted solidly in the reality of our times.

Bitching and moaning is great for relieving stress, but eventually it falls to each of us to decide how much time, energy, and money we are willing to give back to the sport. We are the future. In many respects, the demise of steelhead is ultimately the demise of fishermen, wherever the angler resides and fishes. Because life on planet Earth has water for its lifeblood, for better or for worse we are all tied into this together.

Lee Wulff's *The Atlantic Salmon* was originally published in 1958. In his foreword to the 1983 edition he wrote, "In these intervening years salmon fishermen have increased manyfold while the numbers of salmon in the runs and the rivers suitable for their spawning have dwindled. Because there are so many more of us to call for good management of the salmon stocks we are certain to be heard and heeded. We can reclaim the salmon rivers. We can bring the runs back to something like their old-time glory. But we can never give again to anglers the opportunities available in my youth to catch, and if one wished to, keep or kill so many salmon. Even as we rebuild the stocks the number of anglers will grow at an even faster rate than the numbers of fish.

"The average angler cannot hope to increase his opportunity to take more salmon. His increase in pleasure must come from enjoying each salmon he catches more or by having each salmon spread the pleasure it can give to more than one angler. Each salmon angler needs to develop a deeper understanding of the fish and the intriguing angling problems involved to gain a growing pleasure from each fish as he casts and retrieves through his allotted time. Then his last salmon can give him as much pride, satisfaction, and wonder as his first."

It boils down to you and I and the values and attitudes that we embrace that will determine the quality of our steelhead fishing experiences.

On a recent float trip down the Deschutes my partner and I came upon a run that had no anglers in it; the other group was out of their waders, rods propped up against nearby trees, and were sitting down to lunch. I anchored the boat along the shore at the bottom of the long tailout and my partner and I went to the top of the run to fish. He started at the very top and I about halfway down. I had fished about 20 feet

---

The author strongly believes in the catch–and–release of all wild steelhead and the preservation of those runs. To a great extent the future of all steelhead rests with its wild fish. Photo by David Lambroughton.
Facing page: *The choices we make by either working together or by not doing anything at all will shape the future for steelhead in the 21st century.*

All of those who fish for steelhead, including Indians netting on the Columbia or at Sherars Falls on the Deschutes, or sportsmen using bait, lures or flies, have all seen far reaching changes in the steelhead fishery. We all have a part in the use and fate of steelhead, for both today and tomorrow.

when a rock sailed over my head and landed in the water 30 feet in front of me. Then another rock followed it.

"Having any luck?" one of the lunchers asked. They thought it was pretty funny, but the rock thrower's face was flushed with anger. He felt that because he had camped along that run, he and his companions "owned" that water and that other anglers were trespassing on his run, even though the land was Bureau of Land Management property. Although he had all the proper accouterments to fly fish, he had left the most important in his tackle bag—the courtesy and restraint that will be even more necessary as time bolts into the next century, just a few years away.

STEELHEAD FEVER

I, too, have been guilty: early in my steelheading years I was seized by "steelhead fever," a malaise that thrusts passion for catching steelhead above all else.

As evening dropped its blanket over the escarpments guarding the Deschutes, I had no trouble taking turns with another angler, drifting wet flies through this one particularly juicy run.

As I arranged my gear in my tent that night I vowed I would be the first one through the run in the morning. When the alarm woke me it wasn't quite dawn yet; I peeked out to see the other angler's camper, which was still dark. I hastily donned waders and vest. As I was jointing up my rod I noticed movement within the camper, which was closer to the river. I finished stringing the rod, tied on a fly and headed for the river. Then the other angler stepped out, grabbing his already strung-up rod that lay on the camper roof, and walked the few short steps to the water, beating me by 30 feet.

Stung, but gripped by the throes of steelhead passion, I went half way down the 80-yard run and stepped into the river.

"I got a nice strike right there last night and would like to try for him again, if you don't mind," he said.

Chagrined by the realization that I had cut the man's water in half, I stumbled back to shore to reassess the situation.

ELBOW ROOM

It is ideal to have the whole river to yourself and your friends. Unfortunately, reality dictates that we need to consider what is the proper and courteous amount of water an individual can "claim" by being first to wade into a run.

Traditionally, the first angler fly fished through the whole run, followed by the second fisherman, then the first would start over at the head of the run. Oftentimes, friends will split a run. The problem occurs when there are more fishermen than spots, which is common on popular rivers such as the Deschutes. Another problem closely related to overcrowding is a conflict in methods. As long as fly fishing steelheaders employed the classic wet fly swing, the rotation system worked fine. Now, however, more steelheaders are nymphing for steelhead, which is not generally a rotation, cover-the-water strategy, but focuses on a specific section of a run with repeated presentations.

I don't believe that a wet fly presentation is more "proper" than a nymphing presentation because we are all trying to stick a fly hook into the fish's mouth. Although it can be irritating when one angler or a group of anglers monopolize a particular run for hours on end, I support the first-in-the-water criterion for first right to the run. Given the fact some runs go for hundreds of yards, you will have to decide for yourself whether wading into the same run will infringe on your fellow fisherman. Since none of us own a steelhead stream, we will all continue to face that question.

You can always ask your fellow anglers—invariably they will be friendly and say, "Sure, go ahead," or they will tell you about another great spot just around the corner that you probably didn't know about. By talking to other fishermen you lower the barrier—instead of a competitor you become just another human being trying to get away from the press and stress of everyday life—you have common needs and seek a common goal of fly fishing pleasure.

I could have probably avoided the rock-throwing incident I described earlier if I had talked to those lunching anglers before I fished "their water." I would have avoided the sick after-feeling of an angry confrontation which most likely would not have developed after conversation between fly fishermen instead of a clash between presumed enemies.

More and more I find less personal enjoyment because of crowded fishing on the more famous steelhead waters, whether from boaters or wading fishermen. And more and more I find myself seeking out lesser known rivers or streams with sparser runs of steelhead. I find more peace of mind when I'm not competing for water with fellow anglers. I covet elbow room more than hooking a lot of fish and I've found that the numbers of steelhead I catch doesn't seem to matter nearly as much as enjoying some space on the river. I go fishing to get away from people, not compete for fish and fishing spots.

As the twenty-first century unfolds, we will see more crowding on our rivers by boaters and wading fishermen, and probably less steelhead, even though hatchery production increases and we release all wild steelhead. Some runs will hold their own and a few will increase, but many will decline because of the compromises our twenty-first century society will demand to meet the needs of progress for our ever increasing population.

You and I are the problem, and you and I will decide what is proper stream etiquette by our behavior while fishing. For me it means turning loose wild steelhead in a wild setting with flies I've tied myself. Your idea of fly fishing for steelhead is probably very similar—don't you think there is room for both of us?

Fly Pattern Listing

A.P. Flash Black Nymph—Dave Hall
Tail: Black hackle fibers, several strands of pearlescent Flashabou
Body: Black dubbing
Rib: Pearlescent Flashabou
Hackle: Black soft hackle wound through thorax
Shellback: Black feather
Legs: Two strands of pearlescent Flashabou wrapped around rear of head and extending down in front of hackle

Aztec—Dick Nelson
Tail: Acrylic knitting yarn
Rib: Optional, silver tinsel
Body: Acrylic knitting yarn or tinsel
Wing: Acrylic knitting yarn

Bi-Color Hairwing—Dave McNeese
Tag: Flat silver tinsel
Tail: Golden pheasant crest dyed purple
Rib: Flat gold tinsel
Body: Rear half, purple seal; front half, hot orange seal
Hackle: Palmered the length of the body, rear half, purple; front half hot orange
Wing: Polar bear dyed purple on top, hot orange on the bottom
Eyes: Jungle cock
The single palmered hackle is dyed two colors: top half of hackle is dyed purple; bottom half hot orange. The same technique is used to dye the wing material two different colors.

Bi-Color Polar Bear Matuka—Dave McNeese
Tag: Flat silver tinsel
Body: Hot orange seal
Hackle: Light guinea dyed hot orange
Wing: Polar bear dyed purple on top, hot orange on the bottom
Eyes: Jungle cock

Black's Buster Leech—Bill Black
Tail: Black or purple marabou; Flashabou or Krystal Flash optional
Body: Black or purple chenille
Legs: Two sets of gray medium sized rubber legs about hook shank length
Eyes: Nickel plated lead eyes

Black Crawler—Dave Hall
Tail: Chicken tail feather fibers
Rib: Flat black monofilament
Body: Black dubbing
Hackle: Black chicken tail feather, trimmed top and bottom

Black Gordon—Clarence Gordon
Rib: Narrow oval gold tinsel
Body: Rear 1/3 red yarn, front 2/3 black yarn
Hackle: Black
Wing: Black bucktail

Black Marabou
Tail: Black marabou
Body: Black yarn, chenille, or dubbing
Hackle: Saddle hackle, pheasant rump, guinea, or grouse dyed black

Wing: Black marabou

Black Phase Spey—Joe Howell
Body: Rear half flat gold tinsel, front half black floss
Tail: Short orange polar bear tuft at junction of tinsel and floss
Rib: Oval gold tinsel
Spey Hackle: Black heron
Wing: Orange polar bear
Jungle cock eyes are optional

Black Soft Hackle
Body: Black yarn, chenille, or dubbing
Hackle: Saddle hackle, pheasant rump, guinea, or grouse dyed black

Black Stonefly Nymph—Charles Brooks
Tail: Black Goose biots
Rib: Copper wire
Body: Black or dark brown yarn
Hackle: Grizzly and brown grizzly and gray ostrich

Blue Max—Mark Melody
Tag: Copper wire
Rib: Copper wire
Body: Rear half, burnt orange yarn; front half black chenille
Hackle: Silver doctor blue
Wing: Orange calf tail over black calf tail; wing should be 1/4 orange, 3/4 black

Bomber
Tail: White bucktail
Body: Spun deer hair
Hackle: Palmered grizzly
Wing: White deerhair

Boss
Tail: Black bucktail at least as long as hook shank
Rib: Silver tinsel
Body: Black chenille
Hackle: Extra long red or fluorescent red
Head: Red tying thread with bead chain eyes

Brad's Brat—Enos Bradner
Tail: Orange and white hackle fibers
Body: Rear half orange chenille or yarn; front half red
Rib: Gold tinsel
Wing: Orange over white bucktail
Hackle: Brown

Brown Heron—Syd Glasso
Rib: Wide or medium flat silver tinsel, overlay with narrow oval silver tinsel
Body: Rear 2/3 orange floss; front 1/3 hot orange seal
Spey Hackle: Gray heron, one side stripped
Throat: Teal flank
Wing: Bronze mallard or widgeon flank
Head: Red

Bucktail Caddis
Body: Orange yarn or dubbing
Rib: Palmered brown hackle
Wing: Brown bucktail
Hackle: Brown rooster

Clark's Stonefly—Lee Clark
Thread: Orange
Body: Flat gold tinsel
Underwing: Sparkly yarn, orange or rust colored
Overwing: Deer hair; can substitute elk or moose
Hackle: Brown

Coastal Skunk—Alec Jackson
Thread: Fluorescent red 6\0
Tail: Red hackle fibers
Rib: Silver tinsel
Body: Peacock herl twisted with rib and wrapped
Hackle: Soft black hackle
Wing: White polar bear, sparse

Cole's Comet
Tail: Hot orange polar bear, long
Body: Wide oval gold tinsel
Hackle: Extra wide orange and yellow
Head: Brass or gold finish bead chain eyes, tied down with orange thread

Copper Top—Brian Silvey
Tail: Gold Krystal Flash
Body: Rear 2/3 copper wire; front 1/3 black chenille
Hackle: Black
Wing: Gold Krystal Flash

Courtesan—Syd Glasso
Rib: Flat silver tinsel
Body: Fluorescent orange floss
Spey Hackle: Brown
Wing: Four matching hot orange hackle tips
Head: Red

Dahlberg Diver—Larry Dahlberg
Tail: Rabbit fur strip, strands of Flashabou
Body: Rabbit fur strip, wrapped (excess becomes tail)
Wing: Long spun deer hair collar on top, clipped
Head: Spun deer hair

Dark Caddis—Mike Kennedy
Tail: Golden pheasant tippet fibers
Rib: Narrow flat gold tinsel
Body: Orange wool
Hackle: Cock-Y-Bondhu or brown
Wing: Red fox squirrel tail

Dean River Lantern Series
Tail: Squirrel tail dyed black, as long as the body
Body: Edge Bright dyed fluorescent green, orange, red, yellow, or chartreuse
Hackle: Matches body material

Deep Purple Spey—Walter Johnson
Rib: Flat silver tinsel
Body: Purple floss
Spey Hackle: Brown Chinese ringneck pheasant rump, started at end of body of fly
Throat: Purple hackle
Wing: Reddish golden pheasant body feather

Del Cooper—Mike Kennedy
Tag: Flat silver tinsel
Tail: Red hackle fibers
Rib: Narrow silver tinsel
Body: Purple wool
Hackle: Red
Wing: White bucktail

Deschutes Madness—Dave McNeese
Thread: Fluorescent red
Tag: Flat silver tinsel
Tail: Hot pink floss
Body: Hot pink or fluorescent red floss
Rib: Dark purple plastic chenille
Wing: Purple or fluorescent blue polar bear, then purple Crystal Flash over the wing and as a sparse collar around the front of the fly
Hackle: Dark purple
Jungle cock eyes optional

Deschutes Skunk—Forrest Maxwell
Tag: Flat silver or gold tinsel
Butt: Red floss
Tail: Golden pheasant crest dyed red
Rib: Oval silver or gold tinsel
Body: Black dubbing
Hackle: Chinese pheasant rump feather, teal in front
Wing: Bronze mallard or dark turkey or substitute

The Deschutes Skunk can be made into the Deschutes Skunk Spey by adding a palmered Chinese pheasant rump feather as the Spey hackle.

Evening Coachman—Walter Johnson
Tag: Flat silver tinsel, florescent orange floss wrapped over
Tail: Golden pheasant crest feather
Body: Peacock herl divided by a narrow band of fluorescent red floss
Hackle: Grizzly

Eyed Shrimp—Mark Bachmann
Hook: Eagle Claw L1197N size 4 or 6
Tail: Thick short bright red marabou
Rib: 16/18 or fine oval gold tinsel
Body: Lead wire .035 covered with flat flame yarn
Wing: Fluorescent white calf tail, body length
Head: #503 Danville flat waxed thread (flame orange, matches body color; head is tied large enough to accommodate the eyes
Eyes: Painted enamel; yellow iris, black pupil

Fall Favorite
Body: Flat, oval, or embossed silver tinsel
Hackle: Red
Wing: Orange bucktail or polar bear fur

Feather Strip Wing Spey—Joe Howell
Body: Rear half embossed silver tinsel, front half claret seal
Rib: Oval gold tinsel
Spey Hackle: Black heron
Wing: Outer strips speckled turkey, inner strips bronze mallard
Jungle cock eyes are optional

Flame—Gary Alger
Tag: Flat gold tinsel
Body and Hackle: Hot orange marabou,

red marabou in front
Wing: Bronze mallard

Flashdancer—Larry Dahlberg
Tail: Red marabou
Body: White chenille
Wing: Gold, silver, or pearlescent Flashabou
Head: Spun deer hair and a deer hair collar on top

Glasso's Grizzly—Syd Glasso
Body: Rear 2/3 fluorescent orange floss, front 1/3 hot orange seal fur
Rib: Flat silver tinsel
Body: Grizzly saddle hackle palmered
Wing: Four matching hot orange hackle tips
Topping: Hot orange golden pheasant crest
Head: Red

Golden Demon
Tail: Golden pheasant crest
Body: Gold tinsel
Hackle: Orange
Wing: Brown mallard or natural brown bucktail

Golden Purple Spey—Gary Alger
Tag: Flat gold tinsel
Butt: Hot orange floss
Body: Purple dubbing
Rib: Fine oval gold tinsel
Spey Hackle: Reddish-brown golden pheasant
Front Hackle: Guinea
Wing: Two reddish-brown golden pheasant breast feathers

Golden Spey—Walter Johnson
Rib: Flat gold tinsel
Body: Golden yellow dubbing
Spey Hackle: Black tipped white feather from the Great Blue Heron dyed golden yellow, started at end of body of fly
Throat: Golden yellow hackle
Wing: Matched brown hackle tips
Topping: Golden pheasant crest

Golden Stone Tie-Down—Dave Hall
Tail: Deer hair dyed golden cinnamon color
Body: Golden stone dubbing
Hackle: Golden cinnamon soft hackle wound through thorax
Wing: Deer hair dyed golden cinnamon color tied down at head and end of thorax, forming shellback over thorax and wing over rest of body and tail

Gold Heron—Syd Glasso
Rib: Narrow oval gold tinsel
Body: Rear 2/3 flat gold tinsel, front 1/3 hot orange seal
Spey Hackle: Gray heron, one side stripped, or brown heron
Throat: Widgeon flank
Wing: Widgeon flank
Head: Orange

Gold Hilton
Tail: Grizzly hackle fibers
Rib: Gold tinsel
Body: Black chenille
Hackle: Brown

Wing: Mallard flank, divided

Gold Hilton Spider
Tail: Wood duck, widgeon, shoveler, or bronze mallard flank fibers
Body: Black chenille
Rib: Gold tinsel
Wings: Flared out grizzly hackle tips
Hackle: Wodduck, widgeon, shoveler, or bronze mallard flank feather

Gray Orange—Syd Glasso
Also called Grizzly Orange or Glasso's Grizzly. See Glasso's Grizzly

Grease Liner—Harry Lemire
Tail: Deer hair
Body: Dubbing; black, dark brown, gray olive, burnt orange, yellow orange
Wing: Deer hair
Beard: Sparse grizzly
Head: Cinched-down deer hair

Green Butt Skunk—Dan Callaghan
Tail: Red hackle fibers
Rib: Oval silver tinsel
Body: Rear 1/4 florescent green chenille; front 3/4 black chenille
Hackle: Black
Wing: White calf tail, bucktail, or polar bear substitute

Green Butt Spey—Gary Alger
Tag: Flat silver tinsel
Butt: Fluorescent green floss
Rib: Small oval silver tinsel
Body: Black dubbing
Spey Hackle: Black heron, blue eared pheasant, or substitute
Front Hackle: Guinea
Wing: Bronze mallard

Grizzly Orange—Syd Glasso
Also called Grizzly Orange or Glasso's Grizzly. See Glasso's Grizzly.

Halloween Matuka—Deke Meyer
Body: Black chenille, yarn, or dubbing
Rib: Gold or silver oval tinsel
Wing/Tail: Orange hackle tips, two pair matched
Hackle: Orange

Halloween Spey—Deke Meyer
Rib: Silver or gold oval tinsel
Body: Black dubbing
Spey Hackle: Orange goose flank feather
Wing: Black hackle tips
Front Hackle: Dark guinea

Hyatt's Steelhead Caddis—LeRoy Hyatt
Body: Dubbing or sparkly yarn, varied colors
Wing: Separate stacks of deer or elk hair
Hackle: Brown, grizzly, or a mixture, can substitute creme
Can substitute a spun deer hair head for the hackle.

Inland Skunk—Alec Jackson
Thread: Fluorescent red 6/0
Tail: Red hackle fibers
Rib: Silver tinsel
Body: Rear half, black ostrich twisted with tinsel and wrapped; front half, black seal twisted with tinsel and wrapped
Hackle: Black soft hackle
Wing: Sparse white polar bear

Lady Caroline
  Tail: Reddish-brown golden pheasant breast feather
  Rib: Flat gold tinsel and fine oval silver tinsel
  Body: Olive brown dubbing
  Spey Hackle: Great blue heron
  Front Hackle: Reddish-brown golden pheasant
  Wing: Bronze mallard
Lady Coachman—Walter Johnson
  Tag: Flat silver tinsel with fluorescent red floss wrapped over
  Tail: Cerise hackle fibers
  Body: Peacock herl divided by a narrow band of fluorescent pink wool
  Hackle: Light fluorescent pink
  Wing: White bucktail
Leggo-My-Eggo
  Hook: Short shank reversed drift hook or short shank streamer hook
  Body: Glow yarn of various colors tied on and trimmed to a round shape or an acrylic puff ball of yarn slipped on the hook. Effective colors include white, orange, red, pink, and pearl in "regular" and dyed fluorescent.

Lemire's Fall Caddis—Harry Lemire
  Rib: Flat orange monofilament
  Body: Burnt orange dubbing
  Wing: Matched golden brown grouse feathers
  Hackle: Sparse deer hairs
  Head: Spun deer hair
Marabou Madness—John Shewey
  Tag: Flat silver tinsel
  Tail: Purple hackle fibers
  Body: Underbody of fluorescent orange single strand floss; then front half of body of dark purple plastic chenille
  Hackle: Purple
  Wing: Purple marabou, then purple Krystal Flash, then purple marabou, then 4 or 5 strands of purple Flashabou tied on each side of the wing
Marabou Paintbrush—Gary Alger
  Tag: Flat gold tinsel
  Body and Hackle: Hot orange marabou, red marabou, pale blue marabou, dark blue marabou in front
  Wing: Bronze mallard
Marabou Streamer
  Tail: Tuft of marabou
  Body: Chenille or yarn
  Wing: Marabou

Migrant Orange—Walter Johnson
  Tag: Copper tinsel, fluorescent orange floss wrapped over
  Tail: Fluorescent orange bucktail or hackle fibers
  Rib: Copper tinsel
  Body: Fluorescent orange wool
  Hackle: Fluorescent orange
  Wing: Fluorescent orange bucktail
  Topping: Strand of fluorescent orange wool

Mr. Glasso—Dick Wentworth
  Thread: Wine colored 6/0
  Tag: Flat silver tinsel
  Rib: Flat silver tinsel
  Body: Rear half hot orange floss, front half hot orange seal
  Spey Hackle: Black heron
  Throat: Guinea dyed orange
  Wing: Matching hot orange hackle tips
  Topping: Golden pheasant crest dyed hot orange
Muddler—Don Gapen
  Tail: Brown turkey
  Body: Gold tinsel, flat or embossed
  Wing: Brown turkey enclosing gray squirrel tail
  Hackle: Brown deer hair
  Head: Brown deer hair
Natural Crawler—Dave Hall
  Tail: Chicken tail feather fibers
  Rib: Flat clear or gray or tan monofilament
  Body: Squirrel body fur dubbing
  Hackle: Chicken tail feather, trimmed top and bottom

October Caddis Spey—Gary Alger
  Rib: Fine oval gold tinsel
  Body: Rusty orange dubbing
  Spey Hackle: Reddish-brown golden pheasant
  Front Hackle: Yellowish-brown golden pheasant
  Wing: Bronze mallard
October Caddis Tie-Down—Dave Hall
  Tail: Black deer hair
  Body: Burnt orange dubbing
  Hackle: Furnace hackle wound through thorax
  Wing: Black deer hair tied down at head and end of thorax, forming shellback over thorax and wing over rest of body and tail
Orange Heron—Syd Glasso
  Body: Rear 2/3 fluorescent orange floss, front 1/3 hot orange seal fur
  Rib: Flat silver tinsel, overlay with oval silver tinsel
  Spey Hackle: Gray heron, one side stripped
  Throat: Teal flank
  Wing: Four matching hot orange hackle tips
  Head: Red
Orleans Barber—C. Jim Pray
  Tail: Barred wood duck flank
  Body: Red chenille
  Hackle: Grizzly
Peacock Woolly Bugger—Mark Bachmann
  Tail: Kelly green marabou with dark olive Super Fly Flash
  Rib: Green wire
  Body: Peacock herl
  Hackle: Grizzly dyed olive, palmered
Pink Prancer—Gary Alger
  Tag: Flat silver tinsel
  Body and Hackle: Pale pink marabou, hot pink marabou in front
  Wing: Bronze mallard

Pink Puff
  Hook: Eagle Claw L254N size 2
  Thread: White
  Body: Pink Super Fly Flash tubing wrapped around the hook
  Wing: Pull up the end of the Fly Flash tubing and tie it back for the wing, fraying it out with a dubbing needle.
  Eyes: Large nickel plated bead chain
  Head: Cross wrap around the eyes with fine fluorescent pink chenille.
Pink Shrimp—Bill Chinn
  Rib: Oval gold tinsel
  Body: Hot pink dubbing
  Spey Hackle: Heron or pheasant dyed hot pink
  Wing: Bronze mallard

Plastic Polar Shrimp—Dave McNeese
  Thread: Fluorescent red
  Tag: Flat silver tinsel
  Tail: Red hackle fibers
  Body: Gold braid
  Rib: Fluorescent shell pink plastic chenille
  Hackle: Fluorescent orange
  Wing: White polar bear, then fluorescent orange Crystal Flash, then fluorescent pink Crystal Flash, then more white polar bear
  Jungle cock eyes optional

Polar Bear Spey—Dave McNeese
  Thread: Orange
  Tag: Flat silver tinsel
  Body: Rear 1/2 hot orange floss, middle 1/4 purple dubbing/polar bear Spey hair, front 1/4 hot orange dubbing/polar bear Spey hair
  Beard: Bleached golden pheasant tippet dyed purple
  Wing: Purple mallard flank
  Topping: Golden pheasant crest dyed purple
Polar Shrimp—Clarence Shoff
  Tail: Red hackle fibers
  Body: Orange or fluorescent orange chenille
  Wing: White polar bear or substitute
  Hackle: Orange or fluorescent orange
Polar Shrimp—Syd Glasso
  Tag: Flat silver tinsel
  Tail: Red hackle fibers
  Rib: Oval silver tinsel
  Body: Rear half fluorescent orange floss, front half fluorescent orange seal (can substitute hot pink)
  Spey Hackle: Long wide red hackle (or substitute hot pink) or reddish golden pheasant body feather
  Wing: White feather
  Head: Red
Popsicle—George Cook
  Body: None
  Hackle: Marabou in several color schemes, such as orange, cherry, and purple; salmon egg color and orange; white and red; with Flashabou or Crystal Flash

Prizm—Mark Bachmann
Tag: Copper wire
Tail: Golden pheasant tippet
Rib: Copper wire
Body: Peacock herl
Hackle: Brown
Wing: Red fox squirrel tail

Mark says, "Since 1975 I've used this pattern in size 6 with success on the Deschutes during periods of low warm water when all else failed."

Pseudo Spey—Alec Jackson
Hook: Alec Jackson Spey hook
Thread: Hot orange
Tail: Hot orange hackle fibers
Body: Rear half, peacock herls twirled around oval tinsel and wrapped as dubbing, front half hot orange ostrich twirled around oval tinsel and wrapped as dubbing
Hackle: Hot orange hackle, then blue eared pheasant, then hot orange hackle

Purple Deceiver—Gary Alger
Tag: Flat silver tinsel
Body and Hackle: Light purple marabou, dark purple marabou in front
Wing: Bronze mallard

Purple Goose Spey—Deke Meyer
Butt: Hot pink floss
Body: Black dubbing
Rib: Oval silver tinsel
Spey Hackle: Purple goose
Wing: Hot pink hackle tips
Front Hackle: Hackle or guinea dyed red

Purple Matuka—Forrest Maxwell
Tag: Flat silver tinsel
Rib: Oval silver tinsel
Body: Black seal or dubbing substitute, chenille or yarn; or substitute flat gold or silver tinsel
Wing/Tail: Purple hackles, two matched pair
Hackle: Purple

Purple Moose Bomber—Bob Clay
Tail: Purple moose
Body: Purple moose, flared on top of the hook shank, not spun (bottom of body and head area well cemented to keep the body from spinning on the hook)
Wing: Purple moose

Purple Muddler—John Hazel
Body: Purple plastic floss
Wing: Gray squirrel dyed purple, purple Crystal Flash, brown oak turkey.
Red dubbing wrapped over wing tie down area
Hackle: Purple deer hair
Head: Purple deer hair

Purple Peril—Ken McLeod
Tag: Flat silver tinsel
Tail: Purple hackle
Rib: Silver tinsel
Body: Purple floss, yarn, chenille, or dubbing
Hackle: Purple
Wing: Brown deer hair

Purple Phase Spey—Joe Howell
Body: Rear half flat silver tinsel, front half purple floss
Rib: Oval silver tinsel
Spey Hackle: Black heron
Wing: Purple polar bear
The Red Phase Spey is the same except the body floss and the wing are red.

Purple Spey—Keith Mootry
Rib: Flat silver tinsel
Body: Rear 1/2 orange floss, front 1/2 purple seal
Spey Hackle: Black heron or substitute
Throat: Guinea
Wing: Matched purple hackle tips
Dave McNeese adds a flat silver tinsel tag, jungle cock, and substitutes bleached golden pheasant crest dyed purple for the wings in his version.

Quillayute—Dick Wentworth
Tail: Red hackle fibers
Body: Rear half orange floss, front half hot orange seal fur
Rib: Flat silver tinsel
Spey Hackle: Large teal flank
Front Hackle: Black heron
Wing: Four matching reddish golden pheasant body feathers
Head: Red

Red and White Puff
Hook: Eagle Claw L254N size 2
Thread: White
Body: White everglo tubing wrapped around the hook
Wing: Pull up the end of the Fly Flash tubing and tie it back for the wing, fraying it out with a dubbing needle.
Eyes: Large nickel plated bead chain
Head: Cross wrap around the eyes with fine fluorescent red chenille.

Red Phase Spey—Joe Howell
Body: Rear half flat silver tinsel, front half red floss
Rib: Oval silver tinsel
Spey Hackle: Black heron
Wing: Red polar bear (orange is an alternative)
The Purple Phase Spey is the same except the body floss and the wing are purple.

Red Shrimp—Walter Johnson
Rib: Flat silver tinsel
Body: Fluorescent orange floss veiled with thin red dubbing
Spey Hackle: Brown Chinese ringneck pheasant rump, started at end of body of fly
Beard: Red hackle
Wing: White turkey or similar dyed red
Topping: Golden pheasant crest

Rooster Spey—Richard Bunse
Tag: Flat gold tinsel
Rib: Flat gold tinsel
Body: Rear half hot orange floss, front half black seal
Spey Hackle: Brown Chinese pheasant rump feather
Wing: Matched hot orange hackle tips enclosed in iridescent black rooster chicken tail feather

Rusty Bomber—John Hazel
Tail: Red fox squirrel tail
Rib: Palmered brown hackle to front of body
Body: Spun rusty deer hair
Wing: Red fox squirrel tail

Sauk River Shrimp—Alec Jackson
Tail: Orange calf tail, bucktail, or polar bear
Body: Separate segments of spun red ostrich
Hackle: Separate segments of orange hackle

Silver Demon—C. Jim Pray
Tag: Oval silver tinsel
Tail: Wood duck flank
Body: Oval silver tinsel
Hackle: Orange
Wing: Gadwall flank
Tail is often orange hackle fibers and wing is mallard flank. Another alternate is tail, orange polar bear fur; body, flat silver tinsel; wing, guinea strips with golden pheasant topping or silver squirrel tail wing.

Silver Heron—Syd Glasso
Body: Rear half flat silver tinsel, front half black seal or substitute
Rib: Oval silver tinsel
Spey Hackle: Gray heron or black heron or substitute
Throat: Guinea
Wing: Gray or black feather

Silver Hilton
Tail: Mallard flank fibers
Body: Black chenille
Rib: Silver tinsel
Wings: Flared out grizzly hackle tips
Hackle: Grizzly

Silver Hilton Spider
Tail: Mallard, pintail, or gadwall flank fibers
Body: Black chenille
Rib: Silver tinsel
Wings: Flared out grizzly hackle tips
Hackle: Mallard, pintail, or gadwall flank feather

Silver Streak Spey—Joe Howell
Body: Flat silver tinsel
Rib: Oval gold tinsel
Spey Hackle: Gray heron, started at end of body
Beard: Guinea dyed pale blue
Wing: Bronze mallard
Jungle cock eyes optional

Skunk—Clarence Gordon
Body: Rear half yellow yarn, front half black yarn
Hackle: Black
Wing: White bucktail with black bucktail on top

Skunk
Tail: Red hackle fibers
Body: Black chenille
Rib: Silver tinsel
Wing: White calftail
Hackle: Black

Skunk Spider—Forrest Maxwell
Tail: Red hackle fibers
Body: Black chenille
Rib: Silver tinsel
Wing: Brown mottled feather such as turkey
Hackle: Pheasant rump

Soft Hackle Spey
Tail: Soft webby feather fibers (optional)
Body: Yarn or dubbing
Rib: Flat or oval tinsel or wire (optional)
Spey Hackle: Wide leggy hackle palmered; hackle extends past rear of hook
Front Hackle: Wide leggy hackle
Fly can be tied in various color schemes. This design could also be called a Spider Spey or Spey Spider or Spey Soft Hackle. (See Steelhead Soft Hackle.)

Sol Duc—Syd Glasso
Tag: Flat silver tinsel
Tail: Golden pheasant crest
Body: Rear half fluorescent orange floss, front half hot orange seal fur
Rib: Flat silver tinsel
Spey Hackle: Yellow chicken hackle
Throat: Teal
Wing: Four matching hot orange hackle tips
Topping: Golden pheasant crest
Head: Red

Sol Duc Dark—Syd Glasso
Tag: Narrow oval silver tinsel
Tail: Red golden pheasant body feather
Body: Rear half fluorescent orange floss, front half hot orange seal fur
Rib: Flat silver tinsel, overlay with narrow oval silver tinsel
Spey Hackle: Yellow chicken hackle
Throat: Teal
Wing: Four matching red golden pheasant body feathers
Head: Red

Sol Duc Spey—Syd Glasso
Body: Rear half fluorescent orange floss, front half hot orange seal fur
Rib: Flat silver tinsel
Spey Hackle: Long webby yellow chicken hackle
Throat: Black heron
Wing: Four matching hot orange hackle tips
Head: Red

Spawning Purple—Dave McNeese
Tag: Flat silver tinsel
Tail: Orange polar bear
Body: Hot orange polar bear
Hackle: Hot orange hackle, then dark guinea in front
Wing: Matched purple hackle tips, flared out

Steelhead Bee—Roderick Haig-Brown
Tail: Red fox squirrel, quite bushy. Slightly longer than hook shank
Body: Equal sections dark brown, yellow and dark brown silk
Hackle: Brown, sparse

Wings: Red fox squirrel, quite bushy and slightly longer than the hook shank, tied forward, divided and straightened back within about 10 degrees of upright

Steelhead Caddis-Bill McMillan
Body: Rust colored dubbing
Wing: Slips of mottled turkey wing feather
Hackle: Sparse deer hair
Head: Spun deer hair

Steelhead Charlie—Bob Wagoner
Underbody: Flat silver tinsel
Body: Edge Bright dyed fluorescent red, orange, green, yellow, or chartreuse
Wing: Squirrel tail dyed black or to match body
Bead Eyes: Nickel plated, on top of the fly

Steelhead General Hairwing—Deke Meyer
Tail: Red hackle fibers
Rib: Oval silver tinsel
Body: Purple seal substitute
Hackle: Red
Wing: White polar bear substitute
The idea behind the Steelhead General series is that the colors are an integral part of fly design, but not the only ingredient. For example, you can reverse the colors with a red body and purple tail and hackle, or use an orange/black combination.

Steelhead General Matuka—Deke Meyer
Rib: Oval silver tinsel
Body: Purple seal substitute
Hackle: Red
Wing: Red hackle fibers

Steelhead General Simplified Spey—Deke Meyer
Rib: Fine oval silver tinsel
Body: Rear half, red or hot pink floss; front half purple seal substitute
Spey Hackle: Palmered natural gray heron
Front Hackle: Light guinea

Steelhead General Skater—Deke Meyer
Tag: Flat silver tinsel
Body: Rear half, red seal substitute; front half purple seal substitute
Wing: Cinched down deer hair or atural brown bucktail

Steelhead General Soft Hackle—Deke Meyer
Tail: Red hackle fibers
Rib: Oval silver tinsel
Body: Purple seal substitute
Hackle: Large webby soft hackle dyed red, then dark guinea dyed red

Steelhead Sculpin—Harry Lemire
Tag: Wide pearlescent mylar tinsel
Tail: Continuation of matuka wing, badger orgrizzly hackle
Rib: Wide pearlescent mylar tinsel; counter-ribbed with fine copper wire
Body: Dark gray yarn or dubbing
Gills: Red yarn
Beard: Sparse grizzly orbadger hackle
Head: Deer hair
Wing: Badger or grizzly hackle as

matuka wing; black deer hair tied in as overwing after head is tied so top of head is also black

Steelhead Shrimp
Thread: Pale salmon colored, or light pinkish yellow
Hook: English Bait Hook style, Tiemco 207BL, Mustad 37160
Underbody: Optional, lead wire on shank, flips fly upside down
Body: Pale fluorescent salmon colored chenille
Tail: Tip of palmered hackle
Hackle: Palmered pale fluorescent salmon color, clipped on top

Steelhead Soft Hackle

Tail: Optional, soft hackle fibers as listed below
Body: Dubbing, yarn, or chenille
Rib: Tinsel is optional
Hackle: Natural grouse, pheasant rump, guinea, duck flank feathers or large saddle hackle; or dyed bright colors

Steelhead Spey—Bill Chinn
Butt: Hot orange floss
Rib: Oval gold tinsel
Body: Red seal or substitute
Spey Hackle: Palmered red hackle
Front Hackle: Gray heron
Wing: Bronze mallard

Steelhead Woolly Bugger
Tail: Marabou
Body: Chenille or yarn
Body Hackle: Palmered saddle hackle Varied color schemes, including black, olive, purple, pink.

Stewart—Marty Sherman
Tag: Flat gold tinsel
Tail: Golden pheasant tippet
Rib: Fine oval gold tinsel
Body: Black yarn
Hackle: Black
Wing: Black calf tail with a wisp of orange calf tail on top

Summer Fling—John Shewey
Thread: Orange or red
Tag: Flat silver tinsel
Tail: Hackle fibers, purple over orange
Body: Underbody of lead wire, then 1/4 hot pink plastic chenille, 1/4 hot orange plastic chenille, 1/2 purple plastic chenille
Rib: Small oval silver
Hackle: Dark purple, then two turns of red guinea
Wing: Polar bear, purple over orange

Surgeon General—Dr. Robert P. Terrill
Tag: Fine oval silver tinsel
Tail: Fluorescent red hackle fibers
Rib: Silver tinsel
Body: Purple yarn
Hackle: Fluorescent red tied as a collar
Wing: Fluorescent white bucktail
Throat: Guinea fibers

Teeny Leech—Jim Teeny
- *Tail:* Chinese ringneck pheasant tail feather fibers
- *Body:* Chinese ringneck pheasant tail feather fibers
- *Beard:* Two clumps of ringneck tail feather fibers form two separate beards

Leech is tied in natural, black, insect green, antique gold, flame orange, hot pink, hot green, ginger, and purple.

Teeny Nymph—Jim Teeny
- *Body:* Chinese ringneck pheasant tail feather fibers
- *Beard:* Two clumps of ringneck tail feather fibers form two separate beards
- *Wing:* Optional; same material as above

Nymph is tied in natural, black, insect green, antique gold, flame orange, hot pink, hot green, ginger, and purple. Teeny also adds Crystal Flash for his two-toned Flash Flies with a black body and ginger, fluorescent orange, hot green, or purple wing; or a ginger body and fluorescent orange, hot green, hot pink, or purple wing

Telkwa Stone—Mike Maxwell
- *Egg sac:* Black poly dubbing
- *Tail:* Dark brown goose biots
- *Rib:* Dark orange heavy thread
- *Body:* Bottom, golden stone dubbing; top, moose hair
- *Head:* Black poly dubbing
- *Antennae:* Dark brown goose biots
- *Wing:* Elk hair, cinched down

Thor—C. Jim Pray
- *Tail:* Orange hackle fibers
- *Body:* Red chenille
- *Hackle:* Brown
- *Wing:* White bucktail

Trophy Hunter—Gary Alger
- *Tag:* Flat gold tinsel, then hot orange floss
- *Rib:* Oval silver tinsel
- *Body:* Red seal substitute
- *Spey Hackle:* Black heron or substitute
- *Front Hackle:* Dark guinea
- *Wing:* Red body feather from golden pheasant

Umpqua Red Brat—Polly Rosborough
- *Tail:* Gray mallard flank
- *Rib:* Silver tinsel
- *Body:* Red chenille
- *Hackle:* Gray mallard flank
- *Wing:* Red bucktail

Umpqua—Don Harter
- *Tail:* White bucktail
- *Rib:* Silver tinsel
- *Body:* Rear 1/3 yellow wool, front 2/3 red wool or chenille
- *Hackle:* Brown
- *Wing:* White bucktail with wisps of red bucktail on each side

Umpqua Special has jungle cock cheeks added.

Wag's Waker—Bob Wagoner
- *Tail:* Elk or black moose
- *Body:* Spun natural or dyed deer hair; peacock herl; pearlescent Flashabou
- *Hackle:* Brown or grizzly or grizzly dyed brown (one size smaller than usual; you can eliminate the hackle)
- *Wings:* Elk or black moose (tied in upside down and splayed out)

Waller Waker—Lani Waller
- *Tail:* Black moose
- *Body:* Spun deer hair
- *Wing:* Calf tail or elk hair
- *Beard:* Black moose

The "Standard Waker" has white calf tail wings and mixed black and gray body hair for a mottled effect. The "Bee" has tan elk hair wings and a black deer hair body with a band of orange spun deer hair in the middle. The "High Visibility Moth" has fluorescent yellow calf tail wings and a banded body effect, starting at the back with white, gray, white, then gray deer hair.

Wet Spider—Al Knudson
- *Tail:* Optional, mallard flank
- *Rib:* Optional, silver tinsel
- *Body:* Yellow chenille
- *Hackle:* Very wide mallard flank

Winter's Hope—Bill McMillan
- *Hook:* 3/0 to 6/0
- *Thread:* Burgundy 6/0
- *Body:* Flat silver tinsel
- *Wing:* Hackle tips, orange enclosing yellow (can substitute pale orange for yellow)
- *Overwing:* Sparse pale olive calf tail
- *Hackle:* Deep blue, then purple

Selected Bibliography

BOOKS

Attenborough, David, *Life On Earth*, Little, Brown, 1979.

Balfour-Kinnear, G.P.R., *Flying Salmon*, Longmans, Green and Co., 1937.

Bates, Joseph D., Jr., *The Art Of The Salmon Fly*, David R. Godine, 1987.

Combs, Trey, *Steelhead Fly Fishing And Flies*, Frank Amato Publications, 1976.

Crossley, Anthony, *The Floating Line For Salmon And Sea-Trout*, Methuene Publishers London, 1939, 1944.

Curtis, Helena and N. Sue Barnes, *Invitation To Biology*, Fourth Edition, Worth Publishers, 1985.

Downes, Stephen, *The New Compleat Angler*, Stackpole, 1983.

Falkus, Hugh, *Salmon Fishing*, H.F. & G. Witherby Ltd., 1984.

Haig-Brown, Roderick L., *The Western Angler*, William Morrow and Company, 1947.

—*A River Never Sleeps*, Collins, 1944, 1946; Crown, 1974.

—*Fisherman's Spring*, Crown, 1951, 1975.

—*Fisherman's Summer*, Crown, 1959, 1975.

—*Fisherman's Fall*, William Morrow and Company, 1964; Crown, 1975.

—*The Master And His Fish*, University Of Washington Press, 1981.

Hickman, Jr., Cleveland P., Larry S. Roberts, Frances M. Hickman, *Integrated Principles Of Zoology*, Seventh Edition, Times Mirror/Mosby College Publishing, 1984.

Hugo, Richard, *Selected Poems*, W.W. Norton & Company, 1979.

Kelson, George M., *The Salmon Fly*, Angler's and Shooter's Press, 1979.

McMillan, Bill, *Dry Line Steelhead*, Frank Amato Publications, 1987.

Mortenson, Josesph, *Whale Songs and Wasp Maps*, E.P. Dutton, 1987.

Oglesby, Arthur, *Fly Fishing For Salmon And Sea Trout*, The Crowood Press, 1986.

Rosborough, E.H. "Polly", *Reminiscences From 50 Years Of Flyrodding* Caxton Printers, 1982.

Scott, Jock, *Greased Line Fishing For Salmon*, Seely Service & Co. Ltd., 1935, 1982.

—*Fine And Far Off*, Seely Service & Co. Ltd., 1952.

Sosin, Mark and John Clark, *Through The Fish's Eye*, Harper & Row, 1973.

Stewart, W.C., *The Practical Angler*, Adam & Charles Black, 1857.

Taverner, Eric, *Salmon Fishing*, Seely Service & Co. Ltd., 1931.

Wulff, Joan, *Fly Casting Techniques*, Nick Lyons Books, 1987.

Wulff, Lee, *The Atlantic Salmon*, Nick Lyons Books, 1953, 1983.

—*Lee Wulff On Flies*, Stackpole Books, 1980.

—*Trout On A Fly*, Nick Lyons Books, 1986.

—*The Compleat Lee Wulff*, Truman Talley Books/E.P. Dutton, 1989.

VIDEOS

Krieger, Mel, *The Essence Of Fly Casting*, 1987.

Swisher, Doug, *Advanced Fly Casting*, Scientific Anglers/3M, 1987.

Teeny, Jim, *Catching More Steelhead: Breaking Traditions With Jim Teeny*, Scientific Anglers/3M, 1988.

Waller, Lani, *Fly Fishing For Pacific Steelhead*, Scientific Anglers/3M, 1987.

—*Advanced Fly Fishing For Pacific Steelhead*, Scientific Anglers/3M, 1987.

—*Fly Fishing For Trophy Steelhead*, Scientific Anglers/3M, 1987.

Index

Photo Credits

Frank W. Amato, 2 and 3, 8, 12, 15, 28, 30, 38, 42, 43, 44, 46, 48, 55, 59, 61, 63, 65, 70, 77, 78, 96, 121,

Pete Anderson, 27

Dick Evans, 13

Dave Hall, 104

Joe Howell, 66

Brad Jackson, 6 and 7, 52, 61,

David Lambroughton, 68, 113, 149

Denise Maxwell, 21

Bill McMillan, 1, 4 and 5, 56, 94, 108

B. J. Meiggs, 10, 58

Barbara Meyer, 122, 126, 127

Deke Meyer, 9, 10, 11, 16, 17, 18, 20, 21, 22, 23, 24, 25, 26, 27, 28, 29, 31, 32, 33, 35, 39, 40, 41, 45, 50, 53, 55, 67, 71, 76, 98, 101, 102, 103, 105, 107, 110, 111, 112, 116, 117, 119, 121, 130, 137, 138, 139, 142, 144, 146, 148, 150

Steve Probasco, Front Cover

Ted Richter, 115

Scott Ripley, 13, 37, 49, 54, 74, 99, 131, Back Cover

Jim Schollmeyer, 79 thru 93

Carolyn Z. Shelton, 95

Craig Shreeve, 34

Randy Stetzer, 20

Gene Trump, 100, Back Cover

Lani Waller, 71, 72

Howard West, 69

Joan Wulff, 76